⸱ ⸱ ⸱

PRACTICING SECTARIANISM

⸱ ⸱ ⸱

PRACTICING SECTARIANISM

Archival and Ethnographic Interventions on Lebanon

Edited by

LARA DEEB,
TSOLIN NALBANTIAN,
and NADYA SBAITI

STANFORD UNIVERSITY PRESS
Stanford, California

Stanford University Press
Stanford, California

An earlier version of chapter 3, "The Archive Is Burning," appeared in *Sextarianism: Sovereignty, Secularism, and the State in Lebanon* by Maya Mikdashi,
published by Stanford University Press. © 2022 by Maya Mikdashi.

Printed in the United States of America on acid-free, archival-quality paper

Library of Congress Cataloging-in-Publication Data

Names: Deeb, Lara, 1974- editor. | Nalbantian, Tsolin, editor. | Sbaiti, Nadya,
    editor.
Title: Practicing sectarianism : archival and ethnographic interventions on
    Lebanon / edited by Lara Deeb, Tsolin Nalbantian, and Nadya Sbaiti.
Description: Stanford, California : Stanford University Press, [2022] |
    Includes bibliographical references and index.
Identifiers: LCCN 2022008364 (print) | LCCN 2022008365 (ebook) |
    ISBN 9781503631090 (cloth) | ISBN 9781503633865 (paperback) | ISBN
    9781503633872 (ebook)
Subjects: LCSH: Communalism—Lebanon. | Communalism—Religious
    aspects. | Sects—Political aspects—Lebanon. | Sects—Social aspects—
    Lebanon. | Lebanon—Ethnic relations.
Classification: LCC DS80.4 .P73 2022 (print) | LCC DS80.4 (ebook) | DDC
    302/.14095692—dc23/eng/20220701
LC record available at https://lccn.loc.gov/2022008364
LC ebook record available at https://lccn.loc.gov/2022008365

Cover design: Rob Ehle
Cover art: Jana Traboulsi
Typeset by Elliott Beard in Minion 10/14

In solidarity with everyone who has ever dealt
with sectarianism and refused to bend.

CONTENTS

ACKNOWLEDGMENTS

OUR GRATITUDE GOES TO all the authors in this volume for their intellectual camaraderie, both recently and over the years. Insightful comments from the anonymous reviewers as well as from Andrew Arsan helped to make this volume stronger. We are indebted to Jana Traboulsi's creativity and grateful for the thoughtful cover art she provided for this book. The intellectual groundwork for this book solidified over many years of conversation with myriad scholars, friends, colleagues, and comrades. You are too many to list, but we appreciate the discussions, critiques, encouragement, and exchange of ideas immensely.

We thank Kate Wahl for her support, and especially for believing in this project from the moment we first described it to her. Caroline McKusick, Cat Ng Pavel, and Tiffany Mok at Stanford University Press have been tremendously helpful. We appreciate Renaldo Migaldi's careful copyediting and Kate Mertes's indexing skills. We also thank Mariana Nakfour for her work on the bibliography, and Scripps College for the research funds that made it possible for us to hire her. The Leiden Institute for Area Studies at Leiden University generously provided funds to help index the work.

Gratitude and love from Lara to Qutayba, and to Hadi, Hera, and Ziad; from Tsolin to Cyrus, and to Rostom and Nazani; from Nadya to Omar, Mona, and Ziad. Finally, we want to thank one another. Working on this volume together across multiple time zones has been a source of joy, companionship, friendship, humor, and sanity, especially during the uprisings in Lebanon, the aftermath of the Beirut port explosion, the country's ongoing criminal economic collapse, and the covid-19 pandemic, with all its anxieties and isolation. We came to depend on one another as this project became the backdrop of our relationships, which formed, developed, and nourished us during these very strange times.

NOTE ON TRANSLITERATION

WE HAVE USED A simplified version of the *International Journal of Middle East Studies* system for transliterating Modern Standard Arabic and Arabic dialect. We have omitted indications of long and short vowels, and any distinctions between "hard" and "soft" letters, trusting that specialist readers will be able to follow our transliteration by relying on context. Proper nouns and place names are rendered in their common English spellings when available, or their most common spellings in Lebanon. The transliterations of all Armenian sources are based on the *Armenian Review* key (modeled on the Eastern Armenian pronunciation), and include diacritics. Names of the Armenian political parties have been given in Armenian. Common spellings of Western and Eastern Armenian names have been used.

. . .

PRACTICING SECTARIANISM

. . .

INTRODUCTION

PRACTICING SECTARIANISM IN LEBANON

LARA DEEB, TSOLIN NALBANTIAN,
and NADYA SBAITI

SECTARIANISM IS A CONCEPT that simply won't die. Scholars, pundits, and journalists turn to it again and again to describe and explain violence and political strife in the Middle East. Some of the most nuanced of these evocations—those that insist that sectarianism is neither essential nor primordial—still rest on the idea that sectarianism is an indelible constant in the region. Lebanon represents an exemplary case that both generates these assumptions and suggests paths to overcoming them. Lebanon's seemingly inextricable link with sectarianism led us to this book via a series of conversations across disciplines and time frames, underpinned by questions about how people practice sectarianism: how they use it, live it, and maintain it in their daily lives.[1]

This recurring conversation was different and, frankly, more interesting than one structured by the perennial question "What do we do *about* sectarianism?" and its corollary, "What's the alternative?" These questions have plagued scholars, researchers, and activists working in and on Lebanon and the region more broadly. Both questions fail to consider how and why sectarianism moves through the everyday lives of the region's inhabitants. This volume aims to change the parameters of scholarship on the subject by engaging with the varied ways in which people *live* sectarianism daily, in meaningful albeit inconsistent ways. *Practicing Sectarianism* intervenes directly at this juncture by bringing together scholars from history and anthropology—two disciplines that take as a priori the idea that sectarianism is contingent and constructed—in order to explore the imaginative and contradictory ways in which people engage with sectarianism in the social realm. This volume contends that sectarianism can be more fully understood if we take it seriously *as* a set of practices, and models a way of doing so in scholarship.

Each scholar whose work is featured in this book uses sectarianism as an animating principle through which to investigate how it is conceived of and practiced within a variety of sites across Lebanon and its diasporas, and over a range of historical periods. By considering how productive the destabilization of sectarianism can be, this volume magnifies how actors in various times and spaces have used the concept to exhibit, imagine, or contest power. What forms of affective pull does sectarianism have on people and communities? What epistemological work does sectarianism do as a concept? How does sectarianism function as a marker of social difference? How is sectarianism mobilized as a multivalent signifier or value claim to convey disagreement or discrimination?

A Materially Impactful, Socially Constructed Sectarianism

Scholars and nonspecialists alike use the term "sectarianism" to refer to at least three different ways in which sect has come to permeate life in Lebanon.[2] In its most common usage, the term denotes the imbrication of sect and politics as it manifests in Lebanon's form of parliamentary democracy, in which all elected and appointed government and public positions are allocated by sect. This deployment of the term is best captured in its specific, modified form: "political-sectarianism." Second, "sectarianism" is used to describe the Lebanese state's categorization of its citizens and the country's personal status laws, which require a citizen who wants to marry, divorce, manage child custody, or distribute inheritance to follow the laws of their official state-designated sect.[3] While this aspect of sectarianism is linked to the political-sectarian system, Maya Mikdashi reminds us that it demands attention to sex as well.[4] Finally, many Lebanese use the term "sectarianism" to signal how people treat one another based on their sect, whether through discrimination or favoritism, negative stereotypes, or generalized positive regard. This usage intersects with notions of *wasta* (connections) in ideas about the flow of economic or social or political resources within sect-based networks. These three strands of sectarianism are braided tightly together, sometimes so tightly that their distinctions cannot easily be seen. They cocreate and shape one another.

This book focuses on how these intertwined forms of sectarianism are lived in the everyday. By focusing on the microlevel of social interaction, the chapters that follow add texture to how people live sectarianism inconsistently: resisting it, evading it, and deploying it strategically, sometimes all at once. The everyday is most readily evident in the third form of sectarianism, that of interpersonal interactions. Yet it is also a part of sectarianism's structural and institutional forms, as it reveals how people interact with the political-sectarian and personal status categories that affect their lives. As Suad Joseph notes, sectarianism is a process of differentiation "that operates through the everyday—through socialization, through family systems, and through various other aspects of social organization in both systematic and erratic or contradictory ways."[5] Each contribution to this book explores how different social actors consider, negotiate, and/or use sectarianism in daily interactions with a variety of effects and often unintended consequences. The authors follow how power moves through sectarian communities in practice; and in so doing, they reveal how sectarianism travels across spatial and temporal boundaries. They highlight a variety of institutions that both limit and expand sectarian belonging and practice, and they show how sectarian identity is complicated by class positioning, historical change, diaspora politics, gender and sexual identities, ideas about religiosity, personal status law, and regional location within Lebanon. By exploring everyday practice, we aim to provide a new model for scholarship—one that understands sectarianism as simultaneously constructed and experienced, as imagined yet materially impactful.

Our intervention adds the dimension of daily experience to a body of scholarship that should have understood sectarianism as constructed, especially since the publication of Ussama Makdisi's *Culture of Sectarianism*—a foundational, widely read work that argues that the development of sectarianism in Lebanon was a distinctly modern phenomenon.[6] Indeed, scholars have gone on to show that sect should not be treated differently from other communal identities, and is likewise a social and historical product.[7] Accordingly, they have argued that political-sectarianism is hardly an inevitable outcome of age-old divisions. Even before the publication of Makdisi's book detailing the process of sectarianization, Suad Joseph's dissertation argued that because sects are politicized, they are constructed through social and political processes, and scholars publishing in Arabic addressed sectarianism as thus constructed.[8] Historians, anthropologists, and political scientists have continued to explore how sectarianism in Lebanon is produced and reproduced at various local and state levels, including civil society, elite networks, citizenship, urban space, personal status law, and infrastructure.[9]

Nevertheless, in one recent wave of sectarianism studies, many of the lessons of Makdisi's pioneering intervention have been lost. These publications tend to focus on only the political-sectarian dimension, and specifically on sectarianism's deployment by governmental figures, institutions, and ideologies. They exhibit a drive to connect violence (and peace, for that matter) to religion irrespective of time, place, and local struggles for power—ignoring Elizabeth Hurd's important plea to dethrone "religion as a singular and stable interpretive and policy category."[10] Many analyses of the 2003 US-led war on Iraq, the continued instability and violence in its wake, the disintegration of Syria, the ongoing Saudi-led war on Yemen, the counterrevolution and reinforcement of military rule in Egypt, the crushed uprising in Bahrain, and the concern for the dwindling numbers of Christians in the region have diagnosed sectarianism as the problem.[11] And due to an assumption about the "indigenous" nature of sectarianism, some of these takes have ironically designated it as the cure for the region.[12]

The year 2003 marked the "transferability" of political sectarianism from Lebanon to Iraq. Other locations have also "qualified" or met "eligibility" requirements for the deployment of sectarianism as cure. This use of sectarianism certainly replicates the narrative of authoritarian rulers, as Hurd warns; but perhaps more importantly, it flattens an understanding of populations as passive, timeless victims of their ancestry and origin. It negates people's self-identifications and their understandings of their own societies, as seen in the cases of Bahrain, Egypt, and Israel/Palestine.[13] Further, it overlooks the interdependent relationship between sectarian and national identities, as Fanar Haddad noted in his investigation of the prominence of identity politics in post-2003 Iraq.[14] Omar AlShehabi also argues that it obscures other political thoughts, discourses, and movements of the period.[15] We are left with a patronizing hypothetical of the Middle East as it could or should be. This hypothetical often emerges from ideas about an earlier, often idealized "nonsectarian" era, an imagination that exposes misunderstanding and ignorance of how inhabitants of the region actually lived and coexisted.[16] Those who have contributed to this form of sectarianism's conceptual resurgence assume that the Middle East and its inhabitants are unwittingly entangled in essentialized identities that lead to political-sectarianism as the only possible form of governance,[17] or that sectarianism is the primary reason for enduring systems of power in the region.[18] This body of work reproduces the very assumptions it attempts to deconstruct.[19]

Practicing Sectarianism, refuses both ahistorical and recent starting points, as well as the notion that historical processes are so easily rendered into predictable and fixed "outcomes." The contributors fold significant events and periodic markers into a larger continuum of Lebanese history, during which sectarianism has been practiced in varied ways. Nearly every chapter reveals paths to sectarianization: the mechanisms by which people start to see others through the lens of sect, or come to act in ways deemed sectarian. By unpacking the (re)production of sectarianism in specific times and places, the authors show how practices of sectarianism that emerge from the ground up, including in interpersonal interactions, affect and effect institutions and structures. Thus they contribute to a growing body of work that has similarly examined the agency of those who enact sectarianism in the realms of political economy and ideological hegemony,[20] or within clientelism and political-economic networks.[21]

Existing works provide strong explanations for how sectarianism is reinforced and reproduced at the levels of the state, civil society, and elite networks. The contributors to this volume insist that even where sectarianism is facilitated or nurtured in top-down ways, its development is never unidirectional and can never be fully understood without deep attention to the everyday. In other words, sectarianization is produced neither solely by structures nor by people on the ground, but through dialectical processes that require the entanglement of the two levels of life and analysis. Political elites in power use sectarian discourses to maintain that power, deploying sectarianism—too often successfully—as a weapon to divide people. As sectarianism in all its forms has been constructed and molded over time, it has shaped the ways people think and live, and has fostered new practices of identification and discrimination. Those practices, in turn, continue to fuel sectarianism's institutionalized forms. Overall, these ground-up dimensions of sectarianism's persistence have been understudied in the copious scholarship on its various consequences and manifestations. This book thus adds to this rich but incomplete conversation about *why* sectarianism is such a persistent part of modern identity and *how* it is maintained, by focusing on its quotidian, mundane, intimate aspects that are practiced every day.[22]

The construction of sectarianism does not make its practice any less legitimate as a collection of forces, nor does it dilute its impact on people's lives.[23]

Many of us scholars of Lebanon have long shared this unpopular idea among ourselves. But we often hesitate to bring it into our work—not because it is untrue, but because we fear that acknowledging the realities of sectarian experience will only serve policymakers' erroneous ideas about sectarianism as an essential and primordial characteristic of Lebanon and the Middle East more broadly. In this volume, we collectively insist that one can understand sectarianism as socially constructed *and* materially impactful at the same time. The chapters by Joanne Nucho and Lara Deeb capture the ways in which sect is co-constituted with other social categories, identities, and practices. Along with Roxana Arāṣ's chapter, they also explore how sectarian structures are produced affectively and have affective impacts on people's lives. Disrupting scholarly tendencies to focus on the perspectives of one sect at a time, Nucho, Tsolin Nalbantian, and Linda Sayed each write about the contestation of sectarian belonging within communal groups, while Deeb, Reem Bailony, Maya Mikdashi, and Nadya Sbaiti each address the uses, limitations, and practices of sectarianism across various Lebanese communities and institutions.

Historiography and Ethnography Juxtaposed

Practicing Sectarianism disrupts ideas about Lebanese institutions and society as being forever entrenched in sectarianism. It offers nuanced analyses of the fissures and inconsistencies through which people practice their identities in far more complex ways. Each contributor approaches Lebanese historiography and/or ethnography without assuming the meanings held by sect as a signifier, and in doing so, links the volume's theoretical interventions to its methodological approach. Each chapter takes the archive or field site as a key focus for investigation and rereading. While the individual contributions are grounded in disciplinary methods, this volume as a whole considers the relationship between the ethnographic and the archival, and shows how a variety of disciplinary conventions can be mobilized in interdisciplinary ways to shed new light on sectarianism's many lives. The authors collectively demonstrate how scholarship can break sect open as a category, rethinking Lebanese history and contemporary social dynamics.

By juxtaposing the archive and the ethnographic field site, we highlight a key juncture at which history and anthropology present innovative research possibilities. We raise new questions about what constitutes valid historical records and ethnographic terrain, and about how that legitimacy is determined in the first place. Historians Bailony, Nalbantian, Sayed, and Sbaiti reimagine what comprises the archival terrain for Lebanon. By using or rereading archives that have been overlooked, deemed irrelevant, or explored perfunctorily, they elicit subtleties in how sectarianism offers both opportunities and limitations. They demonstrate that archives are not merely repositories of a finitude of knowledge, but sites that can free scholarship from the restrictive binary of either complicity or insufficiency in relation to conventional sectarian narratives. They argue that much of the way sectarianism has been framed has resulted from historians' selective reading of the archival terrain around issues of education, law, gender, and diaspora.

Similarly, the contributions by anthropologists Ārāṣ, Deeb, Mikdashi, and Nucho rethink the relationship between their discipline's key methodological driver—the ethnographic field site—and sectarianism. They refuse to accede to the fear that acknowledging sectarian practice in contemporary life will fuel a political rhetoric that perpetually insists upon sectarianism's inescapable presence in the Middle East. These ethnographers harness spaces and daily activities that are often overlooked as sites of sectarian practice, and analyze how people mobilize them to diverse ends in arenas such as law, marriage, neighborly relations, and the sensorium. As such, they open new possibilities for articulating the everyday with sectarianism while refuting essentialism and attending to historical shifts.

Temporality is often viewed as the domain of history, yet it shapes this book as a whole, regardless of each chapter's disciplinary inclinations. Attentive readers will note that most chapters focus on either the Mandate era or the late twentieth and early twenty-first centuries. To a certain extent, this limitation is related to norms within our disciplines, or to the accessibility of archives and field sites. In the late 1990s, historians of Lebanon began reassessing the Mandate era not merely as an explanatory vehicle for some inevitable sectarian future, but on its own terms as a period of society and politics in formation.[24] This research has since been buoyed by the unprecedented expansion of Lebanon's archival terrain particularly since the mid- to late 2000s, with the most accessible archives and materials primarily informing the interwar period.[25] The depth and scope of work on the Mandate period has broadened and nuanced the study of Lebanon in critical ways. By excavating the everyday lived experiences of sectarianism, historians in this volume build on that scholarly focus while also pushing research on this period in new directions. In doing so, we also look forward to future research on the 1943–90 period that will take up the methodological questions raised in this volume.

Ethnographic research on Lebanon has increased exponentially since the mid-1990s,[26] and anthropologists have begun asking the kinds of questions addressed in this volume more recently. The ethnographic chapters (Arāş, Deeb, Mikdashi, Nucho) are also saturated with temporality in another way: they remind us that despite disciplinary claims to be studying "the present" as opposed to history's "past," anthropology is always about the recent past. The rapidity of social change triggered by compounding forms of devastation in Lebanon has underscored the relationship of ethnography to time. There is something especially jarring about reading (or writing) about people's contemporary practices of sectarianism while knowing that in the moment between research and writing, their lives have been upended in catastrophic ways.

Similarly, spatiality is often imagined as anthropology's domain, yet it infuses this book as a whole, as the authors raise questions about how sectarian practices shape and are shaped through space. In their chapters, anthropologists Mikdashi, Arāş, and Nucho evoke the resonance of specific places (court archives, ritual sites, workshops) and neighborhoods with ideas about sect, while historians Sayed and Sbaiti render the courtroom and the school, respectively, as spaces for both producing and restricting sectarian ways of being. These details about the relationship of particular physical encounters with ideas about belonging and difference make evident the critical ways in which daily practice matters to understanding sectarianism. Even while Beirut continues to offer the greatest research accessibility for both historians and anthropologists, the city is not one homogenous space. The chapters in this book by Sbaiti, Arāş, Mikdashi, and Nucho reflect complex webs of neighborhoods, networks, and experiences as their work moves through multiple diverse areas of the city. The capital is often imagined as Lebanon's center, at the expense of attention to its so-called peripheries; yet none of these chapters, though set in Beirut, are solely "about" Beirut. Going further, Sayed's chapter leaves the capital entirely and moves to Lebanon's south, while Deeb questions the relationship between Beirut and other regions of the country, especially as it manifests in stereotypes about Ras Beirut as a "mixed" space. The contributions by Nalbantian and Bailony travel still further, dislodging sectarianism from Lebanon and the Middle East (and in Nalbantian's case, even from the Lebanese) by highlighting its transnational flows and demonstrating how it is used by inhabitants in other geographies, most notably in the United States.

The thematic and methodological interplays between the two disciplines and across time and space shape our organization of these chapters in a roughly chronothematic order. Sbaiti and Sayed provide critical rereadings of different archives in their analyses of community formation in Mandate Lebanon. Sbaiti attends to the ways in which people used schooling, and circuits of education more broadly, to transgress allegedly impermeable communal boundaries that revolved around the intersection of sect and socioeconomic status. Sayed shows how religious courts became a site where Shiʻi litigants enacted, contested, and reproduced notions of citizenship, sectarian identities, and gendered norms. Mikdashi's anthropological reading of archives follows, bridging mandate law with contemporary state building in ways that connect to Sayed's analysis of Jaʻfari court records and Bailony's focus on state building. Mikdashi presents an ethnographic journey into a Lebanese legal archive, excavating sectarian and other forms of power through archivists' practices, and considering those practices as part of the archive itself. The contributions by Bailony, Arāş, and Nalbantian cohere around interwoven themes of diaspora and transnationalism, and analyses of specific sectarian and confessional communities.[27] Bailony discusses sect and sectarianism in diaspora as processes through which people negotiated nationalism vis-à-vis the homeland, one another, and French colonial and American authorities. Arāş demonstrates how members of the Rum Orthodox community use sensory experience and sensibilities, specifically scent, to negotiate and embody sectarian and intersectarian identities, spaces, and encounters. Nalbantian focuses on the productive nature of sectarianism, analyzing an intra-Armenian conflict related to Cold War geopolitics in order to disabuse the notions of a united Armenian diaspora and of Lebanon as the origin and site of sectarian struggles. The final two chapters, by Nucho and Deeb, provide critical ethnographies of postwar social dynamics that disrupt sect as a coherent category by linking it to class and geography, whether that of neighborhood or of region of origin in Lebanon. Nucho shows how class and sect are mutually constituted categories through her ethnography of work and social welfare practices in an Armenian neighborhood of Beirut. Finally, Deeb analyzes region or neighborhood as a key source of anxiety about sectarian difference in mixed marriages, and considers how "exposure" to various people and places in Lebanon may influence the expression or suppression of sectarian bias.

Lebanon and Beyond

To fully grasp the various ways people practice sectarianism in Lebanon today, we must attend to the historical production of Lebanon as a political terrain. The Ottoman state's decrees, culminating in the Tanzimat reforms during the mid-1800s, applied to the area that is now Lebanon, as part of the Ottoman Empire. But how inhabitants of the empire "practiced" those decrees varied across the empire. Tanzimat reforms in what is now Lebanon upended the prioritization and practice of "rank rather than religion" as the key social structure of power.[28] Ottoman, foreign, and religious authorities such as the Maronite Church reacted with punitive force to these new forms of local organization and knowledge that hinged on sectarian difference—thus exposing a visceral yearning for an imagined yesteryear when elite power was absolute. When that proved impossible, they adapted to and co-opted the new order.[29] The combustion of this nostalgic view with the modernization reforms of the Tanzimat, religious violence, and new administrative sectarian structures led to the establishment of Mount Lebanon as an Ottoman *mutasarrifiyya*, a semiautonomous administrative district, in 1861.

In 1920, following World War I, the French Mandate combined the formerly Ottoman Mount Lebanon with surrounding areas to shape the borders of the contemporary Lebanese nation-state. Over the next two decades, Mandate authorities and local elites cultivated sectarian differences of the late 1800s and enmeshed them into Lebanon's political, economic, cultural, and social institutions—and, by extension, into daily life. "Only" eighteen sects made the cut: Alawite, Armenian Catholic, Armenian Orthodox, Assyrian, Chaldean Catholic, Coptic Orthodox, Druze, Greek Catholic, Greek Orthodox, Isma'ili, Jewish, Roman Catholic, Maronite, Protestant, Sunni, Shi'i, Syriac Catholic, and Syriac Orthodox. Many of the multiple ways in which sect shapes Lebanese life have grown out of this institutionalization. For example, Lebanon's political-sectarian system was partly imagined in the National Pact, a 1943 tacit agreement between Maronite and Sunni confessional leaders meant to maintain sectarian political balance, and then was delineated for the Parliament in the constitution. Since then, the prime minister has always been Sunni, the president Maronite, and the speaker of Parliament Shi'i. Moreover, nearly every position, from member of Parliament to mayor to public university professor, has been distributed by sect. Lebanon's sectarian personal status laws build on these divisions: the state assigns each citizen their father's sect at birth—unless the parents were not married and the father does not claim the child, in which case the child is assigned the sect of the maternal grandfather.[30]

While these various forms of institutionalized sectarianism (especially the personal status laws) have been on the table for revision at different times since Lebanon's establishment, the October 2019 uprising in Lebanon brought the political-sectarian system to the foreground. Explicit calls to dismantle the system were both a culmination of the growth of multiple activist movements over the past decades—including the intersection of antisectarian, feminist, environmentalist, and queer rights strands—and an echo of earlier movements on the left. The strength of these calls in the fall of 2019 demonstrated the need to understand how sectarianism is selectively and strategically practiced by Lebanon's inhabitants in the everyday. Sectarianism—even in its political-sectarian or legal forms—is not simply a removable frame that, once "dismantled," would allow Lebanon to "be" like other presumably "normal" nation-states that supposedly have perfected the separation of church and state.[31] The popular uprising during the fall and winter of 2019, along with its predecessors and the ensuing demonstrations, confrontations, conversations, and frustrations, emphatically demand that researchers and activists engage with sectarianism as a complex constellation of institutions, ideas, and practices.[32] Its collision with the global covid-19 pandemic, Lebanon's economic collapse, and the brute criminality of the Lebanese government that led to the August 4, 2020, port explosion necessitates more imaginative studies to understand and counter the myriad ways people, especially political elites, redeploy sectarianism.

These crises have confirmed the impossibility of framing Lebanon along sectarian lines. While protesters around the country and across sects called for an end to sectarianism and for the downfall of its representative leaders, they did not all do so for the same reasons. Many called for the dismantling of sectarianism as a system, along with its handmaidens: patriarchy, racism, and economic injustice. Others cited its failure to live up to its promises of resource allocation. At the same time, sectarian leaders cynically used the covid-19 pandemic relief efforts to shore up their constituencies. The ensuing disasters of economic collapse and the port explosion thus helped renew the conditions for sectarian support while simultaneously laying bare the instrumental and malleable ways in which citizens and residents in Lebanon continue to understand the uses and limitations of sect as an identity, and of sectarianism as a communal sphere.

While *Practicing Sectarianism* takes Lebanon as the crucible for its exploration, by bringing together scholarship focused on a variety of sites, including the diaspora, it seeks to help dislocate sect and sectarianism from Lebanon, and to question the physical and ideological contours of the nation-state. Indeed, this volume's insights into how people's practices contribute to sectarian dynamics are relevant beyond Lebanon.[33] Just as politicians and policy makers invoked Lebanon to model the political-sectarian system in Iraq, Lebanon can be used to unravel assumptions about sectarian workings elsewhere in the Middle East and beyond. At the same time, we aim to draw attention to how narrow understandings of sectarianism that persist in some disciplines other than anthropology and history—such as psychology, political science, and public policy—muddle rather than clarify the topic.[34]

We hope that the theoretical and methodological interventions presented here inspire scholars and students both familiar and unfamiliar with the region to carry our arguments to other contexts and geographies where scholarship has drawn on the frame of sectarianism to understand conflict—such as the Central African Republic, Ireland, Indonesia, Kashmir, the Balkans, India, Pakistan, and Sri Lanka.[35] To the extent that insights about sectarianism translate to contexts where other forms of social difference, such as racism, dominate, these arguments may resonate with scholars working on the United States and parts of Europe as well. Our interventions on sectarianism will fall short if iterations of Lebanese exceptionalism prevent comparisons and interconnections—particularly with areas outside the Middle East—from even being considered. At the same time, the consideration of connections across time and space must proceed with care. Our call to take sectarianism seriously as a practice is not a call to merely replace political-sectarian readings, which would lead to even more homogenization. The chapters in this book show how, by counterintuitively *expanding* how sect operates, people can exert pressure from below on systems that assume it to be a fixed category. People live sectarianism in imaginative and innovative ways.

Whether thinking about Lebanon or elsewhere, the contributors to this volume write about sectarianism in order to disrupt its epistemological and discursive hegemony. Some chapters show how sectarianism is used in nonbinary ways, moving away from the simplistic paradigm of "sectarian" versus "antisectarian," which has imprisoned us in the face of the inequality, corruption, and criminal behavior of political sectarian leaders in Lebanon. Many of the people and institutions described in this book deploy sect at various points between these poles, and complicate it as an identity and a practice. Other chapters show how deeply ideas about sect, as well as other forms of difference, are internalized. This forces us to confront the inconsistencies in antisectarian calls that still view certain members of society through a sectarian lens. We see the limits of solidarity—whether in the form of sect, class, or race—and we must address them. We can do better.

This book insists that we set aside the naive notion that dismantling a sectarian system will necessarily lead to the disappearance of sectarianism in people's daily lives. However, unlike Lebanese politicians who use the idea that sectarianism already exists in society to justify the political-sectarian system, we emphasize that sectarianism's diffusion into the everyday means that we must work against the social categories it creates, and against the impulse to simultaneously fall back on them to succeed. This is a call for change in *all* of sectarianism's forms—political-sectarian, personal status, and interpersonal—in structures and institutions as well as the everyday, with our eyes wide open to the multiple challenges it presents, and to possibilities of empowerment we may not want to see. Such change must include working against other forms of discrimination and deployments of power through identity in Lebanon: gender, class, and—less frequently discussed but no less important—race. *Killun ya'ni killun*—"All of them means all of them"—may also mean "All of them means all of us." With that in mind, we look to Joanne Nucho's use in this volume of the notion of "doing collective" as a potential way forward. If we hold to the notion that communities, including sectarian ones, are created through collective labor, we can also hold a vision of collective labor that unravels or challenges sectarian ways of being and creates more capacious and empowered kinds of communities.

1 NO ROOM FOR THIS STORY

Education and the Limits of Sectarianism
during the Mandate Era

NADYA SBAITI

THIS CHAPTER EXPLORES EDUCATION in Lebanon as a critical historical lens to reveal the Mandate era as a time of dynamic and diverse potentialities. Such potentialities complicate conventional narratives of historical inevitability and the foreclosure of alternative futures. By examining the role of education and schooling in French and Lebanese visions of communal belonging and exclusion, and by attending to colonial and national commonalities and divergences, historians and other scholars of Lebanon can begin to transcend trite interpretations that reduce community formation to primarily sectarian affiliation situated within immutable bounds.

In this vein, I am calling for a critical rereading of the archive around education that destabilizes categories often taken for granted in research on and in Lebanon,[1] thus opening new avenues of historical inquiry. This chapter involves such rereading of archives in order to attend to evidence that, I argue, has been largely overlooked or dismissed, in part because it has not fit within conventional narratives of Lebanese history. Those narratives understand sect and sectarian affiliation to have indelibly shaped unfolding dynamics. In addition to documents from the French Mandatory archives, this chapter closely engages with sources that for Lebanon remain relatively unexplored, namely those in "unofficial" school archives: correspondence, curricula, speeches, textbooks, and oral accounts. This rereading ruptures, in particular, metanarratives of sect and on "sectarian culture" in which so much of Lebanon's history is mired. Attending to these sources reveals a hidden or alternative narrative, comfortably nestled in the domain of education, about how parents, teachers, and students crossed allegedly impermeable boundaries that have been ascribed to sectarian community. One of the implications of studying how education became a site of such boundary transgression is to take a more expansive view of the definition of "community," and to explore how new community identities began to form in the interwar years: two and a half decades during which Lebanon transitioned from postwar Mandatory territory to institutionalized nation-state.

Scholars often emphasize political rhetoric, official acts and declarations, laws, and public demonstrations of national allegiance or discord to trace the process of state building and nation making.[2] But there are other sites and sources through which to explore this process: the "informal," often intangible, but equally politicized channels of language, history writing, and notions of civic duty incubated in classrooms, as well as in broader debates over the intellectual value versus the material instrumentality of education. This chapter intervenes in this literature, arguing that these experiences and experiments unfolded in the domain of education and the institutional space of the school, and were just as foundational in forging and contesting the parameters of national subjectivities. Perhaps more importantly, the domain of education exposes the "grey spaces" in which people forged new social and politico-national subjectivities in strategic ways.

I highlight such subjectivities at the primary and secondary levels of private education because during the interwar years, French Mandate and Lebanese officials, school principals, parents, teachers, and students themselves identified these strata of education as the most essential building blocks to nation making, rendering them the focus of their educational energies. Debates raged in the Arabic-language press in particular over what the purpose and content of education for a newly minted state should be—and for whom.[3] Given that the number of private schools established in Lebanon eclipsed that of public schools, private schools were a main site for contestations over investing education with new meanings for social mobility and national inclusion.

As World War I ended, former Ottoman allegiances were reformulated. Internal migration and mobility increased, and questions of resources, employment, and professionalization came to the fore in stark ways. The imperatives and aspirations of social mobility and the training of young minds were not new for educational professionals and institutions. What *was* new was the need to shape a collective future that paralleled shifting conceptions of the newly territorialized nation-state of Lebanon. Over the course of the Mandate, educational practitioners and the wide range of schools that proliferated helped shape the epistemological infrastructure en route to creating this entity. By "epistemological infrastructure," I mean the vast array of ideas that become validated as truths and convincing explanations.

Much of the historiography of education in Lebanon contends that schools were established whose educational content responded to the needs of already existing, pre-formed and bounded communities[4]—what I call "pedagogical constituencies." In this work, missionaries, local religious leaders, and members of the urban and rural elites understood various pedagogical constituencies as communities connected mainly by a religion or sect, while also using such identity to negotiate ideas and practices of social mobility.

France's position on educating the inhabitants of its new mandates of Syria and Lebanon followed what Alice Conklin shows was a broader imperial policy shift at the turn of the twentieth century, from acculturation to accommodation. In practice, it meant that "natives" were not to be educated outside their class.[5] As it did in France's other colonies,[6] this approach confounded and contradicted dreams of the social mobility and general betterment with which newly minted Lebanese invested education. However, a closer look at sources on education in this era reveals that students, parents, and teachers created educational *content* through curricula, and educational practices so as to produce *new* "communities of knowledge." These communities of knowledge, connected as they were by worlds of ideas and networks of knowledge, often transcended confessional, sociopolitical, and even at times regional subjectivities.

In the neighboring mandates, as well as in other newly minted postwar states, efforts were already underway to shape history, culture, law, and language in ways that would be defined as "authentically" Lebanese, Syrian, or Iraqi, for example. In Lebanon, sectarian community leaders (*zuʿama*) strove to delineate distinct sectarian histories which would situate their sect squarely within or as the locus of a broader Lebanese identity. They did this through institutions such as schools and religious centers as well as courts and municipalities, as Linda Sayed and Maya Mikdashi also illustrate in this volume. Lebanon's sectarian political structure would coalesce over the course of the Mandate period and would be further entrenched with the National Pact in 1943, which designated specific political leadership positions for each sect for the postindependence period.

In contrast to this sectarian state structure, at the societal and individual levels sectarian obligations and affiliations were far more muddy, informal, unstructured, and pragmatic—and thus appear less consistently applied. Yet where some see inconsistency, we need to instead see a strategy for living. The analytical concept of "communities of knowledge" reflects the archival rereading underlying this chapter, a rereading that reveals a distinct phenomenon whereby within the domain of private schools, even those that were established to serve a specific sect, people were working *across* communal lines—often in response to the changing needs of students themselves. Rereading the French archives in particular also reveals that students and teachers transferred *between* allegedly different "types" of schools which nonetheless, for example, often used the same history and geography textbooks—which, in other words, taught the same narrative of Lebanon's history and political borders. Ultimately, this rereading compels us to complicate discursive and ideological dichotomies of "secular" and "religious," "Orthodox" or "Sunni" (or any other two sects)—recycled oppositions that buttressed much of educational and institutional discourse during this period, and would animate much of the scholarship on Lebanon.

Education in the Grey Spaces: The Interwar Educational Landscape

In 1920, the French Haut Commissariat established the Service de l'instruction publique (SIP),[7] the Mandate's largest administrative institution for both Syria and Lebanon. Its mission was to oversee all facets of educational policy: school openings and closures, teacher training and hiring, enrollments, school construction, sanitation and hygiene, and curriculum development. Above all, it was to ensure that the French language was being taught in every school, whether public or private, in the Mandate territories. The SIP had various branches for each of the administrative entities in Syria and Lebanon: Greater Lebanon (Grand Liban), and Damascus, Aleppo, Jabal Druze, and the ʿAlawi state in Mandate Syria. The branch in Beirut served as the "headquarters," coordinating the activities of all other branches, highlighting both the mandate's particular preoccupation with education in the capital city and its efforts at centralization.

According to the terms set forth by the League of Nations, mandatory powers were responsible for developing public education, which they also termed *education officiel*.[8] The French Mandate inherited a rather mottled educational landscape in Lebanon. It comprised, first, a previously functioning system of Ottoman public schools, which became the foundation of the new system of public elementary education in Mandate Lebanon.[9] Secondly, the educational landscape included a wide array of foreign missionary schools (American, British, Scottish, Russian, German, Italian, and Swiss), plus a rather extensive network of French schools, both parochial and *laïque*.[10] The latter, in addition to private French religious schools and the public schools, formed part of the network of educational institutions wholly subsidized by the SIP; their existence was contingent on adherence to a Mandate-imposed curriculum. Lastly, this educational landscape also included a third some-what distinctive type of school, neither formerly Ottoman nor religiously framed, which thus often fell outside the funding structure of the Mandate. Perhaps the most well-known of these was *al-madrasa al-wataniyya* (the Na-tional School), founded by *nahda* writer and intellectual Butrus al-Bustani in Beirut in 1863 as a more secular, culturally Arab alternative to both the Ottoman state schools and missionary institutions.[11] By the Mandate era, this genre of school would include the Ahliyya National School for Girls, and the Maqasid Islamic Benevolent Society, among others. I return to these schools below.

Historiographies of education and nation-state building, for places as varied as Algeria, Egypt, India, Indochina, Iran, Kuwait, and Turkey, have illustrated the public and official perception of the centrality of a uniform system of *public* education as both prerequisite for and harbinger of the forg-ing and dissemination of a particular colonial or national ideology.[12] In Leb-anon, however, contrary to the Mandate's purported goal of establishing a unified system of public education as a pillar of nation and state building, the SIP pursued a bifurcated policy vis-à-vis education. Per a clause in what would become the 1922 draft of the constitution, the SIP effectively allowed different religious communities to open their own schools.[13] This was the Mandate's concession to demands arising from those communities (those pedagogical constituencies), as well as a postwar cost-saving measure. Whereas the public schools were brought under the auspices of the SIP's more or less unified cur-riculum and were regularly subject to school inspections, the private schools were largely left to their own curricular devices.

Beginning in 1924, this curricular autonomy would be offered to nonreli-gious private schools, on the condition that a minimum number of hours of French were taught each week. It was through these French language classes that the long arm of the Mandate reached into the private educational domain. In the tight postwar financial circumstances, the SIP capitalized on the fact that many of these schools were in dire need of funds; it tied the granting of subventions and emergency aid (*sécours*) to the installation of at least one French-language teacher in those schools that did not fall under its direct curricular authority.[14] Here, it is important to note that the French Mandate never allotted sufficient funds to allow for the possibility of a fully functioning public school system. By 1938 the Mandate had opened just 177 public schools in the entire territory of Lebanon, educating 18,000 students, in contrast to 1,180 private schools that enrolled 76,196 students.[15]

For the Mandate period, then, what were the implications for Lebanon, whose public school system was overwhelmingly eclipsed by private schools? Historiography on education in interwar Lebanon paints a pedagogical landscape that adapts and reinforces what some scholars have labeled the mosaic paradigm. Individual studies on education generally examine only one piece of the mosaic: *either* American Protestant *or* French—largely in its Catholic or *laïque* iterations—*or* Islamic education, for example. This historical analysis presumes discrete categories or "systems" of education or schooling, and has reinforced the narrative of extant predetermined, fixed communities. In so doing, historiography has often been complicit in reinforcing the notion that French, American, and modern Islamic education were autonomous, impermeable realms linked only or primarily to respective metropoles or homelands rather than to other educational spaces functioning within the same political-cultural landscape. The presumptions about pedagogical constituencies whose boundaries comported with those of the political sectarian system embed a further presumption about some fundamental incommensurability between these "spheres" of Western and Arab knowledge and education—and an ontological and epistemological incompatibility.

This chapter departs from that historiography by examining allegedly different "types" of schools *together* as part of the same colonial-administrative, political-cultural landscape. It foregrounds schools, rather than the state, in the analytical frame that then renders a different picture of the processes of nation and citizenship making. It exposes the ways in which the process of forming new communities of knowledge in schools is inextricable from the co-constitution of what are largely assumed to be different knowledge traditions (French, American, or Arabo-Islamic). Underpinning that are the practical and strategic decisions that families made around school choice and the value with which they vested education. These decisions were just as often *not* in alignment with shifting sectarian affiliations as they were informed by such allegiances. At its core, this chapter asks: Is there room for a narrative that acknowledges that sectarian communal affiliation often played little to no part in people's everyday lives and educational choices? How would allowing for that possibility change how scholars research and write about Lebanon?

School as Community of Knowledge

When researchers delve into school archives, oral histories, and official Mandate records, we see how individuals—administrators, teachers, students, and parents—negotiated practices of inclusion and exclusion, manipulated tensions and alliances, in order to create pedagogical spaces for new communities based not solely on religion or sect, but also on socioeconomic strata, political ideology, or cultural or linguistic affinity. In so doing, this helped make these schools *themselves* into new communities, responding to changing needs on the ground—needs that blurred and challenged the boundaries between communities that were conceived of as bounded confessional entities.

What does the process of creating these new communities of knowledge look like? The French Mandate's policy of allowing a proliferation of private schools not tied to a standardized curriculum meant the establishment of an increasing number of schools whose founders *perceived*—and were responding to—communal demands for education. The contours of those demands often lay along political leanings, or in line with the new cultural or social capital of language. These new communities often included people of various backgrounds—whether familial, religious, socioeconomic, or even regional (villages and towns).[16] Whatever homogenizing aims administrators and education officials might have had in setting up new schools for pedagogical constituencies based on religion or sect, intracommunal differences would invariably be legible on the ground, in the corridors, in classrooms, and in assembly halls.

Two schools offer examples of directions in which people took their schooling and, by extension, the role they perceived education and sect to have in notions of national belonging. While the schools are neither representative nor exceptional, they do offer us an important way of rereading Lebanese history that cuts against the grain of received wisdom about sectarian and metropolitan differences in the domain of education.

The Ahliyya National School for Girls (*al-madrasa al-ahliyya li al-banat*) was founded by Mary Kassab, who wished to educate the daughters of Beirut's mostly middle- and upper-middle-class Greek Orthodox and Sunni families.

Kassab had been herself educated in British Syrian mission schools, and began the Ahliyya school in her living room in 1906 before managing to establish it in a separate building in 1916.[17] In its 1920–21 annual report, Ahliyya was touted as a "*non-sectarian* institution [whose] students could grow with integrity, awareness, and independence of thought, which is what their humanity is based on and what their nation needs."[18] The fact that this annual report was included in the official French Mandate archive says much about the degree to which the Mandate authorities took notice of this institution from its inception. Ahliyya quickly attracted students whose families were interested in a modern nonsectarian education with solid Arabic-language training, all of which comprised the parameters of a new national educational framework. Indeed, the school's cultural politics were rooted in the idea of a Lebanon with an Arabo-Islamic cultural history—one that in its early decades did not exclude a larger-umbrella Syrian identity. Despite having initially been established to specifically meet what Kassab perceived as the demands of Beirut's upper-class Greek Orthodox and Sunni communities, through its curriculum Ahliyya ended up producing a different community of knowledge, one that straddled a nascent sense of "Lebaneseness" with one we might construe today as proto-pan-Arab. It effectively attracted families with similar political bents and goals, from different religions, sects, and, later, nationalities. These families chose Ahliyya explicitly because they wanted their daughters educated in a particular setting, to help shape a new communal space of knowledge and politics. Particularly for Widad Makdisi Cortas, who took the helm of Ahliyya in 1937, an Ahliyya education meant not just the essentials of reading, writing, and arithmetic, but the forging of an awareness of one's position as a female citizen within a national framework, and more broadly with an awareness of that position in a postwar regional order.

As part of the knowledge production and dissemination within the school's walls, the teaching of history was a singular domain in which much of this played out. Given the lack of an official history textbook for Syria and Lebanon during this period, Ahliyya's Arabic teachers were tasked with teaching a history comprising lessons in Arabic philosophy, science, literature, and grammar.[19] This was complemented by excursions. Ahliyya girls were taken by their headmistress on road trips through the new territory of Lebanon.[20] They crossed political borders to visit Haifa, Baghdad, and Cairo (where some would recall getting to hear a young Umm Kulthum perform).[21] These trips were part of an expressed vision for allowing students to get to know their new country in all its multicommunalism, as well as for reminding them that they were part of an Arab world—one whose lessons and delights were still accessible even while territorial boundaries slowly hardened, and documents like passports increasingly were required to traverse them. Nationalist and anticolonial sentiments found space to flourish in Ahliyya's school corridors and assembly hall. The principal and teachers would encourage—sometimes subtly, sometimes not—expressions of disobedience against the French teachers who had been imposed on them (albeit not so easily) by the SIP authorities.[22] These strategies of resistance could take the form of refusal to alter lesson plans, using "aggressive tones," and viewing French-language teaching as "propaganda."

The school's staunch anticolonial bent, folded into its self-declared nonsectarian approach to nation making, provided a model for students to cohere into a community of knowledge. After Widad Cortas became headmistress, the school added a boarding house, at which point girls from other Arab countries were sent to study at Ahliyya. Diplomats and other foreign nationals also enrolled their daughters there, wishing them to be educated in a nonreligious, nonsectarian atmosphere while also gaining Arabic language skills.[23] Throughout the Mandate period, Ahliyya counted dozens of boarders from neighboring Palestine as well as Egypt, Iraq, Syria, and Tunisia.[24] The school furthermore managed to maintain its reputation as an avowedly nationalist and pan-Arabist institution well after independence—so much so that Pierre Gemayyel, founder of the Maronite Phalangist (*kata'eb*) Party, would later opt to transfer his daughter Arzeh from the Catholic school run by nuns, in which she had been enrolled, and place her in Ahliyya.[25] At first glance this may seem an astonishing development, considering the Phalange's well-established position regarding Lebanon as a Christian, non-Arab state. However, it speaks incontrovertibly to the strategic inconsistency of living sectarianism against the more rigid ideological framework of the state—even among those most responsible for its maintenance at that state level.

Ahliyya also counted among its graduates dozens of Palestinian students who had found an alternative to the foreign schools as conditions worsened next door. In fact, Ahliyya's records show that it was fairly common for Palestinian students who had attended French Catholic schools, like the Dames de Zion in Jerusalem, to be sent after 1948 to Beirut to attend Ahliyya, because their mothers or aunts had been Ahliyya graduates.[26] Pre–World War II familial, economic, and intellectual networks boosted Ahliyya's profile as a generative educational space in which not just new Lebanese but also Palestinians could share anticolonial aspirations nourished by a common sense of Arabness that transcended religion or sect. Ahliyya was one of several schools whose first generation of students came from families who had constituted the last Ottoman-era cosmopolitan generation. Those networks endured, and circumscribed putative postwar borders to continue linking urban bourgeoisie and elites between places like Haifa, Jerusalem, Beirut, Damascus, Aleppo, Cairo, and Alexandria.

The community of knowledge that Ahliyya produced would thus include students from various socioeconomic, geographic, and sect backgrounds in Lebanon and around the region. Their families searched for an educational space that would offer a particular political bent. In so doing, they blurred confession, class, and communal boundaries. Upon graduation, this community of knowledge formed around particular ideas: a Lebanon that was entitled to be independent and yet had been part of a larger former Ottoman province of Syria, and which continued to have common cultural ties with the "co-colony." Graduates carried with them a cultural identity rooted in an Arabic language that held significant cultural, political, and intellectual capital, and an intellectual inheritance in part comprising an Islamic cultural legacy as well as the Anglo-American mission teachings to which both Kassab and Cortas had been privy as students. In operating outside the SIP, Ahliyya merged two supposedly incongruous knowledge traditions. Rereading the archives to get at moments of transgression and see how the SIP was often marginalized demonstrates that, while alignment with religion or sect could offer educational opportunities, it would be eclipsed by matters of class, culture, and geography.

But what about schools that already were seemingly nestled in one or another sectarian community? As I have indicated, the demand for such constituency-serving schools was one reason why the Mandate charter of 1922 enacted the clause allowing for private school autonomy. The school records of the Maqasid Islamic Benevolent Society (*jam'iyyat al-maqasid al-khayriyya al-islamiyya*) gives us a glimpse into the situation there. Founded in 1878 by 'Abdel Qadir al-Qabbani, a Damascene notable, and a number of other Sunni Muslim Beiruti notables, the Maqasid was originally part of an Ottoman network of schools before it ran afoul of Ottoman governor Hamdi Pasha, who shut it down.[27] The Maqasid Society reopened its schools at war's end in 1918, intent on serving Beirut's Sunni bourgeoisie in a new postwar Mandate reality with "proper religious and national education [*tarbiya diniyya wa tarbiya wataniyya sahiha*]".[28] For the next several decades, it established boys', girls', and eventually coeducational schools, and also oversaw orphanages, poorhouses, homes for the elderly, clinics, hospitals, asylums, cemeteries, and a publishing house.[29]

The enrollment records and annual reports for the Maqasid illustrate the opportunities that aligning with sect and community offered, and of which Sunni families availed themselves, choosing them over French alternatives. Yet they also reveal communal boundary transcendence within schools. The Maqasid, like other schools in the area, recorded the confessional identity of each entering student. Enrollment records also show that throughout this period, close to 25 percent of enrolled students at the Maqasid were neither Sunni nor even necessarily Muslim.[30] Determining or deducing *why* students were motivated to enroll there is harder to piece together from the archival records. But clearly, given the range of religious backgrounds of students noted—Shi'a, Druze, Greek Orthodox—the Maqasid's ostensibly Sunni Muslim affiliation and curriculum were not deterrents to confessional diversity within the student body.[31] This is likely due to a number of reasons. The Maqasid's extensive network of boys' and girls' schools reached into many of Beirut's neighborhoods, which meant that there was often a school within a short distance of much of the city's growing population. The lack of available boarding houses meant that parents within Maqasid's constituency would have sent their children to schools close to home. Critically, the Maqasid derived most of its income from its *awqaf* and thus was able to maintain more autonomy from the Mandate SIP than other schools: in fact, its budget was at one point ten times that of the Mandate's entire education budget.[32] The Maqasid was thus able to maintain tuition-free elementary and middle schools (*ibtida'i* and *i'adi*) that were better staffed and better funded than other comparable schools. These were key considerations and attractions at a time when the scarcity of public schools meant they were overcrowded, not easily accessible, and underfunded, while comparable American- and French-run private schools charged relatively hefty fees. All of this suggests that while sectarian community affiliation may have been increasingly institutionalized at a state and colonial/national level, families opted out or in depending on circumstance, their children's best interest, and available resources. Sect, therefore, often ceased to matter in light of other more pressing considerations.

What is also important to consider is the knowledge that was produced and circulated in the Maqasid network of schools. The history and geography books and curricula emphasized that Lebanon shared an historical, cultural, and political legacy and affinity with Syria—with Syria being a core part of the region's Arabo-Islamic and Ottoman heritage. To address the lack of history textbooks for students, two teachers at the Maqasid, Mustapha Farroukh and Zaki Naqqash, wrote and published their own textbook for both primary and secondary levels: the two-volume *Tarikh Suriya wa Lubnan al-Musawwar*.[33] These books would also eventually be used in other schools in Lebanon, including Ahliyya. The Maqasid annual reports and internal correspondence reveal that the board, at least, was well aware of the appeal that the Maqasid schools had for families across confessional lines. These were families who sought a modern education that was affordable, couched within a familiar framework that was more culturally and historically rather than doctrinally Islamic, in an institution that took a public stand against French colonial rule. At the same time, the Maqasid Society annual reports also clearly show the intention to educate and expand a Beiruti Sunni Muslim bourgeoisie that could compete both intellectually and practically with graduates of the French schools, who were often favored by French authorities and whose postgraduate futures appeared brighter. Yet the community of knowledge created through the Maqasid curricula crossed confessional lines, and did so in ways that also fostered social and economic mobility for graduates of many different sects. It was an upward mobility that people believed a modern Arabo-Islamic education should offer as part of establishing the new nation-state.

The backgrounds of the Lebanese individuals who established or oversaw schools like Ahliyya and Maqasid were vital in the formation of communities of knowledge. Ahliyya's founder, Mary Kassab, and her successor, Widad Makdisi Cortas, had been products of British and American Protestant schools, but Cortas had been raised in a family of Arab nationalists steeped in the cultural politics of the *nahda*.[34] The board of the Maqasid Society comprised members of Beirut's Sunni urban bourgeoisie who were in no way claiming, as Ahliyya did, "nondenominational" education. According to the historiography, therefore, these two schools shouldn't have anything in common. And yet they do, in various fundamental if not unexpected ways, in the processes of forging national historical imaginings. The socioeconomic networks between private schools crossed boundaries of religion and sect. Just to give two examples, one of the Maqasid's most notable teachers was Julia Tu'ma, who hailed from a Christian family and was founder and editor of the women's magazine *Al-Mar'a al-Jadida*. She met and married Badr Di-mashqiyya, a Muslim who had been a member of the Beirut municipality and later also served on the board of Ahliyya with Kassab. The Dimashqiyyas' son, Nadim, would later serve on Ahliyya's board, under Cortas.[35] 'Umar Da'uq, a political pillar of Beirut's Sunni political community and a leading board member of the Maqasid, also served on Ahliyya's board of consultants and directors.[36] Equally significantly, there was a convergence of the two schools' perspectives on what constituted Lebanon's history and educational future. Da'uq and Cortas would form the Secondary School Principals' Association, and in the years leading up to and following independence, they met regularly enough to cause grumbling in the SIP.[37]

The categories of "Islamic" versus "secular" education that historiography on education in Lebanon has presented and maintained as being so incompat-ible, even impermeable, are further disrupted when we closely examine school enrollment records. Here, French archival documents, local histories, and oral narratives intersect in suggesting people's determinations on where to send their children to school. Parents sacrificed a lot to ensure their children re-ceived at the very least a basic education, enduring privations in the hopes of some incremental if not dramatic betterment. Their decisions often cen-tered around this goal, and evinced less concern with the allegedly "unique" confessional-communal characteristics reflected by a given school.

One way these decisions manifest, clearly and consistently throughout the Mandate, is in the fact that students transferred between the ostensibly differ-ent "types" of schools that were as seemingly opposed as the Islamic Maqasid and the French Collège Protestant; Ahliyya and the Soeurs de la charité; the Maronite al-Hikma school (La Sagesse) and the missionary American School for Boys. The figures are uneven, to be sure.[38] But the fact that it was not at all uncommon to transfer across the supposedly hard and fast boundaries of language or "cultural identity" speaks volumes about the actual porosity of these sect/school communities, and significantly complicates the conven-tional narrative that there existed sectarian ecosystems of knowledge. School memos, official correspondence, and oral histories reveal, for example, that students transferred for a whole plethora of reasons that often had nothing to do with whether a school taught in French, English or Arabic, or whether it was identified as, say, *laïque*, Islamic, or Maronite.[39] Instead, parents chose their children's schools for reasons as practical and commonplace as the ones for which they continue to make those choices every day: proximity to the home or family business, school fees and affordability, siblings attending the same school, formative encounters with teachers or principals. Through this history we see how the heterogeneity of the population was in flux, where one node of affiliation or identity was often highlighted or eclipsed by another depending on circumstances. It also suggests how people, even under newly hardening sectarian affiliations at the state level, opted to live their sect in ways that highlighted the distinctly nonsectarian impetus behind choices they selectively and strategically made.

Official Mandate records similarly reveal how the SIP transferred teachers between putatively "different" schools. Starting in the mid-1920s, the SIP began transferring the French teachers it had "planted" as part of conditions for subventions, as mentioned above. The permits the SIP had granted to individuals to start their own schools exceeded and outpaced the available French teachers. Since the new schools had to have French teachers on staff in order to officially be licensed, these teachers were often spending months at a time in one school before returning to their original post. These teacher transfers were part of a larger regional trend: around this time, a shortage of teachers for schools in the new states led to Lebanese, Palestinian, and Syrian teachers traveling around the Arab world.[40] By the early 1930s the shortage of instructors grew more severe, compounded by the deteriorating economy. More teachers who spoke French and taught a range of topics from science, literature, and math to philosophy ended up transferring between schools like the Maqasid, Soeurs de la charité, the French Collège Protestant, and Ahliyya. As an example, one Mlle Chabanne was transferred from Ahliyya in 1931. She reappears by 1935 at the Collège Protestant school for girls, and then reappears later that year at Ahliyya.[41] In both places she taught the same subject matter. Scholarship on education in Lebanon would have us believe that Collège Protestant and Ahliyya, inhabiting separate French and Lebanese educational "spheres," had mutually exclusive approaches to knowledge production and dissemination among their students. Yet particularly in the absence of a standard curriculum, if teachers were responsible for imparting lessons in history, geography, and language but were being transferred between different types of schools, then what does that imply about these allegedly fixed sectarian boundaries and their accompanying knowledge traditions?

Within the context of the transferring between schools that was occurring, however, one boundary remained constant: that of socioeconomic status. Families would transfer children between schools within socioeconomic lines, unless financial circumstances changed. For example, one Protestant family, who decided to transfer their children after a negative encounter with a teacher, abandoned their long tradition of attending French Jesuit schools and opted for the American school that was a tramway ride away, despite there being a Protestant school nearer home. They made this choice because the American school was of the same socioeconomic background.[42] Attending to these archival records in such a way as to *listen* to why people often crossed sect and confessional community lines also tells us how doing so gave rise to a larger community of knowledge that was simultaneously shaping an educated modern middle class of newly minted Lebanese citizens. This is a counter-narrative to how Lebanon continues to be represented today—with sect and confession as immutable spheres.

What does the phenomenon of teacher and student transfers mean for putatively hard and fast categories between "types" of schools, or "types of education"? The prism of education refracts the specious boundaries that continue to be held up, as the divisions of types of education more often than not incorporate French, American, Lebanese, and myriad other ideas of either secular or religious influence all at once, in varying degrees. Reexamining the official French archive alongside the microhistories of certain schools—found in their annual reports, student records, oral histories, and curricula—illustrates that permeability in a way that has been too often obscured.

Rewriting This Story

Many scholars and education policy makers often ruefully talk about the Lebanese state having been rendered dysfunctional through the consecration of sectarian communities' links to resources and upward mobility. In this narrative, these communities' access to resources during the Mandate and early independence eras often continued late-Ottoman economic and political networks. As such, it privileges the sectarian framework as a way to understand the history, trajectory, and role of education. And indeed, that is part of the reality that was and is Lebanon.

I am asking us to attend to another part of the story: that ordinary people—in their everyday demands, and the dreams they attached to the purpose of education and the "quest for a better life"[43]—had other ideas of what community could and should look like. These ideas transcended—or at the very least placed within a larger playing field—confessional and sectarian communal affiliations. The narrative of Lebanon is one that has mobilized, and been mobilized by, the notion that sectarian communal affiliations had often been imposed by French colonial and Lebanese government officials, rather than being actively and willingly chosen or rejected by people for strategic ends. It is that active choice, however, that rereading the archive tells us existed and that people regularly exercised. Even with its own desire and ambitions for a homogenized yet divided educational system, the Mandate could not escape circumstances that often necessitated the blurring of the very boundaries it had erected.

In many cases, the choices people made about where to go to school and why circumvented the intentions of the government officials or the school founders, and led to the creation of a "community of knowledge" that blurred the lines between what was conceived as French, Lebanese, or American content of knowledge. These choices were part of the process by which a national society in Lebanon was emerging during the interwar period. Thinking about community via the production of knowledge in schools calls into question the ideologically presumptive separation between multiple parts of a bifurcated system of education.

In a larger sense, this chapter asks scholars to push back against the archive that in the Lebanese context is too often read to confirm, rather than question, ideas about how sectarianism manifests and is lived. What if scholars approach these archives differently, to listen for and actually *hear* other voices, experiences, and narratives? If we start to frame things differently, forgoing the explanatory power of the prefabricated pedagogical constituency in favor of supple communities of knowledge, what could we find? If we open Lebanon up past the usual tired tropes, would that allow for new research possibilities for Lebanese history, and for the field of Middle East history more generally?

Approaching Lebanese history in this way, it must be said, is not to deny that community affiliation based on sect or religion existed or mattered as a quotidian reality. But by researching and analyzing the details of the educational landscape—including who attended what school and why, in addition to what was taught and learned—we see that these boundaries were often fluid, porous, permeable, and in flux, responding to particular needs and circumstances that lay well outside any ingrained ideological impetus. This is important for addressing assumptions of scholarship as well as those of present-day notions of community.

Thinking about how knowledge and community constitute one another allows us to reconsider the epistemological infrastructures of the nation-state.

The real question is: Can we make room for this part of the story in the Lebanese context? Can we acknowledge that sectarian affiliation often seemed to play no part at the local everyday level *alongside* a national landscape in which, over the course of the Mandate period, political sectarianism hardened? The coexistence—indeed, coconstitution—of those two narratives is an essential rewriting of this period of Lebanese history, and education is a vital lens through which to rewrite it. Doing so, expanding the archive and repositioning the narrative, allows us to think about all the possible paths and futures that existed over the course of the Mandate period. Thus, it allows us to more seriously consider that what followed was not in fact inevitable.

NEGOTIATING CITIZENSHIP
Shi'i Families and the Ja'fari Shari'a Courts

LINDA SAYED

ON NOVEMBER 18, 1937, Fatima, an Iranian, appeared before the Ja'fari shari'a court in Beirut demanding that her husband, 'Abbas, an Iraqi, provide her with her rightful alimony (*nafaqa*) and pay her remaining dowry.[1] According to the records, the couple had been married in the Ja'fari shari'a court in Beirut, but had then moved to Baghdad, where 'Abbas continued to reside. Fatima had returned to Beirut, recently divorced and with the aims of recovering the monies owed to her by legal right of marriage and divorce in the Ja'fari shari'a court. On the day of the court hearing, 'Abbas did not physically appear, instead sending a letter proclaiming that the appropriate Baghdadi shari'a court had already ruled against Fatima on this matter, and that she should return to him as his wife. In his letter, 'Abbas dismissed the jurisdiction of the Ja'fari court of Beirut and demanded that Fatima return to Baghdad. At Fatima's request, the hearing in Beirut continued with an absentee judgment, ruling in favor of Fatima and her petitioned expenses. The court noted that 'Abbas could appeal this decision if he could bring proof that Fatima had disobeyed him. The court did not address the issue of nationality or residence, Iraqi or Lebanese, and did not elaborate as to why it claimed jurisdiction over this case. However, by sanctioning the Ja'fari shari'a court as an adherent to the Ja'fari *madhhab*, a Shi'i legal school of Islamic jurisprudence, and living in Lebanon at the time, Fatima believed that the shari'a court in Beirut would rule in her favor and grant her the requested alimony.[2] Cases like Fatima's in which citizenship or residence was outside the scope of the courts, were not an anomaly during the French Mandate period.

With this territorial reallocation, a significant number of Shiʻi Muslims found themselves incorporated into the newly formed Lebanese nation-state and a distinct system of political citizenship. With the designation of an officially recognized sect, Shiʻi Muslims in Greater Lebanon were granted distinct shariʻa courts to litigate civil and personal disputes among the population by 1926.[3] How did the creation of these courts under the French Mandate rule of Lebanon complicate and reinforce the legal, political, and national categories of citizenship as practiced by individuals like Fatima who came before the court? Indeed, why would an Iranian national who is married to an Iraqi come before the Jaʻfari shariʻa court in Beirut in 1937? How did she end up in this court, and what purpose did it serve her? More importantly, how did her petitioning before the court reflect a particular notion of subjectivity that questioned national, sectarian, and religious boundaries and gender norms?

Based on archival research conducted at the *sijillat* (court archives) of the Jaʻfari shariʻa courts on matters of marriage and divorce,[4] I demonstrate how cases like Fatima's and their various participants went beyond the regulatory practices of the courts by negotiating and challenging legal categories of Shiʻi sectarian and national belonging. From the thousands of cases examined in the Beirut, Sidon, Tyre, Baʻalbek, Marjaʻyun, and Bint Jbeil Jaʻfari shariʻa courts, cases wherein the nationality, residence, or sectarian identity of litigants was contentious frequently appeared in the records during the Mandate period. From the hundreds of cases of this sort that will be referenced in this chapter, I examine in detail five particular cases that demonstrate the flexibility of identity markers during the Mandate period. While cases like Fatima's may appear merely as personal status matters of everyday private life, analysis reveals that they are significantly intertwined in practices of politics, citizenry, women's agency, mobility, transnationalism, and identity formation in the context of Mandate Lebanon.[5] Through an examination of several cases, this chapter investigates the ways that Shiʻi Muslims enacted, imagined, and challenged the sectarian identities that were set up as legal and political categories of French colonial rule. In making legal claims, Shiʻi individuals—and women in particular—inserted their subjectivity in ways that informed not only familial norms and gender roles but broad notions of political belonging. This chapter highlights how men and women pushed against patriarchal structures, such as those embedded in the institution of shariʻa law, that became intertwined in the Lebanese state-building enterprise and the practice of sectarianism.[6] The complexity of these cases also reveals how litigants used the Ja'fari shari'a courts to delegitimize or legitimize another shari'a court in Lebanon, or in a different nation-state, for citizens outside of the Lebanese political and juridical system. Such engagements expose the subjective and changing meaning attributed to the courts and their authority by the individuals who came before them to dispute familial and marital affairs. This chapter reveals how the domain of the family as seen in the exchanges of the Ja'fari shari'a courts became a space where national, sectarian, social, and gender identities were practiced and contested. It also shows that individuals used the fluidity and contradictory nature of these institutional sites to make legal and political claims. The Ja'fari shari'a courts became a place of strategic practices that enacted, challenged, and reproduced shared notions of citizenry, sectarianism, national, and gendered norms.

Colonial Legacies: The Formation of the Ja'fari Shari'a Court

The formation of the modern Lebanese nation-state in 1920 and its official independence in 1943 were founded on politicized sectarianism as the only form of governance and presumed egalitarianism between individual citizens and recognized sectarian groups. Lebanese citizenship became contingent on sectarian identification. According to the Lebanese state structure, citizens were tied to sectarian categories of identification—designated by citizenship cards, voting rights, and access to social services—that governed both personal and private practices of citizenship in the nation-state. In many ways, sectarian identification converged with personal status, or *madhhab*, whereby the state recognized one official personal status per sect.[7] However, analysis of cases from the Ja'fari shari'a courts demonstrates that this conflation generated much ambiguity and pushback over the meaning of *madhhab* and sect. For Shi'i Muslims living in what would become the Republic of Lebanon in 1943, these administrative reforms imposed by the French Mandate became the first and only form of legitimate and legal representation for the group.[8] Under the Ottoman Empire, Shi'i Muslims were not recognized as a separate group with distinct religious rights or legal status; followers of the Ja'fari *madhhab* had to adhere to Hanafi Sunni courts for official legal matters and jurisprudence.[9] The expansion of sectarian rights under the French Mandate laid the foundation for Shi'i citizens in the postcolonial state, which entailed the formation of Ja'fari shari'a courts.

On January 27, 1926, shortly after the constitution was promulgated, the French high commissioner decreed that the Shi'a constituted "an independent religious community," and that matters of personal status were to be judged "according to the principles of the rite known by the name of the Ja'fari."[10] Article 3 of the decree specified the creation of a Shi'i religious court of cassation, and the hiring of Shi'i *qadis* (judges) to administer this newly founded legal institution. The common colonial practice of designating shari'a law into a separate subdivision of the centralizing state integrated it into the officializing and written documentation procedures of the nation-state.[11] The designation of personal status law and courts contributed to a system of classification based on sectarianism in the case of Lebanon.[12] Separate systems for personal status law contributed in many ways to the segregation of the local population through the same system that sought to give them legal recognition.[13] The personal status courts allowed only "recognized" communities to administer their legal affairs, and defined a place for "religion" to make its public appearance within the state.[14] Religion took on a public presence in an otherwise "secular" nation-state by delineating a sectarian system of political recognition reinforced by personal status courts presiding over marital affairs. Under these new constraints, the political integration of Shi'i Muslims in the Lebanese state was established through sectarian lines, as the imagined nation envisioned a Lebanese Shi'i collective.

Following the formal recognition of the Ja'fari *madhhab* in 1926, the first Ja'fari shari'a courts to administer Shi'i personal status or family law were established. Based on a two-tiered system, the mandatory state established Ja'fari shari'a courts of the first instance (*al-mahakim al-bida'iyya*, equivalent to the French Cour de première instance) in Sidon, Tyre, Nabatiyya, Marja'yun, and Ba'albek al-Hirmil, with Beirut housing the higher appellate court (*al-mahkamat al-'ulya*).[15] As Max Weiss has argued, this marked the first time that the Shi'a in Jabal 'Amil (South Lebanon), the Beqa' Valley, and Beirut were politically and legally identified as citizens of a collective sectarian entity within the borders of the modern nation-state.[16] Within this context, the Shi'a emerged as a nationalized sect among other Lebanese sects, themselves artifacts of new modern political arrangements that had not existed under Ottoman rule.

As citizens of the Lebanese nation-state were defined by their sectarian affiliation, personal status law became the only means of documenting marriages to ensure citizenship to future children of the nation, since civil courts were not established. More importantly, personal status law came to have no meaning independent of the judicial institutions belonging to the Lebanese nation-state.[17] The law created a legal body in which "categories of practices," as defined by Rogers Brubaker, were shaped by both the state and individuals who came before the law as citizens of the modern nation-state, whether or not they supported the initial formation of the shariʿa courts.[18] As an institution of the state, personal status laws became the prime regulators of conjugal affairs in Lebanon, playing an integral role in people's daily lives and producing the institution of the family as an element in the nation-building process. The Jaʿfari shariʿa courts, as well as the individuals who came before them, were inadvertently forced to draw lines of sectarian and national/territorial identification, in acting as newly established personal status courts. With the establishment of the Lebanese nation-state and subsequent Jaʿfari shariʿa courts, Shiʿi Muslims witnessed the nationalization and sectarianization of *taʾifa* and *madhhab*. However, as these court records reveal, citizens practiced sectarianism in inconsistent ways, sometimes rejecting it and sometimes deploying it strategically, to manage and create meaning in their daily lives. It was in this environment that the nationalization of Shiʿi families proceeded, and in which individuals like Fatima were socialized into sectarian citizenship while also disputing the frameworks under transnational attachments to a broader understanding of the Jaʿfari *madhhab*.[19]

From *Madhhab* to *Taʾifa*: The Jaʿfari *Madhhab* as Territorially Lebanese?

What was significant about the recognition of the Jaʿfari *madhhab* (personal status) by the French authorities was the establishment of personal status courts that defined and legitimized the *madhhab* within a nation-state. This recognition gave and assumed Shiʿi Muslims' communal autonomy as a sect. Citizenship, within the modern nation-state, was based on sectarian affiliation, which in turn was contingent on recognition of the *madhhab*. The understanding was that each sect, or *taʾifa,* should only be affiliated with one religious *madhhab*. However, some sects had not been granted their own authorized religious courts, so many sects used the same *madhhab* or personal status courts. Thus, the Shiʿa were recognized as a separate sect by virtue of being a separate *madhhab*, and through the establishment of the Jaʿfari shariʿa court system.

The official recognition of the Jaʿfari sect and the establishment of Jaʿfari shariʿa courts presumed a sense of Shiʿi sectarian identification and unity within the national political system. The Jaʿfari *madhhab* has been used interchangeably with the term "sect" or *ta'ifa* in the context of the newly established Lebanese nation-state. Nevertheless, the Arabic term *ta'ifa*, which today has come to mean "religious political sect," has a longer history of signifying a class of public notables in the eighteenth and nineteenth century.[20] Even when the term *ta'ifa* was used in reference to the Christian Maronite sect, it alluded specifically to Maronite public notables as a group distinct and separate from the rest of the community. As Maronites came to see themselves as a sect, the meaning was still predominantly class-based and not political. It was during the late nineteenth century, with the establishment of Mutasarrifiyya of Mount Lebanon, that a "culture of sectarianism" developed, as argued by Ussama Makdisi. In many ways then, the term *ta'ifa* is specific to Mount Lebanon, and only later to the modern nation-state of Lebanon. The term *ta'ifa* or sect emerged in a specific time and space, and has become synonymous with the Lebanese nation-state despite the fact that the term itself has been used to refer to a greater transnational sect, as will be shown in the cases discussed below.

In the Lebanese context, *ta'ifa* or sect became intertwined and legally synonymous with *madhhab* or personal status. Currently there are eighteen officially recognized sects in Lebanon, with fifteen legally recognized *madhhabs*.[21] Sects that do not have state-appointed, government-subsidized clerical courts that administer personal status law follow the religious courts closest to them, like the Alawites and Isma'ili. However, the term *madhhab* suggests a transnational community wherein members of the Ja'fari *madhhab*, whether in Iraq, Iran, Syria, or Pakistan, share a common religious understanding, history, legal jurisprudence, doctrines, and authoritative institutions. During the French Mandate period, one of Lebanon's leading *marja' al-taqlid*, a religious scholar with established training to issue Islamic jurisprudence and teachings, was Sayyid 'Abd al-Hussein Sharaf al-Din.[22] However, other *maraji'* existed and circulated their teachings during the same period, such as Shaykh Hussein Mughniyya; Sayyid Muhsin al-Amin, who originally hailed from Jabal 'Amil but resided in Damascus after his studies in Najaf; and the *marja'* Sayyid Abu al-Hasan al-Isfahani in Iraq. With the creation of the Lebanese nation-state, the notion of *al-madhhab al-ja'fari* (the Ja'fari *madhhab*) became bounded by a territorial space limiting it to, and making it synonymous with, the politicized form of *al-ta'ifa al-shi'iyya* (the Shi'i sect). This correlation was further heightened with the creation of institutional personal status courts to be administered under the jurisdiction and guidance of the Ja'fari *madhhab* and its religious scholars.[23]

Despite the politicization of sectarianism endorsed by the nation-state, individuals contested the limitations of such categories. As the cases from the Jaʿfari shariʿa courts during the French Mandate show, people appeared before the Jaʿfari shariʿa courts in Lebanon demanding its intervention, asserting themselves as members of the same *maddhab* even though they were citizens of a different nation-state. Similarities are apparent in the experience of Armenians whose Lebanese sectarian identities were welcomed in the United States even though they did not hold Lebanese citizenship and did not always "come" from Lebanon, as Tsolin Nalbantian's chapter in this volume illustrates. In many court cases appearing during the Mandate period, individuals utilized a broader notion of *madhhab* that contested the national limitations imposed by the Lebanese nation-state while others attempted to tighten that notion. The establishment of the personal status system as the authority legitimizing sectarian affiliation and citizenship slowly led to a *maddhab* becoming confined to the boundaries of the Lebanese nation-state. This, the practices of *madhhab* increasingly came to seem limited. Such limitations made by its institutionalization in the Lebanese state can be clearly seen in the early years of Jaʿfari shariʿa courts, as litigants made demands to expand or redefine understandings of *madhhab* or to counter nationalistic claims.

In the court cases analyzed below, however, we see how the notion of *madhhab* is subjective; it is at times expandable and at times constrictive in its territorial and national definitions. Its meaning and definition are made and remade by the individuals who practiced, shaped, and used the sectarian markers of *taʾifa* and *madhhab* to exhibit, imagine, and contest power in their daily lives. *Madhhab*, as the cases reveal, transcends national borders even though the Jaʿfari shariʿa courts were produced as a Lebanese institution within the nation-state and as a legal representation of the Shiʿa as a sect. Litigants use the Jaʿfari shariʿa courts to push back against the legality of another shariʿa court in a different nation-state, and for citizens outside the Lebanese political and juridical system. These cases reveal these tensions, and the performative nature of notions such as *taʾifa* or *madhhab* as used by the litigants who came before the Jaʿfari shariʿa courts during the French Mandate period.

Contesting National and Territorial Borders: Lebanese or Not?

Muhammad first appeared before the Jaʿfari shariʿa court in Beirut on June 13, 1937, requesting that the judge order his wife, Badiʿa, to return to his authority and place of residence, while at the same time he contested their divorce, which had taken place in the Hanafi shariʿa court in Haifa, Palestine.[24] The court proceedings reveal that both Muhammad and Badiʿa were living in Palestine and had been married in Haifa under the Hanafi shariʿa. A lengthy debate between their legal representatives (*wakils*) ensued, concerning whether the Jaʿfari court had the jurisdiction to review this case. In her testimony, Badiʿa argued that all Islamic religious courts are one, and that no differentiation should be made between Sunni and Shiʿa shariʿa courts. She insisted that the case return to the Haifa courts, where the dissension between the couple had originally taken place. Muhammad's legal representative, on the other hand, contended that his client was Jaʿfari, and that only the Jaʿfari shariʿa court thus had the jurisdiction to rule on the matter. He reiterated the provisions of the French High Commission that gave the Jaʿfari *madhhab* the authority to rule on matters of personal status pertaining to its sect, asserting that each sect must follow its own communal courts.[25] During the case it was revealed that Badiʿa had gone before the Hanafi court and divorced herself after Muhammad had sworn *ṭalaq* (divorce) for the third time during an argument. After a lengthy deliberation, the Jaʿfari court argued that since a woman cannot divorce herself, such a divorce was against the Islamic tenets of the Jaʿfari *madhhab*. Thus it invalidated the ruling of the Hanafi court in Haifa. The court ruled that Badiʿa was still married to Muhammad, and compelled her to return to the marriage.

In her appeal (*iʿtirad*) to the court, Badiʿa raised the fact that she and Muhammad had been living in Haifa for the last eight years, held Palestinian identity cards, and thus were married in the Hanafi court in Haifa. For that reason, Badiʿa argued, she should therefore have the right to divorce there. Accordingly, the first president of the Jaʿfari court, Munir ʿUsayran, confirmed the court's previous ruling on the condition that Muhammad verified that his wife was of the Jaʿfari *madhhab*, and that they were both Palestinian. In his final words, ʿUsayran maintained that this was necessary to determine whether the Jaʿfari court had the authority and jurisdictional power to rule on the case.

On July 17, 1938, nearly a year later, Muhammad returned to the court to affirm that his case against Badiʿa fell within jurisdiction of the Jaʿfari court.[26] He asserted that he and Badiʿa were of the Jaʿfari sect and of Lebanese nationality, hailing from the southern town of ʿAynatha in Jabal ʿAmil.[27] Using the Tyre census files, Muhammad confirmed his Lebanese lineage and Shiʿi allegiance. He demanded that the court validate his marriage, as it fell under the precepts of the Jaʿfari *madhhab* and confirmed his sectarian affiliation as Shi'i. Muhammad's legal representative adamantly argued that only this court could rule on the matter of marital separation, since no Ja'fari judge existed in Haifa. Although Badi'a was not present on the last day of the court proceeding, the presiding judge, Muhammad Yahya Safi al-Din al-Husseini, ruled that a wife should abide by the *madhhab* of her husband. He also added that since their marriage in 1929 had taken place after the 1926 establishment of the Ja'fari personal status court in Lebanon, all affairs relating to this case had to be handled only by this court and no other. In his final words, the presiding judge reasserted the institutional authority and jurisdiction that the Ja'fari court held on matters pertaining to Lebanese Shi'a.

The case between Muhammad and Badi'a blends issues of nationality, citizenship, sectarianism, and *madhhab* in that it highlights the gendered aspects of identity formation and categories of national belonging embedded in the institution of the Ja'fari shari'a court.[28] The case also highlights how citizenship and nationality are themselves inextricable from gender and sex as articulated by Maya Mikdashi's notion of sextarianism.[29] Each category is enacting a different understanding of shared identity and citizenry that conflicts with the other. The different meanings are shaped by the imaginative and contradictory ways people practice sectarianism in their lived experiences. Individuals used varying strategies to maximize their chances of supporting their claims. In this case, Muhammad and Badi'a made contradictory claims on the basis of sectarian and national markers before the Ja'fari court, with Badi'a challenging its authority and legal jurisdiction by calling upon oppositional categories and technologies of belonging to the nation-state to question its authority.

On the one hand, the case reveals that understandings of citizenship, place, religious affiliation, and sectarian identifiers were not given or assumed, as is often presumed by state institutions in the case of Lebanon, but rather were subjectively practiced by individuals who made claims to them at a particular moment and time.[30] This subjectivity was shaped by gender and its relationship to the patriarchal institution of the personal status courts that became an embodiment of the Lebanese nation-state during the Mandate period. Women such as Badi'a strategically sought to place their marriage within the Hanafi court, which ultimately forced them to make contradictory claims on the basis of sectarian and national markers. There was an attempt to use the fluidity of these markers, whether national or sectarian or both, to one's advantage, given the male-dominated features of legal stipulation about divorce as enshrined in codified personal status law, which continued to be male patriarchal domains. Badiʿa, aware that the Hanafi court might be more favorable in matters of granting a divorce or obtaining child custody, sought its authority over that of the Jaʿfari courts.[31] Muhammad first appeared in court to sanction the authoritative power of the Jaʿfari court to rule in his favor on the basis of his *madhhab*, while Badiʿa attempted to dismiss the authority of the Jaʿfari court on the grounds that her nationality, or *jinsiyya*, was Palestinian, due to the fact that she resided there and had done so for years. Both *madhhab* and *jinsiyya* came to have new meaning under the Mandate authority and the formation of the Lebanese nation-state that was articulated differently. Written within this ostensibly small, private case of marriage law, the contours of modern sovereignty began to emerge in high relief: The question about legal claims to divorce revealed core debates about what it meant to be a citizen of the Lebanese nation-state, and about how different gendered individuals understood that citizenship, thus reflecting the unfolding process of sectarianization. The issue of citizenship and of which nation-state has claims over citizen rights, along with the documents used, reveals the porosity of the new borders and national identities, and the contested notions of belonging to the nation as a member of an officially designated sect.[32]

For both Muhammad and Badiʿa, everyday practices of sectarian identity were evident in the contrasting claims made in the name of the nation. The Hanafi court in Haifa had already granted the divorce to Badiʿa, and for this reason she wanted to discredit the intervention of the Jaʿfari court in Lebanon summoned by Muhammad. The marriage had taken place in 1929, after the establishment of the Jaʿfari courts in 1926, and Badiʿa and Muhammad had asked the Hanafi court in Haifa to legalize their marriage—an indication of their residence and their endorsement of the court, which had been the site of both their 1929 marriage and their 1937 divorce. However, Muhammad, who was well aware of the French constitutional decree recognizing the Jaʿfari *madhhab* as the legalized personal status of the Shiʿi *taʾifa*, used this in his favor to call upon the court's authority to intervene. Muhammad summoned the Lebanese nation-state through the institutional power bestowed on the Jaʿfari shariʿa courts in order to refute the power of the Hanafi courts in Haifa. It is clear that he realized the Jaʿfari court would rule in his favor on the basis of *madhhab* and nationality, whereby a difference in rulings on verbal divorce existed between Jaʿfari and Hanafi jurisprudence.[33] As seen in this case, the Jaʿfari court requested that Muhammad produce evidence of both their *madhhab* and their nationality. This request for proof legitimized the court's authority over the trial, and enabled it to use its state-authorized power to overrule and reverse the divorce administered in the Haifa Hanafi court by asserting that Muhammad and Badiʿa were not only Jaʿfari but also Lebanese.

Though Badiʿa and her legal representatives asserted that there should be no distinctions between Sunni Hanafi and Shiʿi Jaʿfari courts, the court still demanded the replication of proof of the couple's nationality and *madhhab* on Muhammad's demand, highlighting not only the Jaʿfari shariʿa court's claims to authority via the state, but also the extent to which patriarchy had been institutionalized. Written documentation of national identity based on geographical and ancestral lines through patronal lineage and sectarian lines was requested to establish legitimacy and jurisdiction, further indicating the gender implications in the conflicting demands made by Muhammad and Badiʿa.[34] In Lebanon, political representation and citizenship in the nation-state was based on the 1932 census as the official state record and proof of national belonging and eventual citizenship.[35] Instead of using the 1932 census, Muhammad presented his registration in the 1921 census from the Tyre personal registries as evidence of his Jaʿfari affiliation and his lineage to the town of ʿAynatha in southern Lebanon. Reference to the earlier 1921 census was legal and common, but his submission of the 1921 census record as proof of identification was significant and incongruent on many levels.[36] First, the Tyre census Muhammad provided in his case actually preceded the juridical establishment of the Jaʿfari court that he sought to rule over his marriage. Ironically, to prove his citizenship in the Lebanese nation-state, he reverted back to the Tyre registries of 1921 that preceded both the official recognition of Shiʿi Muslims as a political and legal sect and the formation of the Jaʿfari shariʿa court in 1926. Muhammad retroactively imposed and inscribed sectarian and national identity onto his marriage, using documents that had existed prior to the formation of such legalized categories. Such legalized categories were assumed to be natural and stable by the Mandate authorities, and contingencies in state institutions where they were not. In the case of Badiʿa, the opposite occured and she was less interested in asserting her Lebanese citizenship to enhance her odds of securing a divorce. While the personal status courts could undermine individual claims to rights and belonging, as in the case of Badiʿa, it had the overall effect of crystallizing the state's claims to sovereignty.

Secondly, Muhammad's use of the 1921 Tyre census rather than the national 1932 census suggests that he and Badiʿa most likely had lived in Palestine at the time of their marriage in 1929, and likely had not been present when the 1932 census was conducted as the official determinant for citizenship. The aspect of residence and identity based on locality was an attribute argued by Badi'a. Her claim was not that she did not hail from Lebanon, but that she had been living in Palestine for more than seven years and considered it to be her home and place of residence. It also had been the site of her marriage and divorce. Moreover, she had some form of Palestinian identity card to prove this, and could therefore claim to be recognized as a national of another state. The insertion of an earlier census record over a later one further complicated the boundaries of inclusion and exclusion in a society that was enacting political sectarianism during the early formation of a nation-state. The porosity of borders and uncertainty over document legitimacy, reveals the ambiguity in determining citizenship and the ways in which sectarianism was being selectively lived and practiced by individuals in their daily affairs.[37]

During this period of national formation, the procedure of documentation needed to determine national and sectarian affiliation remained flexible. With the creation of the Lebanese nation-state and the subsequent establishment of the Ja'fari shari'a courts, new markers and boundaries were formed that had not existed before. Conflicting evidence and methods to determine legality were purported during the advent years of the Ja'fari court, as seen in the case of Muhammad and Badi'a. The presumed immutability of these national, sectarian, and *madhhab* categories of identification was evident in how they were practiced and articulated in people's everyday lives. For many people living in what became southern Lebanon, the construction of territorial borders created ambiguity and displacement.[38] Commercial and social exchanges between northern Palestine and Jabal 'Amil have historically been vibrant and fluid. It was a common practice for individuals of what became the Ja'fari *madhhab* who lived in Jabal 'Amil to document their marriages and divorces in Palestine prior to the Mandate, as opposed to the Hanafi courts in Tyre or Sidon, because the Palestinian courts were closer. The construction of borders under the Mandate period only complicated the legal status of these people and the types of documents that were admissible in court.

Muhammad and Badi'a inadvertently used the porosity of these territorial borders to summon different identity markers and citizenship while trying to increase their chances of getting a favorable outcome in the courts. Their case also reveals the gendered inequalities apparent in the epistemic shift in the legal capabilities women had before the codification of the personal status law in the state-authorized shariʿa courts that embodied patriarchal interests. The maneuvering between Hanafi and Jaʿfari courts in Lebanon and Palestine became more rigid with their institutionalization, despite the fact that women like Badiʿa pushed back and perceived mobility in these spaces. Nonetheless, the Jaʿfari court, after receiving proof of *madhhab* and Lebanese citizenship, made arguments to negate the ruling of the Haifa court on several grounds. First, they argued that Badiʿa had been able to go before the Haifa Hanafi judge and divorce herself on one occasion without the presence of Muhammad. The Jaʿfari court's president, Munir ʿUsayran, asserted that this action went against the "Islamic shariʿa of the Jaʿfari *madhhab*," since women could divorce themselves unless their right to do so had been established at the time of the marriage contract, and thus that the divorce in Haifa was indeed invalidated. Second, ʿUsayran added that the divorce in Haifa had come after the creation of the Jaʿfari shariʿa court and the legal recognition of the Shiʿa as a sect, so it was not permissible for the Hanafi court to administer divorce when a court of the couple's *madhhab* was available. Even when the issue of Lebanese or Palestinian nationality was in question, *madhhab* seemed to hold precedence. This was an understanding of *madhhab* that no longer retained its meaning from a transnational framework, but was nationally bound by the Lebanese state. The court seems to have concurred with this stance. Finally, the Jaʿfari court judge remarked that, even without proof of her *madhhab*, Badiʿa had to abide by her husband's religious *madhhab*. The judge ended by confirming that Badiʿa was Jaʿfari. Such a jurisdiction was not common under Jaʿfari jurisprudence, as it implied that women were legally required to adhere to the *madhhab* of their spouses. Something could be said about ʿUsayran's use of this argument to support the court's authority over this case, which strengthened both patrimonial ties and *madhhab* association. By using this logic, ʿUsayran dismissed any claim made by Badiʿa, whether or not she could demonstrate proof of her sect and nationality. *Madhhab*, according to the court ruling, was ultimately determined by the husband, and this determination was reinforced by institutionalized patriarchal shariʿa courts.

In many ways, the case represented an extension of the court's authority and a reassertion of male-dominated patriarchy infused in the institutional frameworks of the state. Oddly enough, Badiʿa's self-identification conflicted with how the court identified her. Due to the nature and limitations of court records, one can witness why Badiʿa made claims that promoted her desired outcomes when it came to matters of child custody and alimony under Hanafi jurisprudence, which was deemed more favorable in these matters than Ja'fari personal status law.[39] What is most revealing is how women like Badi'a made claims to dismiss the Ja'fari courts, and used sectarian markers to contest power. Not only was the court acting on behalf of its state-endorsed authority, but individuals like Badi'a pushed back against its authority and indirectly rejected the Lebanese nation-state in their efforts to attain their desired outcomes. However, this case, like many others, revealed how uncertain these modern boundaries (territorial, national, sectarian, *madhhab*) were during this initial period, as individuals attempted to claim or reject different aspects of the nation-state's authority that regulated who belonged and who did not. Regardless of how Badi'a identified herself, the Ja'fari shari'a courts through the authority of the state began to follow specific legal procedures and codes rooted in a system of institutional documentation and legitimacy that both limited and expanded ideas of *ta'ifa* and *madhhab*. Significantly, these court records reflect how the categories continued to be debated and mobilized.

At a time in which the Lebanese nation-state was formulating and solidifying its physical boundaries, the Ja'fari shari'a court extended its authority beyond the borders of the nation-state. The court became a space where Shi'i sectarian identification, national affiliation, *madhhab* association, and maternal, paternal and religious norms were debated and deployed within its legal jurisdiction as the prime authority over personal status law. As seen in the case that opened this chapter—of Fatima and 'Abbas, neither of whom were Lebanese citizens—the extraterritorial jurisdiction points to the ways in which people could question the state mechanism of identification that imposed meaning in their daily lives on the grounds of personal status law.

Beyond the Nation-State: Extending the Boundaries of the Ja'fari Shari'a Court

On May 17, 1938, Musa came before the higher appellate Ja'fari shari'a court of Beirut with a rebuttal summons from the Damascus court in Syria. It was to negate a divorce granted to his wife, Wat'a, on April 5, 1938, in the Ja'fari court of Ba'albek, a town in central Lebanon close to the border of Syria.[40] In the decree from the Damascus court, Musa demanded that the ruling from Ba'albek be nullified and voided since he and his wife were from *ahali Dimashq* (the people of Damascus), and thus were not Lebanese. Musa refuted the authority and jurisdiction of the Ja'fari court of Ba'albek over his marriage, claiming that he was from Damascus, where he and Wat'a had married and still lived. According to the Jaʿfari court records, Musa had not appeared before the court on the court date set for their divorce. Thus, an absentee ruling by the Baʿalbek court had granted a divorce to Watʿa, who had apparently been living in Baʿalbek at the time, on the basis of testimonies of six witnesses she had put forth. In his rebuttal, Musa demanded that the case go back to the Damascus court, where the witnesses could be reevaluated under the appropriate legal authority. In its final ruling, the higher appellate Jaʿfari court sustained the divorce granted by the lower Baʿalbek court on the grounds that Watʿa supported her claim with six testifying witnesses while Musa provided no reason for his absence. Thus it dismissed the rebuttal made by the Damascus court on Musa's behalf.

In this case, the Jaʿfari shariʿa court extended its authority beyond the Lebanese borders on behalf of Watʿa by ruling on a marital case between two people who hailed from Syria and self-identified as such. In so doing, the Jaʿfari court completely rejected the claims made by the Damascus court. Musa presented written proof from the Damascus court affirming its legal rights over the case on the basis of nationality and previous site of marital contract. In the court proceedings, Watʿa never denied that she was from Damascus, but rather called on the court on account of a transnational notion of Jaʿfari affiliation and legal jurisprudence. Evident from the records in Baʿalbek, Musa and Watʿa adhered to the Jaʿfari *madhhab*, and hence Watʿa mobilized the court to rule on her marriage on this accord.[41] What legal authority did the Jaʿfari shariʿa courts have to rule on this case? And on a deeper level, how did women use these courts to obtain their desired outcome? How did the tradition of *madhhab* permit them to do this? The site of the couple's marriage, their residence, and their nationality lay outside the scope of the Jaʿfari shariʿa court and the newly defined Lebanese nation-state that had granted it authority. Both Watʿa, in this case, and Fatima, in the case described earlier, sanctioned the court to rule on their marital status on the grounds of their being followers of the Jaʿfari *madhhab* despite not being legal "citizens" of the Lebanese nation-state.[42] The cases reveal how women could navigate, manipulate, and challenge a judicial system in a way that was particular to this historical moment—one that sustained remnants of the former Ottoman legal jurisprudence just as nation-state shariʿa courts were being newly established. The Mandate period reflects the possibilities that litigants, particularly women, sought in the hope of obtaining the most favorable outcome as they pushed within and against these institutional frameworks.

In these cases, women tried to mobilize courts to rule in their favor, petitioning for their self-interest, subjectivity, and desired outcome regarding their marriages and divorces. The imposition of family law onto religious courts, as established in the Lebanese context, embedded a patriarchal bias that institutionalized "the preferential treatment of men in sectarian codes."[43] However, these cases can also be seen as women exercising different interpretative frameworks of *madhhab* during the Mandate period to push back against these sectarian codes. In these cases, it would seem that categories of religious "belonging" or *madhhab* superseded those of national demarcations, despite the fact that the Ja'fari court sanctioned the authority granted to it by the Lebanese nation-state to rule over the cases. Individuals declared a particular understanding of subjectivity that was not defined by the modern nation-state and its parameters of citizenship, by appealing to *madhhab* affinity. Cases of this sort showed and questioned the limitations of national frameworks just as *madhhab* was becoming restricted by its institutionalization to the state. Just as *ta'ifa* and *madhhab* were naturalized, people sought ways to expand and push against these categories, highlighting the practice of sectarianization in everyday marital affairs. As *madhhab* became confined to the boundaries of the Lebanese nation-state through the establishment of personal status courts that legitimized sectarian affiliation and citizenship, the practices of *madhhab* became limited. It was for this reason that people, particularly women, appearing before the Ja'fari shari'a courts of Lebanon demanded its intervention as members of the same *madhhab*, even though they were citizens of a different nation-state. As the cases reveal, women in particular made demands to expand or redefine understandings of *madhhab* to counter state claims. Both Fatima and Wat'a asserted their agency—as members of the Jafari *madhhab*, which had a longer discursive legal tradition—to push against state-asserted categories of sect or nationality. In many ways, these cases reveal how the Ja'fari shari'a courts and its constituents questioned the very nature of the territorial boundaries created by the nation-state, while at times reaffirming the powers of the nation-state that established and granted power to the Ja'fari shari'a courts. They also reflect how their understanding of *madhhab* was not limited to nation-state borders, but had a longer and deeper historical connotation connected to Ja'fari jurisprudence that made extraterritorial assertions on the Lebanese nation-state through these personal status courts.[44]

Whether or not litigants intentionally sought to redefine their citizenry, they used any method possible to have the court rule in their favor, and inadvertently made claims to these modern categories of identification. This was also telling of the period in which such categories of national and sectarian belonging were relatively new structures of institutional significance. This is to say not that notions of sectarian affinity had not existed earlier, but rather that the categories took on political, social, and cultural significance as part of the rise of the modern nation-state. Even though *madhhab* had became incorporated and entangled in the institutional framework of the nation-state, these women redeployed it so as to create new meaning and mobility, reflecting the performative nature of such identity categorizations. In petitioning for a particular notion of subjectivity, they resisted the limitations of the nation-state framing that were rooted in sectarian affiliations.

Wat'a, Fatima, and other litigants who came to the court questioned the legality of such national distinctions and citizenry by asserting their desire to identify with the Ja'fari shari'a courts and the Ja'fari *madhhab*, and hence inserting their social and political representation in this national space. What it meant to be a Lebanese (sectarian) citizen of the nation-state remained highly contestable and open for interpretation shaped by lived experience. The transnational imagined community of the Ja'fari *madhhab* allowed people to question the centrality of the nation-state vis-à-vis *madhhab*. Ironically, the very authority of the Ja'fari shari'a court was based on Lebanese citizenry and political representation in the nation-state. Such categories were not fixed, as is seen in these cases. Dealing with two individuals of differing nationalities and citizenship who lived outside the borders of the Lebanese nation-state, the Ja'fari court extended its authoritative boundaries and interceded in the case of Wat'a and Musa on the grounds of Ja'fari jurisprudence.

Contesting Madhhab within National Borders: Being Ja'fari or Not

The cases discussed thus far reveal elements of resistance to national, sectarian, and *madhhab* characteristics as they appear in personal marital disputes. However, such contestation was not always the case. Throughout the court records, cases reappeared pertaining to marriages that had been performed outside of the judicial body of the Ja'fari shari'a courts, yet within the Lebanese national context. In most cases, individuals came to the courts to certify or refute the tenets of their marriages according to the Ja'fari *madhhab*. In one such case, found in the Ja'fari shari'a court in Beirut and recorded on March 7, 1938, Hussein appeared before the court to confirm the legality of his marriage (*thabat al-zawāj*) to Na'isa.[45] Hussein claimed that they had been married in a Sunni shari'a court in Beirut, and wanted to make certain that the marriage was legitimate under the Jaʿfari *madhhab*. In its final ruling, the Beirut court judge, Muhammad Yahya Safa al-Din al-Husseini, maintained that it did not matter under what *madhhab* a marriage occurred, and thus certified the legality of the marriage even though it had taken place in a Sunni court. In this case, Hussein found it necessary to come before the Jaʿfari shariʿa court to reconfirm his marriage simply because it had taken place in a Sunni shariʿa court in Lebanon. There was no evidence of any legal contestation between Hussein and Naʿisa argued before the court, other than the requested affirmation that their marriage was indeed legitimate under the Jaʿfari *madhhab*. In such cases, the authority of the court, the nation-state that granted the Jaʿfari shariʿa court legitimacy, and the *madhhab* as defined by the authority of the state were all aligned and reaffirmed. Hundreds of cases of this nature appeared before the Jaʿfari courts during the Mandate period, when the nationalization and sectarianization of *taʾifa* and *madhhab* took place within the courts and people's daily lives.[46] Individuals like Hussein came before the Jaʿfari shariʿa court to probe and legitimize decisions made in the Sunni courts, thus imbuing the Jaʿfari court with power over the marital relationships of Lebanese Shiʿi citizens.

In another case, ʿAli came before the court on December 10, 1932, alleging that he had been married to Zahra in Beirut a year before. After four months of marriage, he had traveled to Baghdad to visit his ailing father. Upon his return, he had found Zahra married to another man. In his testimony, he requested that the court order Zahra to return and honor their marital relationship. When Zahra appeared before the court on December 24, she affirmed that she had married ʿAli a year before, but that after a month of marriage they had divorced before a Sunni Hanafi judge in Beirut. Zahra claimed that the Sunni judge had decreed it *haram* (forbidden) for her to be with ʿAli since he was of the Hanafi *madhhab*. ʿAli rebutted this allegation, arguing that he was indeed Jaʿfari and held a Shiʿi identity card. The court judge, ʿAli Fahs al-Husseini, then ordered ʿAli to bring proof of his Jaʿfari identity. On the last day of the trial, ʿAli did not appear. The court adjourned with an acquittal ruling.[47]

In this case, Zahra used the court to affirm her Jaʿfari *madhhab* which subsequently determined her sectarian affiliation, as defined by the state, to differentiate her from ʿAli, whom she claimed was Hanafi Sunni. Although it was unlikely that the Hanafi court had prohibited her from marrying ʿAli simply on the grounds that he was Sunni, Zahra made claims to the Jaʿfari court on the basis not only of her *madhhab* but of Ali's as well, in order to justify the suspension of all marital ties. She used state institutions such as the shariʿa courts not necessarily to uphold the sectarian markers the state authorized, but to obtain her desired outcome. In summoning the courts, however, she deployed sectarian markers to regulate her marital state. She marshaled the Ja'fari court on the grounds of her *madhhab* in the hope that it would rule to her advantage.[48] Although the Ja'fari court did not extract the history of the case from the Hanafi court, it adhered to Zahra's claims by demanding that 'Ali bring proof of his Ja'fari affiliation. 'Ali never did so, but the fact that regular requests for written proof of *madhhab* identification were continuously made reflected the court's proliferation of politicized sectarian lines. By doing this, the Ja'fari courts and the litigants who came before them engaged in practices of sectarianism and in the inconsistencies of its interpretation.

Cases like Zahra's appeared in the records, wherein Lebanese Shi'a came before the shari'a court to assert their Ja'fari *madhhab* so that the court could intercede on their behalf in personal matters. In many ways, these people imposed on the court to legitimize the identity and *madhhab* they had defined unto themselves and wanted the state to recognize as well. Nonetheless, even when they contested the nation-state, Shi'i individuals reproduced the lines of difference it proclaimed. The very existence of a Shi'i sect was contingent on a Sunni other, which the state and the Ja'fari shari'a courts perpetuated in the Lebanese case.[49] The sectarian recognition of the Shi'a created the appearance that a collective Shi'i category and entity was a constant, ever-present practice of society outside of or external to the state, without acknowledging the institutional effect of the Ja'fari shari'a courts in perpetuating this category of identification.[50] Through the examination of these cases, we witness the structural impact of the state that produces the effect that the law exists as a formal framework without witnessing the social practices that push back and yield these spaces.[51] Sectarianism as a political system was established as the rule of governance, while practices of the Ja'fari shari'a courts and the individuals who daily called upon them reproduced and rearticulated Shi'a as sectarian citizens of the Lebanese nation-state. Not only did Shi'i individuals come to reaffirm marriages that had happened in shari'a courts other than the Ja'fari courts; they came to define, reinterpret, and even dispute the sectarian and national markers while they sought to obtain favorable outcomes in their marital affairs. What was most significant about these cases was not that sectarian differences were downplayed in some cases and accentuated in others, but rather that such claims of sectarian belonging or not belonging were readily brought before the court to mediate the everyday affairs of Shi'i

Muslims who contested those very categorizations. The court records reveal the ways Shiʻi Muslims practiced sectarianism: at times as Lebanese citizens, at times as Shiʻa and often across state boundaries, they created a push-pull effect, pushing against circumscribed national borders and pulling within Lebanese society.

The creation of the Jaʻfari shariʻa courts by the mandatory authorities and the subsequent cases that appeared before them reflect a constant negotiation of power relationships and boundaries, particularly in the domain of the family, that took place just as Shiʻi Muslims were being collectively recognized as a sect in the Lebanese nation-state. Most cases that appeared before the court, like those of Muhammad and Badiʻa and of Fatima and ʻAbbas, addressed similar concerns, such as terms of divorce, controversies over inheritance, child custody and support, obedience suits, and requests for alimony or unpaid dowry. As this chapter reveals, however, these personal status matters were sites of struggle over identity formation and the petitioning of demands, whether they were sectarian, *madhhab*, or national in the deployment of Lebanese Shiʻi citizenship, community, and family. It is also in these very spaces that many Shiʻi women pushed back against gendered norms, and against the patriarchy of the state that solidified the authority of the Jaʻfari shariʻa courts.

What these cases clearly reveal is that understandings of sectarian and national belonging were constantly changing and were always under negotiation. The cases expose the tension between how nation-state and broader "cross-border" *madhhab* communities were understood both by individuals and the courts. Communities were not bounded and natural, but rather were loose and shifting, according to historical context and time. As a space regulating the daily lives of Lebanese Shiʻa, the Jaʻfari courts in many ways negotiated and constructed sectarian and national markers while also normalizing familial and social norms within Shiʻi civil society. Categories of belonging or not belonging to the nation-state affected the familial affairs of individuals who came before the court demanding its intervention during the Mandate period.

This research sheds light on the legal and political construction of sectarian identities and the ways in which they were practiced and performed in the French Mandate period, and what this meant for Shiʻa living in this period of nation-state formation. Shiʻa were actively defining their civil status and colonial civil order as "colonial citizens" living under the French Mandate, and as citizens engaging in the power dynamics of the state that defined their legal rights.[52] The penetration of the state into the lives of Shi'i Muslims led to the nationalization of the family along sectarian lines, while the practices of the courts questioned this nationalization by either refuting it or making transnational claims. Thus, this nationalization was not merely a top-down state mechanism of institutionalization, but rather was a site of struggle that contested the very nature of the nation-state. During this formative period, the norms and practices of sectarian and national identification were continuously being debated and shaped through the Ja'fari shari'a court and the individuals who came before it. Although sectarian and national boundaries were negotiated and many times resisted per the contents of the court cases, modes of resistance were formed within the institutional space of the court and colonial state, and not outside it, much like the contestations illustrated by Nadya Sbaiti that similarly occurred within the institutional space of the school.[53] However, these court cases show how the state was challenged, whether by having its territorial authority contested or by having its transnational or imagined notions of Ja'fari Shi'ism highlighted through the broader notion of *madhhab*. While new state structures created categories where none had necessarily existed, the Ja'fari shari'a courts and their litigants still saw movement and volatility within them.

3 THE ARCHIVE IS BURNING
Law, Unknowability, and the Curation of History

MAYA MIKDASHI

I CALLED YOUSSEF WHEN I arrived home in Beirut for research. I had met him months earlier, in New York, when he gave a presentation at Columbia University's law school. At the time, Youssef was president of the State Shura Council, one of the many high posts he has held in the Lebanese judiciary. He invited me to his office at the Beirut Courthouse, which would become the scene of our meetings, alongside long lunches at nearby cafes. On one of those occasions, we were sipping coffee in his office when he called the archivists at the Court of Cassation and introduced me as a PhD researcher. Once I arrived there, the chief archivist and clerk of the court, Evelyn, then introduced me to Mona, the archivist of the Plenary Assembly of the Court of Cassation and the person with whom I ultimately worked most closely during my research.

I have been conducting ethnographic and archival research at the judiciary on and off for more than a decade. Mostly, this has meant spending time in the archives and clerk's offices at the Courts of Cassation and the law library of the lawyer's syndicate.[1] Although I began my research focused solely on religious conversion and its relation to sectarianism and secularism, my interests expanded and shifted the more research I conducted—the more I saw something I had not anticipated and thus had not looked for: sextarianism.

Early on, I asked my interlocutors—archivists, judges, and lawyers—to share case files that they thought were important or that had occupied and weighed on them. What case files did *they* think reflected the work of law and of the court system, the aporias of sovereignty, and the stakes of religious conversion? I developed this praxis to recognize that knowledge production and theorization are always already collaborative efforts that are embedded in power relations. It was also an attempt to think through the different ways in which expertise functions and shapes any given arena of research; a court clerk or archivist might illustrate the workings of the Lebanese state through a different case file than an anthropologist, a historian, or a nonacademic activist would. Marking this difference places academic expertise alongside, and not above, a different form of expertise that makes much of our work possible: that of archivists themselves. Giving up control or, perhaps, giving up the *fantasy* of control can potentiate research as a line of flight,[2] rather than as a goal or a point of departure.[3]

Sectarianism

Mona and I quickly discovered that we were from the same neighborhood in Beirut, Tariq al Jadida, known as the city's "Sunni bastion" of the working and middle class. In fact it is a multinational area, a place where Lebanese, Palestinians, Syrians, and non-Arab migrant workers live and work together. It has a highly rated public high school and a university that brings in students from all over the country. In 2008 a fight in the university cafeteria between pro- and antigovernment students, in this case a designation that mapped onto Sunni and Shi'i political schisms, led to armed clashes in Tariq al Jadida that killed at least four people. The inhabitants of Tariq al Jadida are as diverse, and as not diverse, as the rest of the city. There are multiple ways to describe Tariq al Jadida, and indeed all the different areas of Beirut, but sectarian and classist discourse fixes the neighborhood as a tight-knit community wary of outsiders. In this discourse there is only one kind of insider or outsider: a sectarian one.

It turned out that Mona had been my aunt's neighbor for years and knew my cousins, most of whom still lived only a block away from her. This neighborly connection shaped our interactions at the archives. I was now accountable to my family for my comportment at the judiciary, a form of accountability more immediate and pressing than my distant institutional review board or dissertation committee. To Mona, I represented someone from the neighborhood she could be proud of for getting a PhD abroad (and *living all by herself!*). Our exchanges folded us deeper into an archive of shared experience and an economy of favors that had linked our families for years.[4] Mona and I formed an "us" that debated the best bakeries in Tariq al Jadida and was about specific forms of rootedness despite our different mobilities. Mona and I were not only from the same sect; we were both women in that sect. We shared a "sextarian," as opposed to a sectarian, positionality vis-à-vis the state.

Sextarianism emphasizes how state power articulates and manages sexual difference bureaucratically, ideologically, and legally.[5] Sovereignty is performed at the intersections of sexual and sectarian difference. The Lebanese state is exemplary, not exceptional, in how it ties sect and sex. It represents an intensification of the foundational relationship between political and sexual difference. Lebanon's laws, bureaucracy, and political system are grounded in sextarian logic and praxis. At times, Mona seemed to be offering me advice on how to navigate our shared sextarian positionality. For example, she once outlined the specific clauses Sunni women could add to marriage contracts to make them more equitable, as she handed a divorce case file to me. Another time, when we were discussing a particularly nasty custody case, Mona remarked that only women with more wealth or status than their husbands stood a chance at evening out the sextarian system. "Make sure to marry a poor man," she said to me, laughing.

Youssef and I had a different kind of "us"—one based on social class, educational status, and transnational mobility, even though Youssef and I did not share the same sectarian or sexed positionality vis-à-vis the state. His sextarian position came with more civil, political, and economic rights than either Mona or mine. When I asked Youssef and Mona separately about the necessities of legal reform, at the forefront of Mona's mind was nationality law. She was angry that a group of her relatives were not Lebanese because their mother had married a Palestinian man. On the other hand, Youssef believed administrative reform was necessary to bolster the efficiency, transparency, and legitimacy of the judiciary. They were both right, but their delivery also told a story. Mona was angry, and personalized the effects of the nationality law; Youssef, who shared with Mona a loud and gregarious personality, was coolly analytic. Both Youssef and Mona were powerful figures at the judiciary. One had control over the archive of Lebanon's highest court, and the other had control over an entire regulatory branch of the legal system. Their power manifested, circulated, and was compensated for at different scales, but both were critical figures in the state apparatus. Some mornings I would shadow Mona as she worked, breaking for cheap coffee poured into a small plastic cup, and then I would have lunch with Youssef at a chic café near the ministry. Both were decades older than me and were invested in teaching me the ways of their world. This intimacy allowed us to broach difficult subjects that often became heated disagreements about contemporary politicians and political issues. With both Mona and Youssef it was intimacy that facilitated argument, and argument that facilitated more intimacy.

This chapter focuses on two case files held in the Cassation Court archive—cases that Mona suggested to me. She offered one case file of a notorious civil war militia leader who is currently the leader of a political party well represented in the Lebanese Parliament. This case was decided by the Judicial Council. The other file Mona shared to help me illustrate the work of archivists and was from the Plenary Assembly at the Court of Cassation. Mona was the archivist of both courts. The latter case began in 1982—the year the Israeli army occupied Beirut. It concerns inheritance claims heard and decided at Roman Catholic and civil personal status courts before being appealed and finally decided at the Plenary Assembly. After a decision was issued, the case was burnt in a fire at the court archives following a night of intense fighting and rocket barrages. The family began a new case, asking for certification of their personal photocopy of the decision as an original (and thus actionable) legal document, one that must be re-filed in the archive in order to become a citable source for both addendums to the case itself, and to jurisprudence and the record of the Assembly. In its 1992 iteration, the case focused largely on bureaucratic practice—the Assembly's ability to differentiate, decide between, and authenticate legal documents. The other, Judicial Council, case is infamous in the contemporary history of Lebanon; it was the case against Samir Geagea for crimes committed during and after the civil war. To date, Geagea is the only militia leader or member to have spent time behind bars. Almost every leader in the civil war era has either been assassinated, died of natural causes, or is "in" politics.[6] Upon being pardoned in 2005, Geagea joined his war-time brethren as a post-war political leader. In both the Plenary Assembly case and the Judicial Council case, that of the photocopy and that of Geagea, the civil war is an active subject, setting and experience.

In this chapter, I draw attention to the multiplicity of narratives, social worlds, and actions as they relate to war, archives, and ethnography. Meaning is indeterminate, opaque, and unknowable. Indeterminacy opens insights into the historiographic, political, and affective realms of archival research and theory. By indeterminacy I mean the multiple and sometimes contradictory meanings, intentions, and effects that exist within one interaction, action or statement,[7] and the ways that multiplicity is often disciplined into linear and professional productions of history and anthropology through technologies of archival and ethnographic curation—or the archival and ethnographic disciplining of *what might have happened* and *all that happened* into regimes of truth.[8] I suggest that sectarianism is one technology of archival and ethnographic curation that vibrates with the prehensive force of historicity and futurity. Everything that has happened, everything that may happen, and even things that did not happen—can be, are, and will be curated through the lens of sectarianism.

A Life in the Archives

Mona began working at the judiciary in 1985, the year in which a large portion of the Cassation Court archives and the ledgers that corresponded to them were burned in a fire. She is a trained archeologist and classicist, a mother, and a grandmother. During the years I conducted fieldwork, Mona was responsible for maintaining the archives and the ongoing cases of the Plenary Assembly at the Court of Cassation, the highest civil court to which ordinary citizens have access, and the Judicial Council, an originating and final criminal court that has jurisdiction over crimes committed against the internal or external security of the state, such as political assassinations, as well as crimes against the public, such as terrorism. The judges who sit on the Plenary Assembly and the Judicial Council are both drawn from the Cassation Courts and overlap, and the same clerk works in both courts and their archives. But this was an incomplete picture of Mona's professional responsibilities. She spent hours offering legal advice, quoting jurisprudential tenets, remembering the history of the court and its jurists, and providing a shoulder to cry on. Everybody—from jurist to lawyer to clerk to coffee delivery boy to plaintiff—knew that she was powerful.

Later, I learned that Mona herself was soon to become a convert from Sunni to Shi'i Islam. I told her that I found her impending conversion to be a strange coincidence, given that the case files I was researching, which she was helping me find, were specifically about religious conversion and the Plenary Assembly's role in arbitrating between personal status courts. She threw up her hands and said, "What can we do? We only had girls, and I'm not going to allow my husbands' brothers to take my money." She was referring to the different inheritance laws practiced by these two Muslim sects. As an archivist of Lebanon's highest civil court, she knew very well that conversion can be the easiest and cheapest way to adjust the inheritance she will leave to her daughters, and to ensure that they actually inherit the entirety of her and her husband's estate. In this regard, Mona and her husband were not alone.

While there is a regional and national fear in Lebanon over Sunni-Shiʿi *fitna* (a sectarian Muslim civil war), I know few married Sunni couples who did *not* convert to Shiʿism if and when they had "only" daughters. I also do not know a Sunni couple who have a son and *have* converted to Shiʿism, because in the presence of a son the inheritance rules of Shiʿi and Sunni Islam are the same. The banal, sextarian nature of religious conversion troubles narratives of hardened sectarian difference, and simultaneously reveals how state practices of religious coexistence and secularism in Lebanon function through the maintenance of unequal regimes of sexual difference.

The archive of the Court of Cassation is not a room you can enter and exit—except that, of course, it is. You could identify a case, ask an archivist for it, watch her walk into a room, emerge with a file, and then read that case alone at a desk in the Beirut Courthouse. But instead of staging archival and ethnographic research as a set of extractive and authorial encounters, I suggest a research and writing practice that centers not the archival object itself, but the assemblage that makes *that thing*, the archival object, both legible and knitted into a larger economy of knowledge production.[9] Archives *are* this assemblage of people, paper, processes, temporalities, desires, economies, memories, arguments and affects—all open to the reversals of time.[10]

Tracing the lifeworlds of the archive challenges the dominant historical narrative of Lebanon and of the role of state bureaucracies during times of civil war and/or occupations and invasions, by emphasizing the daily workings, as opposed to the failings, of a wartime state.[11] For fifteen years the warring factions killed upward of 150,000 people, mostly civilians; maimed many more; and led to massive levels of displacement and emigration. Thirty percent (about 772,800 people) of the prewar population of 2.576 million emigrated, and another 33 percent (approximately 850,080 people) were internally displaced. Independent research groups have estimated that 4 percent of the resident population, another 103,040 people, were wounded, and about 19,300 people were forcibly disappeared during the civil war.[12] Throughout these years, citizens continued to turn toward the judiciary to adjudicate the mundane and the quotidian—and the judiciary continued to answer that call. Wartime legal argumentation and the lifeworld of the judiciary's Cassation Court archives reveal the place of memory, or the act of remembering, of constructing and living continuity in Lebanese jurisprudence and history. They unfold archives as thresholds of war and peace, of history and anthropology, and of theory and methodology.

The analytic and political common sense has been to layer a history of destruction, invasion, war, and authoritarianism in the Middle East alongside a history of destroyed, constructed, weaponized, strategically deployed, colonized, and kidnapped archives. The relationship of violence to history making appears linear through this layering, and archives serve as a metaphor or as a coherent technology for historical processes and the consolidation, ruptures, and machinations of political regimes. And yet archives, people, and power are never as coherent as the stories they tell about themselves. In the case of archives, they are never as coherent as academics present them to be. I gesture toward an archival and ethnographic theory that centers the lifeworlds and knowledge production of archivists, and argue that archival destruction, corruption, and recuperation reveals archives as abundant, contradictory, lacking, intimate, and indeterminate spaces. Law, history, jurisprudence, method, theory, and violence curate truths out of abundance, destruction, and indeterminacy.[13] What we make of archives, and what archives make of us, reflects and inflects the impossible desire to render the unknowable rational and predictable—and to fix that meaning in time.[14] Seen this way, historical or theoretical coherence is in fact the compulsive drive *to cohere*, to epistemologically and ideologically fold the reversals and unpredictability of life, death, and everything in between into a narrative that stresses continuity, predictability, and the surety of a recognizable future.

An ethnography of the archive as a physical space, coupled with an ethnographic reading of the archival files they also hold and circulate,[15] troubles the division of labor between cultural and academic production, as well as between the disciplines of history and anthropology.[16] Such an approach presents embodied knowledge, memory, abundance, and affect as sites for research, and the writing and reading of history and ethnography. As the practices of the Atlas Group, the art collective led by Walid Raad, have shown, the distinctions between historical and fictional narrative, on the one hand, and historical events and subjective *experiences* of those events on the other, are multiple, compulsive, and contradictory. There is a constitutive contradiction: a lack of organized historical and archival documents and a lack of a public history of the civil war, coupled with the hyper-presence of civil war in the built environment of Lebanon and within the memory and futurescapes of people who live in Lebanon or are from there. How can war be both everywhere and nowhere at the same time? How can war and violence continue to animate political, social, economic, and urban fabrics across the country, and yet be excluded by official narrations of history, including national history curricula? Omnia El Shakry has persuasively demonstrated that to perform decolonial history is to grapple with destruction—a lack of documents—and to turn toward other sources, methods, and affects of history making.[17] The burning of the Cassation Court archives during the civil war was a catastrophe—and yet catastrophe, as Sherene Seikaly reminds us, is never an ending. Catastrophe is a temporal, affective, and archival order.[18]

Lebanon is not an exceptional site of archival destruction. The Middle East is a space where archives and documents are routinely damaged and targeted by war and occupation practices—most infamously the targeted removal of the Iraqi state archives from Baghdad to Qatar by US occupation forces, and the targeted removal of the PLO archives from Beirut to Tel Aviv as a tactic of Israeli warfare during the invasion and occupation of Lebanon. I join Shakry, the Atlas Group, and Seikaly in arguing that a *lack* of organized sources and official archives is motivation for thinking otherwise, for looking elsewhere, and for writing and creating multiply about and for history. In line with Marisa Fuentes, Anjali Arondekar, Saidiya Hartman, and Michel-Rolph Trouillot,[19] I also suggest that factual fictions, or what we might call historical "ficticity," are often constructed not through a lack of documents, but within an *abundance* of historical documents, narratives, and archives. Desiring or mourning the archive and documents as unique and prized sources for passive, "lying in wait" truths or facts recirculates the power and coercion upon which colonial archives and authority both construct and are constructed.[20] Destruction, in fact, is a process of abundance. I mean not only the way archival destruction and creation is a theoretical metonym for an origin story about sovereignty or a metaphor for power more broadly, but also the abundant affect of mourning and loss that animates much writing and reading about archival destruction and creation.[21]

Lebanon is a site of archival aporia and absences, on the one hand, and a surfeit of documents on the other. Lack and excess exist at the same time, and this is neither a contradiction nor a unique feature of archives, or of archival research in Lebanon. The abundance of archives—even as they are being destroyed or are serving as sites and technologies of destruction—is tied to their material and immaterial forms. Archives are lifeworlds, and thus even the material destruction of an archive facilitates abundance and creation—the work needed to save, remember, reorganize, re-curate and substitute originals for copies. And in this vein, archivists, and not only archives, are the repository

of institutional memory and of history making. While academics are obsessed
with lost and found archival objects, it is archivists who are curating and em-
bodying the relationship of archives to power.[22] Moreover, the destruction or
loss of archives and archival objects are quotidian events; archivists and academics curate, rearrange, forget, stain, steal, and lose archival objects all the
time. Archives are places of work, and archivists are public employees who
in many parts of the world, including Lebanon, are chronically underpaid,
threatened with layoffs and digitization, and accused of everything from corruption to government bloat, inefficiency, and being holdovers from an analog
past. The material conditions of the archives of the Court of Cassation are
inextricable from their geopolitical context. The documents have been burned
in a fire; they are housed in a dark and musty room in a building—the Beirut
Courthouse—that has been deemed structurally unsound by civil engineers
and is literally sinking into the ground. The archival files are inseparable
from the embodied expertise of archivists and clerks like Mona, whom lawyers, plaintiffs, judges, and researchers such as myself call upon to explain the
significance, logic, system, and history of this or that case file. They mediate
and shed light on the relationship between truth and violence, a relationship
that functions through multiple scales: the social, material, methodological,
epistemological, and ideological. Archives continue to function even when
destroyed, kidnapped, transplanted, or burned because their power is immaterial: an empty archive is still full, as Arondekar writes.[23]

The ethnographic space of the archive,[24] moreover, is an actual physical
space; it does not exist without an archivist who shares a file or a document
with a researcher, whether by delicately holding a case file about custody or
throwing a war crimes file on the floor. It is government employees who have
already curated the material we use to curate truths out of an archive. What
if our theory centered the material conditions and experiences of those who
curate and create the spaces that academics conduct research in: archivists,
clerks, employees? At the very least, academics—and nation-states—are not
the only, the primary, nor even the most authoritative victims of archive fever.
Archive fever appears here less as a theoretical metonym for compulsion and
desire than as people working tirelessly to save an archive from fire: in Beirut
in 1985, in Nablus in 2002, in Baghdad in 2003, or Rio de Janeiro in 2018,
people putting themselves in danger of mortars and flames and smoke and
water damage. These images and memories are indicative of the power of
archives, both practically and ideologically, in their role as warehouses for

the curation of multiple futures. As Mona explained it to me: "If *we* didn't rescue files there would be no record of anything left—and then what would happen?" Archives, after all, do not merely produce and perform sovereignty; they are also archives of sovereignty.[25] Merely having them is a claim to power and, importantly, to a history of power and the power of history and historical coherence.[26] The working conditions of government employees who run archives are part of that history and the fabric of knowledge production. We see them—we rely on them—pushing their desks away from a window before it shatters, driving through a checkpoint to get to work, walking into a room of embers, inhaling smoke, pulling smoldering files with their bare hands, breaking bones while retrieving documents, collapsing feverishly and in pain. None of this is metaphorical.[27]

A Fire in the Archive

At the time of my research, the archive of the Cassation Court was divided into three locations. The first, containing the most recent and active case files, was a large L-shaped room facing the archivists' office, which was also L-shaped. The lip of the "L" housed the archival files of the Plenary Assembly, with the much smaller archive of the Judicial Council on one side of the hallway, and the office of Evelyn, the head archivist of the Cassation Court, on the other. Both Evelyn's office and the Plenary Assembly archive are alcoves jutting out from the large shared room of both the archives of the different branches of the Cassation Court and the archivists of those courts, mirroring each other across a hallway. In a space between the second and third floor—something between an attic and a crawl space—was another set of archival files from the Cassation Court, these dating from the 1940s to 1967. Getting to those files required a chair or stepladder, and Mona had once broken a bone in her hand while jumping down from the attic with a file tucked under her other arm. A third set of files, dated from 1967 to 1985, was stacked in an underground depot near a parking lot and the judiciary café—a "mountain of case files" (*jabal malafat*, according to Mona), which I saw on the first day of my research at the judiciary. Evelyn had asked for the files to be taken to this separate location, but she was furious at how the workers had treated them, saying that it was as if they had "worked for Sukleen," the dominant waste removal and treatment company in Lebanon. She accused the workers of treating historical documents as refuse, but there is another story here. The men who collect trash for Sukleen are mostly migrant workers, and they are subjected to racism, classism, and xenophobia. When I returned to this room in 2020, it had become an archive that joined and housed all but the most recent and active Cassation Court cases in filing cabinets organized by year (figure 1). This had been Evelyn's project, her passion, for more than a decade, and she was proud of her work's fruition. The Assembly files that Mona had tended to had been given their own locker, just as they had previously been granted their own shelves and mountains and piles apart from the Cassation Court writ large.

For stretches of time, there was no working lightbulb in the small room that houses the case files of the highest civil court to which civilians have access, the Plenary Assembly, and the case files of the Judicial Council, tasked with ruling on crimes against the state. When the electricity would cut, or the lightbulb would not turn on, Mona and I used the weak flashlights built into cigarette lighters. The files were arranged on metal shelves roughly by decade, and each case file was summarized on the manila folder that contained it. The case files contain all pertinent material from lower courts, including lawyers' briefs, testimony, medical records, copies of evidence, and the notes and decisions of the judges who sit on the Assembly. The thinnest file I saw while

Figure 1. Cassation Court archival files in a room lined with the metal cabinets that will eventually hold them, 2020. Photo by Maya Mikdashi.

conducting research contained only five pages, but the fattest had more than three hundred pages and bulged against the many layers of twine that held it together. It was dusty, dark, and smelled like old paper. My eyes were peeled for inevitable cockroaches. When I asked Mona why there was no lightbulb in the room, she remarked that the archivists had collectively decided to stop buying lightbulbs until the state had reimbursed them for past purchases. That had been months ago, she added. Archivists also pay for the upkeep and cleaning of their bathroom and their offices, she told me.

The case files contained in this section of the archives correspond to the period "after the fire of 1985," Mona explained. The fire in question had begun after a vicious bout of shelling during the civil war, a night when three people were killed and seventeen were wounded—one night in a two-week battle in Beirut that killed 89 and wounded 467. Amin Nassar, then president of Lebanon's Supreme Judicial Council (*majlis qada' al 'a'la*), described the fire as "the greatest catastrophe" of the war until that point[28]—a period that included massacres, aerial bombardment, invasions, occupations, and mass displacement all over the country. He continued, "All files without exception have been burned, and the rights of citizens from all religions and sects have turned into ashes."[29] The burning of legal paper was equated with the ashes of citizenship—and not just any citizenship, but the community of citizens from different religions and sects who are diverse but equal as *citizens* before the judiciary, and perhaps nowhere else, during a civil war. It was a gaping, burning hole in the heart of Lebanon, its legal history and capacities, and its promise of citizenship as the protector of religious difference, harmony, and coexistence.

Given the centrality of Palestinians in Lebanon during the civil war period, and indeed their role in Lebanese history, statements that center "citizens" are not neutral—they construct the history of civilian life in Lebanon, especially during the war, as particularly *Lebanese* rather than multinational and multiple. Nabih Berri, currently the speaker of Parliament and then the leader of the wartime militia Amal (now a political party), was Lebanon's minister of justice at the time.[30] He has been the speaker of Parliament since 1992. The year 1985 saw the fire at the Ministry of Justice, but it also saw Amal launching "the war of the camps" against Palestinian refugees. This included fierce fighting in Tariq al Jadida, not only because it neighbored the Shatila refugee camp, but because it mirrored it: Lebanese and Palestinians living together and in many cases fighting together for what they perceived to be common causes against common enemies.[31] This is one multinational history that frames Lebanese and Palestinians as symbiotic, as part of a common project and lifeworld, rather than as adversaries. This is decidedly *not* the historical narrative highlighted in the postwar era.

From 1975 to 1990, state institutions regularly came under fire by design and mistake. Still, the barrage of mortars that struck the second floor of the Ministry of Justice and the Cassation Court Archives in 1985 seemed, to the archivists, to be aimed at the archive itself. When they discuss the fire that resulted, archivists at the court refuse to speculate on where the shelling came from. Such speculation would implicate "which side" shelled the Ministry of Justice—and the six archivists come from all possible sides in Lebanon. They share one large room, with their boss, Evelyn, the court's head archivist, occupying the only separate office within that space. They are each in charge of a different branch of the court and are diverse in terms of gender, sect, age, and regional origins. In fact, their sectarian diversity is engineered—keeping in line with state practices that ensure equitable sectarian representation in lower-level state bureaucracy and institutions.[32] The principle of sectarian "diversity" and the aversion to monosectarian state life extends from the highest offices of the state to the higher posts in the judiciary, including the one occupied by Youssef, the man who made the phone call that got me into the archivists' offices. Despite the sectarian "diversity" of the archivists of the Cassation Court, there is a unifying characteristic: they are all from middle- and working-class backgrounds, and many are of the generations who remember when a government job guaranteed entry into the professional middle class, economic stability, and a stable retirement. Some were hired during or before the civil war, some before the devaluation of the Lebanese pound and its pegging to the US dollar in 1997, and many during and after the neoliberal market reforms introduced by then Prime Minister Rafik al Hariri, which helped to destroy the middle class. These reforms led to Beirut consistently ranking as one of the most expensive cities in the world. In 2020 the dollar peg collapsed, followed by hyperinflation and shortages of medicine, fuel, and food. The spending power of everyone except those who were already very wealthy or had foreign income streams disappeared, and 75 percent of the country lived below the poverty line by 2021.[33]

When I pressed the archivists about the 1985 fire, refusing to believe that they had no idea who had shelled them, a collective story emerged: Whoever had given the order to shell the archives had a divorce or criminal case file they wanted expunged from the record. The archive must have been targeted in its capacity *as* an archive. The archivists thus rendered the shelling personal, impossible to rationalize, and safe from political affiliation or implication. Perhaps they didn't want to get into an argument in front of me, so they settled on a narrative they could perform together. I was skeptical of this story of sour divorces and notoriously imprecise mortars precisely aimed at the Cassation archives, and I said so. In response, the court archivist waved vaguely westward and said that the shells must have come from West Beirut.[34] Mona immediately slapped my shoulder and joked, "See? She thinks it came from *our* side [of the city]." The stakes of this interaction are clear. While war requires the mobilization of collective memory, postwar terrains—particularly post–civil war terrains—require either a selective forgetting or a necessary lie.

It may not be true that these archivists have no opinion as to where the shells came from that night, or that the culprit would be difficult to uniquely identify. *Making* it true and insisting upon that truth enables the room to function and the archivists to remain friendly coworkers. They perform post–civil war coexistence. The idea of "coexistence" itself is implicitly sectarian. In a postwar political order rededicated to coexistence, sectarian political difference must be maintained—a process in which sectarianism is key. The refusal to remember, or the insistence on creating a memory together, the highlighting of a collective feeling and experience of war—these are all political choices, though they are meant to avoid discussion of politics. A sociability is built around a collective sense of what cannot be said, and of how in fact it *can* be said. Of course a militia leader managed to precisely aim his rockets at the archive, and of course he did it to expunge one particular file from history. The personalization and the intentionality of the violence is perhaps more comforting than the alternatives. After all, the use of rockets could have been a political decision taken by a wartime leader who may be a politician currently supported by an archivist in this postwar work environment. Worst of all, they could be evidence of violence *without* intentionality, a reminder of life lived within the reality of death without consequence, the life of your loved one and death as someone else's mistake, a mechanical error, one of the 150,000 deaths for which a blanket amnesty has been issued. Perhaps the militiaman giving the orders that night didn't care about the archive at all. Maybe he didn't even know it was there; the rocket just happened to start a fire in that room. Maybe it was just someone manning the rockets who got carried away, or maybe two defective rockets malfunctioned and we are still here decades later, finding and performing narratives, making this room—and the Cassation Courts, and the Ministry of Justice—work.

The ministry sat at the seam of (majority-Christian) East and (majority-Muslim) West Beirut, and formed part of the "Green Line"—a makeshift border lined with checkpoints, snipers, overgrown trees, car bombs, mines, and barbed wire that separated the two halves of the city at varying levels of intensity during the civil war. To get to work, Mona would cross Barbir Bridge—a checkpoint I remember crossing with my family as a child (figure 2). The place of the ministry on the Green Line, between warring halves of the city, is key to Mona's memory of her work life during the war.

> *Mona*: We were used to the bombing. We used to go to the parking garage, and when the shelling got worse, we would go *under* the garage. When all of this was burned [*points around the room*], we sat in the big hall over there [*points across the hallway*], we put our desks and our files and our cabinets, and we sat; and we would be exposed to sniper fire there.

Figure 2. Barbir Bridge, 1984. The sign reads: "We must exit the borders of sectarianism to enter the nation, for the nation is more welcoming and dignifying and capacious." Photo by Zaven Kouyoumdjian, from *Lebanon Shot Twice* (Beirut: Dar An Nahar, 2002).

Maya: Here? [*points across the hallway*]

Mona: We were sniped at. Because around here [the Beirut Courthouse and the Ministry of Justice] it is East/West. We were in the middle of the Green Line.

Mona: You used to come here every day?

Mona: Yes. I would come walking from Tariq al Jadida. From my house . . . sometimes my husband would give me a ride to Barbir, Barbir was all sandbags. Sandbags up to here [*points to her neck*]. You remember, right? They must have been taller than you!

Maya: Yes, I remember that. Was it the same for those coming from the East side?

Mona: No; from the East side they come in their cars, it is close [*laughs*]. Not like us; they didn't have to do that zigzag [of open and closed streets, official and unofficial checkpoints].

Maya: I see.

Mona: It was normal [for them] to come to work. But those in the East side, if they wanted to come to the West side, yes, it was the same. . . . The same process, same problems.

Figure 3. Barbir Tunnel, August 2021. The former bridge has been destroyed by postwar redevelopment. Photo by Maya Mikdashi.

Maya: But not to the judiciary.

Mona: No.

Maya: And was there ever . . . I mean, did you use to tell the *shabab* [militiamen and -boys] that you worked at the judiciary? Did you have any problems or . . . ?

Mona: No, nobody ever assaulted me or shot me, I was never exposed to anything dangerous. Ever. Quite the opposite. Maybe they used to make it easier on government employees. . . . I don't know . . . there are people . . . maybe they were crossing, but they weren't employees with a purpose, those who used to pass through these places could have been kidnapped, robbed, exposed to sniper fire. . . .

Maya: I see.

Mona: I don't know. But for me, thank God [*hamdillah*], not one day; and throughout the entire war I would cross.

Maya: Thank God [*hamdillah*].

Mona: Yes I was never exposed to anything, not one time.

Maya: Did you ever have to sleep here?

Mona: No, when the bombing would let up [even if late at night], I would leave. Sometimes . . . there is a day I will never forget. It was a Monday. The shelling started from the mountains to here [*points out the window and mimics the trajectory of a mortar, tapping her finger on her desk to illustrate impact*]. We went down [to the parking garage]. I had my transistor radio. They always used to give out the flashes [on the radio]. You remember those, right? So we went downstairs. And my car was here that day because I was sick, and I drove. I waited a little bit until 11 [p.m.]. It was quieter, so I got into the car. I drove on to the museum. Once I got to the military court, a shell landed near the museum [*a distance of about three hundred meters*] . . . then another. I felt as if the ground under the car was opening up. How I got through, I don't know—but I did. I got there. There was a checkpoint there. I stopped. I just stopped the car and, as if I was feeling as if . . . there was a mountain on my back and I wanted to . . . I wanted to bring it down. . . . I couldn't anymore. I wanted to just throw that mountain off. . . . I arrived yellowed. The militiamen and boys ran to me. They asked me, "What's wrong with you, auntie? What happened? Are you okay, auntie?" I told them nothing. I crossed the road, and a shell landed behind me. But as you know, all of this was nothing compared to the experiences of others. We are very lucky.

This moment and others like it made it clear to me that Mona considered herself and me to form an "us," particularly when talking about the past and specifically when discussing the violence of the civil war. This "us" was tied to our neighborhood with all of its sectarian, political, and class connotations, but was not contained by it. The intimacy of sharing civil war memories is a larger "us" that many in Lebanon construct, conversation by conversation. There is an "us" here to share stories, an ability informed by the contingency of our presence and, hence, our luck. Mona's narration also reveals contradictory intimacies that flourish around violence; the militiamen who may have extorted Mona or harassed her at a checkpoint called her "auntie" when they thought she might be having a heart attack. Or perhaps she actually was their auntie: someone in their neighborhood whom these militiamen believed, or willed themselves to believe, they were protecting by terrorizing others. She hated them, or at least she said she did; but in that moment their concern stood out to her enough that she remembered and narrated it to me more than twenty years later.

Throughout our conversation, Mona kept asking me whether I understood the language she was using; whether I remembered checkpoints, sandbags, transistor radios, and the feeling of luck, then and now. This was an "us" that she did not have to explain. Mona and I were a different "us" when discussing the 2006 Israel-Lebanon war. In that context, "we" represented everyone who had stood against Israel during the war and remained "steadfast," with the implication that there were other Lebanese who had in fact supported Israel, echoing earlier experiences of war when some Lebanese allied with Israel or with Syria against other Lebanese. Sometimes "us" was anyone who had not left Lebanon to live abroad during the civil war,[35] and at other times "us" didn't include me at all—it referred to the "us" of civil servants when I was a researcher in their workplace. When Mona would use this last "us," it was to describe the unique challenges and responsibilities that structure the work of civil servants in the Lebanese state.

Digital Transparencies

Before I began my research, Lebanon had received a grant from USAID to further "the rule of law" in Lebanon. Digitizing court archives, substituting handwriting for type, and standardizing the filing and retrieval system was part of the vision of increasing transparency and judicial independence.[36] Mona's boss, Evelyn, was in favor of these reforms, but her subordinates were not. They feared they would lose their jobs because they could not master the new computer programs. Mona had an additional, more political concern, telling me that she would not allow "other governments," meaning the US government, to control how Lebanese court files were managed, retrieved, or categorized.[37] She would not trust Lebanese politicians, let alone those of another state, to understand or change the system or logic of the archive.

Digitization takes archivists whose handwriting, legal advice, and memories cannot be disambiguated from court files, and transforms them into workers who adhere to international standards of training and professionalism. This process of digitization and the economy of digital knowledge moves power away from middle-class government employees such as clerks and archivists, and into the hands of "experts." The experts' job description will be clear, their hours and tasks regimented, and they will be easily fired, hired, and replaced—or, most likely, *not* replaced. Debates about digitization and standardization are sites of power struggle. The stakes of this struggle are the regime of the archive, the way research is conducted, and the relationship of memory and feeling—shared or oppositional—to knowledge production.[38] The debates and practices implicate and threaten jobs and socioeconomic class. Neoliberal visions of the public sector contain fewer employees and different forms of employment; they shift embodied expertise to contingent forms of labor. Digitization is not merely a copy; it is a new economic and epistemological order. Under digitization, the possibility of loss, of losing this or that file, is assumed to disappear. In this way, the files will no longer be texts that can only be comprehended by acts of active and ethnographic reading.[39] They will circulate outside the lifeworlds in which they reside. They will become texts that can be removed from their immediate physical context and still be comprehensible to readers who are rendered more passive.[40] In addition to reshaping research methods, these changes will have an effect on jurisprudence itself, which at times requires acts of collective memory and sensitivity to life's contingencies and reversals, to be experienced emotively and collectively rather than electronically. Digitization promises immortality but cannot deliver it. It promises transparency and openness, but works to censor and erase.[41]

One day, to illustrate the effects of the 1985 fire on the archive and the need for digitization, Mona handed me an inheritance case file that included decisions from Roman Catholic and civil personal status courts. In 1992 a group of siblings presented a case to the Plenary Assembly. In his brief, their lawyer wrote that his clients were the heirs of a man whose case had been presented to the assembly in 1982—the year the Israeli army occupied West Beirut. That was also the year of the Sabra and Shatila massacre, in which members of Lebanese Christian militias raped, murdered, and mutilated thousands of Palestinian refugees and Lebanese under the watchful and capacitating eye of both Israel and the United States.[42] The siblings' case, which concerned ownership of land upon which a beach resort rested, had been decided in 1985. Their father had won,. but the case file had then burned in the 1985 fire, and now the siblings needed the case to ward off a group of cousins who were suing them for shares of the resort.

The Legal Life of Memory

The case file had consisted of the legally binding ruling, arguments by both the plaintiff and the defendants, evidence presented to the court, and copies of every step of the case as it was heard and ruled on at two different civil and personal status courts before being appealed at the Plenary Assembly. Because the file had been lost to the fire and, the lawyer argued, the archivists had been unable to find either its remnants or the ledger that indexed its presence, he asked the court to certify a photocopy of the decision, held by the siblings, as legally binding. Presence in the archive—being filed and recorded—is what makes a decision legally actionable. A case file is only definitively closed and enforceable if it can be found in the archive.

To reach a decision in this case, the judges analyzed handwriting, questioned archivists, and both separately and collectively *remembered* the case and the search for fire-eaten remnants of files and ledgers. They also remembered the judges presiding, the archivists employed at the time, and their handwriting in order to decide whether the siblings' copy of the decision was a copy of the lost original that had not been tampered with. The judges wondered about their duty as jurists and representatives of the state regarding documents, decisions, and files lost to the war. In the siblings' copy of the decision. The war and the fire were only referenced in the passive voice. The case was thick with historical narratives. It was the history of a family, a beach resort, and careers made and retired at the judiciary. The same judges climbed the ranks of the judiciary over the course of the case. One can even read the history of Mona's employment and that of her predecessor, as the photocopy of the original file carries the signature of a different archivist, but the pages that certify the copy as the original are marked with her distinctive two-letter imprint.

This and other cases adjudicated during the Lebanese civil war contain lawyers' briefs that directly impress on judges, archivists, and researchers the shared reality of terrifying, and in many cases terrifyingly arbitrary, violence. The cases insist on and call forth an activation of memory, a bubbling up, a breaking of the surface. Reading them, one is struck by the quotidian ways in which life and law continue during a war where an estimated one in eight residents in Lebanon is killed or critically injured—one in three if we include emigration, displacement, and disappearance. Some cases seem tragic and surreal: what is a murder case, after all, in the middle of a civil war, if not an insistence that lives still matter and that killing is still a crime? By referencing the war to judges who were also living and working through it, there is an appeal: *We are in this together.* Statements like this are excess information within the genre of legal writing, and their excess is precisely how I read the community-making of citizenship during a civil war. They represent "acts of citizenship" at a time when formal citizenship, alongside the state, is fraying under a civil war and under foreign occupations.[43] These acts of citizenship insist, moreover, on a community of citizens manifested in a shared lexicon of war regardless of political affiliation, sectarian identification, or regional location. They signal a refusal to seek redress from militia justice at a time of war, a turn toward the state: *We are all in this together, and we all refuse to be in it, together.*

But they are also appeals made on behalf of clients in ongoing court cases where they may be defendants or plaintiffs. They are a legal strategy. "My client could not come to the courthouse because there was a militia checkpoint at the mouth of the road." "This man has perverted Christianity and Islam and turned them against each other through his manipulations of religious conversion—a danger to the spirit of the Taif peace accord that ended our brutal nightmare of civil war." These are statements that activate shared archives of experience and press them into the present,[44] forms of address that both affectively and *knowingly* call a community into being. These statements also place the court in the world and the war, and insist that the law must bend to and acknowledge the realities of the world but at the same time transcend them. The law must be at once impartial to and contingent on life outside the court—life that jurists and ordinary people share when not structured by the context of legal encounter. The "we" of citizens is always exclusionary, however. The price of a post–civil war order is the sanctity of citizenship and the banishing of noncitizens from political community, including the community of legal memory. The files that contain these appeals, moreover, are all in this burned and shelled building, rendering the archive an artifact, a museum, a repository, an abundant affective realm.

Lebanon is an effervescent site for reconceptualizing the relationship between archives, violence, and histories of violence. The order and location of what we consider spectacular and nonspectacular violence shifts when we think, for example, that archives cannot account for people who could not get to court or muster the resources needed to pursue a case, or that public prosecutors do not investigate or charge rape, murder, racketeering, or assault during a war. What cannot be found in wartime is a meditation on the relationship between violence, crime, law, and history. War is often thought of us as a seismic event, a rupture of the everyday. Yet anyone who has lived through a war knows that, given enough time, war and destruction are everyday contexts that people not only die in but live through. Archival absence is overflowing with people surviving war—with the histories of life they cannot contain. Archives—particularly in countries where war is a recursive temporality rather than a rupture in time[45]—may in fact demonstrate an indeterminacy to the temporal and epistemological borders between war and peace on the one hand, and theory and method on the other.[46]

Legal files are a particular genre of writing—modular, highly formulaic, and governed by a different set of rules. Often with the advice of archivists like Mona, lawyers orient their arguments to a particular set of audiences that is both embodied (judges) and temporal. They write and argue their way into a tradition and history via citational logic, and they write and argue with an eye toward the future: an appeal, or a citation in a future case. The record left by legal procedure is necessarily incomplete; we encounter stories in the middle, we start somewhere and never return, and we encounter subjects narrating and being narrated toward archival truths that are violent and violating.[47] The force of the state compels one to narrate according to formal procedures and within particular discourse. In a case file we read the ultimate authority of the state, which can license truth statements and give a document—a photocopy, in the case just described—the force of law.[48] In certifying a copy as the original, the Lebanese state performs its sovereignty and scripts its own history of civil war, of "catastrophe," as a history of legal procedure and the continuation of professional life at the judiciary. In doing so it acknowledges the aporia of sovereignty itself: its power, and its vacuums. The state's lack of sovereign authority to protect its own archive and the Ministry of Justice from a wartime fire engenders new sovereign acts: a photocopy that must be certified by the ministry to stand in for the original. The wartime state is not absent, and nor is it behind us.

Describing War

To understand war in Lebanon, and war more generally, one has to pluralize both the wars themselves and the actors involved in them. In Lebanon, Lebanese nationalists, allied with the United States and in some cases Israel, and Arab nationalists, allied with Egypt and in some cases Palestinians, fought a civil war. Arab nationalists allied with Syria have also fought against Arab nationalists allied to Iraq. Protectors of the political status quo and supporters of Palestinian liberation have fought a war, fascists and socialists have fought a war, people who supported and opposed political sectarianism fought a war, capitalists and communists have fought a war. Christians have fought Christians, and Muslims have fought Muslims for reasons ranging from ideology to the profit margins of racketeering and militia "taxation" of areas under their control. The Israeli, US, French, and Syrian armies were part of the civil war from 1975 to 1990. Yet despite these complex and rapidly shifting alliances and counteralliances, the popular imagination and memory of these wars reduces and simplifies them to Christians versus Muslims—to a sectarian civil war. Memories of shared life during the wars are a tangle of intersecting and diverging descriptions. Some histories of the war—such as that of the sexual violence that made life for Lebanese women "hell," in the curt words of a female militia member I interviewed—have yet to be broached.[49]

The post–civil war era, meanwhile, is also war-filled. Political assassinations inaugurated the Taif Accord peace deal and, with it, the era of the Second Lebanese Republic. A full quarter of the country was under Israeli occupation until the year 2000, while 1996 saw the "Grapes of Wrath" Israeli war campaign against Lebanon. The year 2006 marked yet another Israeli invasion and Lebanon-Israel war, with more than 112,500 Lebanese citizens—the vast majority of whom were civilians and approximately 30 percent of whom were children,[50]—killed during the war. Another 70 percent have been killed by Israeli cluster munitions in South Lebanon since the end of the war. One year later, in 2007, the Lebanese Army launched a military campaign against Fath Al Islam, an Islamist militant group. The campaign lasted for months and included the army besieging and shelling Nahr El Bared, a Palestinian refugee camp that the militants had taken over, with the majority of refugees displaced and traumatized yet again by the fighting. More than five hundred soldiers, militants, and civilians are estimated to have died. In 2008, armed clashes (perhaps a mini–civil war) between pro- and anti-government political parties and militias killed at least seventy-one people over a period of two weeks.[51] No less than thirty bombings, political assassinations, and attempted assassinations seized the country from 2004 to 2015.[52] The Lebanese army and its allies fought a war with ISIL and Nusra from 2014 to 2017, and since 2012 political, social, and economic life in Lebanon has been largely defined by war in Syria since 2012. Amid this past and present multiplicity of violence, the Taif Accord was and is itself a technology of archival curation; the only reforms it has proposed have been limited to sectarian representation, and it has effectively collapsed the thickness of the Lebanese civil war into the bullet points of a negotiated peace deal. [53] The accord produced the authoritative account of the war. The economic, social, gendered, ideological and national "wars within wars" were silenced.[54] Peace deals such as Taif shape and curate the wars that precede them and, as Hiba Bou Akar terms them, the "war[s] yet to come."[55] The history of political violence in Lebanon is recursive and it is tragic, but it is not exceptional. Iraq, Syria, Palestine, and Yemen are also filled with war, and have been for decades. Any Iraqi, Syrian, Palestinian, or Yemeni reading this will recognize how the terms "war," "peace," and "cease-fire" fail to account for experience. These words, if anything, index a vanishing point between violence and stability, rather than a border. If only Lebanon were exceptional.

Ian Hacking suggests that to study events that seem overburdened, or overly signified and saturated with meaning, we should be attentive to the multiple descriptions under which any one act can fall. Only when we start with multiplicity can we understand conditions under which one of these descriptions will become hegemonic or authoritative.[56] Anjali Arondekar has cautioned us away from a heuristic of loss and melancholia—orientations toward the archive that demonstrate our attachment to historical categories (the power effects of the archives)—and instead toward an attentiveness to the abundance of the archival object itself.[57] This attention to abundance may allow us to destabilize not only the singularity of truth but our own investments in the singular nature of truth.[58] With these insights in mind, we turn now to our final ethnographic vignette.

One day while I was at the archives, Mona picked up a file I had not asked for and remarked that it was *the* Judicial Council case of Samir Geagea, a

Maronite militia leader. Geagea is the only wartime leader to have served time for crimes committed during the war and after the Taif Accord. He was arrested in 1994 and faced four separate Judicial Council trials for attempted and completed political assassinations during the civil war, and for the bombing of a church after the war ended, which killed nine people. He was convicted of all the crimes and sentenced to death. He then had his sentences commuted to life in prison, was pardoned by the Parliament in 2005, and then swiftly reentered political life. Geagea, an ally of the United States and Israel during the civil war, and still a political leader and US ally, is responsible for brutal wartime violence. He was a leader of the Lebanese Forces, a group of whom committed the Sabra and Shatila massacre under cover from their allies, the Israeli army,[59] blocks away from where Mona, my parents, and my two-year-old self lived at the time. A few years earlier, a sniper from that same militia had shot my grandfather twice as he went to check on his shops in downtown Beirut (he survived)—shops he would lose not during the war but after it, because of a series of legal decisions that paved the way for a corporation's eminent domain. Geagea was still a militia leader when both Mona's family and my own were displaced, along with many others from West Beirut, when then Army General Michel Aoun, now president of Lebanon, launched a war against Syria, which included a vicious war within a war against the Lebanese Forces led by Geagea.

Mona asked me if I wanted to see Geagea's file. Before I could answer, she threw it onto the dusty floor. I had never seen her handle documents with such disrespect. I was surprised, curious, jolted—emotions I papered over with a performance of professionalism. I told her I was only interested in the files I had actually requested, which were about religious conversion. Why did I not look at Geagea's file? Or rather, *how* did I not look at the file? Was I really worried that she would doubt my professionalism and stated *academic* reason for being in the archive if I took the file or even just looked at it? Perhaps I did not want to know, and could not bear to research a fantasy of only one case of "war crimes" and one alleged "war criminal" in a war that was full of crimes and criminals, all pardoned but never forgotten. How can anyone forget them when their faces and insignias still populate the country, now cloaked in the respectability of electoral paraphernalia? Maybe I did not want to feel all the dust Mona had kicked up inside me, could not dare to breathe it in. I said no. I froze. Mona looked back at me, smiled faintly, and shrugged. She went back to the files.

Years later, I struggle to explain the density of this action and my reaction to it.[60] There are several ways to describe Mona's throwing of the case file of the warlord-turned-politician at my feet, all of which are accurate. For example, "Mona threw this politician's case file at Maya's feet"; or "Mona threw Geagea's file at Maya's feet as a statement of disrespect and dislike"; or "Mona threw his file because he was the most famous name in that archive, the case in question was infamous, and Maya is after all a researcher." Or "Mona demonstrated her unprofessionalism—brought forth by corruption, sectarianism, family connections and *wasta* (nepotism)—by throwing a file at Maya's feet that she had not officially requested." Or, perhaps, "Mona threw Geagea's file because she was building another "us" that could not believe our past was still our future." All of these explanations describe the same act, and all are true. But only some are statements. The discourse that licenses them anticipates the act of throwing a file, and reads it as sectarianism. Moreover, this discourse—truth—can reach back into the past to place previous unrelated action and memory under the twinned signs of sectarianism and corruption—a process that Hacking calls "semantic contagion."[61]

At this ethnographic moment, Mona is throwing the file during an American-led "War on Terror" that has killed more than 1.3 million people in Iraq, Pakistan, and Afghanistan alone (a conservative estimate that does not include killings in Yemen and Syria)—and which has spawned the multiple wars on terror that authoritarian leaders are currently waging against political dissent. A few months after Mona threw the file, uprisings would begin in Tunisia and roll like a wave across the region, just as securitization, authoritarianism, and wars would roll through on the heels of those uprisings. A few months before she threw the file, parliamentary elections had been held in Lebanon, and Geagea had been an ally of the Sunni political leadership— led by Saad al Hariri, son of the assassinated prime minister—that claimed to speak in Mona's name and mine. Mona and I had marveled at the spectacle of the son of an assassinated prime minister allying with a man who had infamously assassinated another prime minister, Rashid Karami—whose murder, in fact, was one of the crimes Geagea was convicted of by the Judicial Council. Geagea currently warns of the "dangers" Syrian refugees pose to Lebanon and regularly threatens to "return" them to Syria, just as he said of Palestinians during the civil war. The more we zoom out of this ethnographic scene, the more the descriptions multiply, intersect, and depart. As I began writing this chapter, a civil and transnational war was raging two hours away, across the border in Syria. That war has killed hundreds of thousands of Syrians. Another eleven million have been displaced, and the war—which began as a brutal authoritarian crackdown against a popular uprising—is increasingly being waged through a sectarian War on Terror framework. Syrian refugees in Lebanon are targeted, securitized, and attacked just as Palestinian refugees were during the civil war and continue to be. At this writing, in 2021, we are in the year of Lebanon's centenary, one year out of a popular uprising, and the country has both exploded and imploded economically, politically, and financially. Geagea is one of the most popular politicians, a perpetual candidate for the Lebanese presidency. Alongside many other politicians who were targeted, he now claims the mantle of the 2019 popular uprising. In this same year I have looked up the Judicial Council's decisions related to Geagea, and have noticed for the first time that Mona was the clerk and archivist for those cases. And again, the descriptions proliferate.

Maybe Mona wanted me to see the role she had played in the case. Maybe she wanted me to see her signature on the conviction of Geagea—one of the most infamous and consequential cases in the history of the Lebanese judiciary. Maybe I hurt her by refusing to see it, by not talking about what she thought or felt as she sat there, taking notes and filing papers during the trial and afterward, tending to the case files' place in the archive. Maybe she wanted to be asked questions. There is indeterminacy, then and now, to Mona's action and my writing of it. One cannot know which combination of motivations made her act of throwing the case file possible—or the motivations that informed my perceptions of that act then and now. Archival context is not only about the past. Archives also function *in time,* as do archival research and ethnography. If the archive is a temporal order, so is our relationship to it.[62] What we look for, what we want to find, and how we conceptualize what we have found, changes in time.

The thickness and complexity of this exchange of gestures—just like the previous thickness of an economy of favors at the archive—is fixed and flattened by the discourses of sectarianism and corruption. Once fixed and curated this way, Mona's action can only be understood as evidence that together we are sectarian toward our common Sunni sect, a sectarianism manifesting in the singling out of one militia leader-cum-politician from a different sect, and that together we perform the corruption in state institutions that this sectarianism fosters. But there is only one such file in this room, and I am only *in* this room because of a meeting at a bar near the Columbia University law school with the president of the Administrative Courts—a meeting mediated by my relationship with a well-respected professor of US constitutional law. This is a connection based on class, professionalism, and success within an economy that is deeply polarized. It is a form of nepotism that circulates within transnational networks of class and privilege (perhaps sites of class warfare) that are read neither as "dangerous" nor as inherently violent or corrupt. After all, there is no transnational industry of expertise devoted to "fixing" the problem of class-based bias, Ivy League networking, or the violent production and circulation of wealth. Academia revels in producing knowledge about a sectarian, authoritarian, corrupt, classed, or monarchical Middle East, yet it almost never addresses the ways in which academics sometimes use these same networks to produce that research. Many books that use archival methods never point to or explain how exactly their authors were able to access particularly hard-to-reach archives. Instead, they reproduce the myth of objective meritocracy, which scaffolds and resignifies individual and structural inequality as individual genius, tenacity, and achievement.[63] These myths do work in propping up a vision of the academy as a meritocracy precisely when—in the face of neoliberal austerity, restructuring, and public defunding—prestige, pedigree, and the class system within academia become ever more pronounced.[64]

The archive is not a room the lonely researcher enters to extract research. Such an approach would ensure that both the archival object and the trope of the intrepid researcher remain stable. Citational practices do much to create this trope. To the extent that archivists, bureaucrats, photocopiers, or cleaners enter the stage, they do so in the form of a good fieldwork or research story, usually via a footnote or during an academic lecture. Yet the conversations I have had with Youssef and Mona are part of what makes the archive a legible object, as are the flashlights we used to look for particular cases, or the toilet paper that archivists buy for their offices because the government does not provide it. The ordinariness of the archive *is* the fabric of knowledge production, and if we shift our attention away from the archival object and toward what makes it archival, we find ourselves in the middle of the story each time—but not as its primary authors, nor even its primary audience.

We will end here, on a performance of indeterminacy: Mona throwing the case file of a warlord-turned-politician across the floor of an archive full of dust, cracked walls, and no electricity. This happened in the archive of Lebanon's highest court, a repository of memory, state action, and networks of living together and apart during war and postwar worlds[65]—a place where judges remember the handwriting of their dead colleagues, and where lawyers construct an affective bridge, a legal strategy. It is a place to which I came to look for insights into the rule and ruptures of law, armed with theory and history and ethnography—a place of work. It is a place I had to unlearn, a room struck by mortars, the site of a fire. It is a room that may soon be replaced by digital files, software, and workers without tenure. I now imagine, or choose to think, that Mona is throwing the file across the threshold between memory, ethnography, and history, between archive and Archive, and between the war and postwar worlds. Mona perhaps knows what her action indexes to readers: corruption, sectarianism, unprofessionalism, the failure of state institutions. She knows because she has been to training sessions, has read the civil society literature, follows the news that corrupt politicians want to cut the benefits of public employees as a first step to fighting their corruption, feels the threat of imminent replacement, and is waiting to retire. But in this moment, in *her* archive, holding the file and looking toward me, Mona does not care.

She throws it anyway.

4 DONATING IN THE NAME OF THE NATION
Charity, Sectarianism, and the Mahjar

REEM BAILONY

IN JANUARY 1926, AS a rebellion against the French Mandatory regime was underway in Syria, one of New York's Arabic-language periodicals, *Mir'at al-Gharb* (Mirror of the West), published an editorial titled, "For Whom does *Al-Huda* Collect Money?"[1] Run by the Greek Orthodox publisher Najib Diyab, the piece took issue with its rival publication—*al-Huda* (The Guidance)—over its charitable campaign to aid civilians in southern Lebanon who suffered from the spreading violence there. In October 1925, just a few months after Sultan Pasha al-Atrash called upon Syrians to rebel against the French, Druze rebels crossed into Wadi al-Taym, the southern valley separating Syria from Greater Lebanon.[2] The region's villages, especially Rashaya, suffered in the crossfire, the civilian victims of which were largely Greek Orthodox.[3] At the heart of the article was not a dispute over the injustice of the violence or the need for relief, but a concern about the political motives *al-Huda*'s fundraising effort, run by Na'um Mukarzil, a Maronite Christian and Lebanese nationalist. While both Diyab and Mukarzil could be defined as Christians belonging to the wider Syrian *mahjar* (diaspora), they had very different visions for the future of their homeland.[4]

This chapter focuses on the debate between *Mir'at al-Gharb* and *al-Huda* to consider how the Syrian-Lebanese diaspora in New York, and the United States more broadly, negotiated their political subjectivities through sectarian belonging in the context of the Syrian Revolt of 1925–27. Rumors of Christian suffering at the hands of the rebels provoked transnational debates about the aim and vision of the anticolonial revolt. For Naʿum Mukarzil, Rashaya's fate raised doubts about the stated nationalist aims of the uprising. In the pages of *al-Huda*, Mukarzil often accused the revolt's Druze leaders with purposefully targeting Christians in southern Lebanon in order to impinge on the integrity of Greater Lebanon.[5] From the moment of General Henri Gouraud's declaration of Greater Lebanon in 1920, to which Rashaya and surrounding towns were annexed, various factions opposed to the French Mandate would challenge Lebanon's separation from Syria.[6] Consequently, as a border town, Rashaya's ruin acted as a siren of impending Syrian encroachment onto Lebanese sovereignty, while also calling into question France's avowed role as the guardian of Greater Lebanon's Christians. Rashaya's suffering would in turn incense the Syrian-Lebanese diaspora, inciting both supporters and detractors of France's mission in the region while stoking the flames of sectarianism.[7]

The sectarian dynamics of the *mahjar*, when studied through the pivotal moment of 1925, demonstrate how sectarian markers did not act in a uniform fashion for members of this global diaspora. World War I marked a transformation in the identity politics of the *mahjar*. Having left before the dissolution of the Ottoman Empire, migrants from the eastern Mediterranean arrived in the United States starting in the late nineteenth century, bringing their particularist loyalties to religion, family, and village with them.[8] This largely Christian and Arabic-speaking diaspora would soon come to refer to themselves as "Syrian," a designation that not only held legal significance but graced the titles of their magazines, letters home, and internal dialogues.[9] Yet, as the contours of the future Syrian and Lebanese states came into view under the French Mandate, this sweeping ethnic category obscured more than just translocal attachments; it also obscured the emerging political identities of Syrian, Lebanese, and Palestinian.[10] As the Syrian Revolt threatened French Mandatory political arrangements, it further undermined the salience of this overarching Syrian identity in the diaspora. In effect, Syrian-Lebanese migrants came to understand and employ sectarian and national allegiances in different ways that produced contending "internal and external politics of belonging" toward both the United States and the homeland.[11] As such, rather than taking for granted divisions within the *mahjar*, this chapter makes the case for the sectarianization of the diaspora as a transnational process that connected both contexts.

Homeland tensions quickly spread to the diaspora, raising the specter of preexisting sectarian and political differences among the communities of the *mahjar.* While the *mahjar*'s Muslims, Druze, and Orthodox Christians generally leaned in favor of an anticolonial and wider Syrian nationalism, most Maronite Catholics tended to support Lebanese separatism (guaranteed through French tutelage).[12] As a Maronite, Mukarzil would use his periodical to take up the cause of Rashaya and its Orthodox Christian victims, later going on to create the Lebanon Relief Committee. Through his charitable campaign, Mukarzil thereby instrumentalized the events of the revolt to advance the cause of Lebanese nationalism while also buttressing his own nationalist credentials. Meanwhile, for *Mir'at al-Gharb*'s Najib Diyab, the events at Rashaya brought to the fore tensions between support for sect and support for the nation. An advocate of Syrian nationalism (as many of Orthodox Christians tended to be), Diyab supported a free and independent Syria.[13] Yet for Diyab and other supporters of the Syrian rebellion, the events at Rashaya were a tragic and painful reminder of the fraught nation-making that followed World War I.

This chapter examines the intersecting dynamics of sect and nation as they were practiced through translocal and particularist diaspora institutions like periodicals, charitable associations, churches, and politically oriented clubs. It analyzes *mahjar* publications like *al-Huda* (c. 1898), *Mir'at al-Gharb* (c. 1899), and *al-Bayan* (The Explanation; c. 1910)—all Arabic-language periodicals published in New York—for their unique perspective on how Syrian-Lebanese émigrés understood, reconfigured, and deployed sectarian loyalties while sketching out the often conflicting meanings of patriotic duty. The *mahjar* facilitated not only transnational debates but also key activities like fund-raising, business, and social networking. Moreover, periodicals were—through links with their owners and publishers—unofficially connected to various sectarian communities and political parties. *Al-Huda,* for example, was connected to *Jam'iyyat al-Nahda al-Lubnaniyya* (Lebanon League of Progress), Mukarzil's pro-French, pro-Lebanese independence party; Diyab's *Mir'at al-Gharb* and *al-Bayan*'s Druze editor, Suleyman Baddur, supported Syrian independence through parties like *Hizb Suriyya al-Jadida* (New Syria Party). As *mahjar* historians have demonstrated, the *mahjar* press consequently acted as an important mode and semiotic field of transnational bourgeois activism wherein Syrian-Lebanese émigrés actively fashioned and shaped nationalist understandings.[14]

While scholars have scrutinized the *mahjar* press as a vehicle for diasporic nationalism, this study uncovers how it also acted as a space for debating the contours of sectarian belonging and the meanings of sectarianism in the United States and beyond. Literature on the 1925 Syrian Revolt as well as scholarship on the history of the *mahjar* have largely avoided analyzing the sectarian discourse that in many ways surrounded both. This has largely to do with scholars' analytical tendency—and desire—to locate the development of nationalist discourse in the Arab world outside the field of religion. Moreover, as James Gelvin argues, inasmuch as the narrative on Arab nationalism "differentiates between nationalist and religious movements, it isolates each from the other, reifies the boundaries of both, and disengages religion from the very historical process that made secular nationalist movements meaningful to the inhabitants of the region in the first place."[15] Focusing on the press and philanthropy of the *mahjar* during the revolt years, this chapter demonstrates how nationalist aspirations and sectarian dynamics intersected to produce nationalist agency in the diaspora.

As Syrian-Lebanese émigrés mobilized to come to the aid of their homeland in 1925, they struggled to articulate the differences between notions of sectarian belonging and the meanings attached to nascent Syrian and Lebanese nationalisms. Since sect and translocal dynamics often defined the core organizations and presses of the *mahjar* as well as the networks that sustained connections to the homeland, charitable activity and journalism became highly contentious activities, the stakes of which were often about the future of the nation and homeland. Advertisements for and debates over donations spilled across the pages of Arabic-language publications. As editors got involved in fund-raising efforts, their personal and political feuds colored the dynamics of charity, delegitimizing their charitable projects and calling into question their capacity to donate in the name of the nation. Donations for those affected by the revolt consequently prompted accusations of sectarian factionalism by opposing camps—those supporting the French imperial project and those challenging it. More important, however, was that both sides leveraged sectarian discourse to gain material support and exhibit their place within the imagined Syrian or Lebanese nation.

An examination of the press coverage on the revolt and pursuant fundraising reveals how sectarian community and transnational charitable activity intersected to produce diasporic nationalist agency in the interwar period. Sectarianism and nationalism therefore emerged as simultaneous processes that played out across a transnational space. When studied through the institutions of the diaspora, the Syrian Revolt of 1925–27 becomes as much a moment of practicing sectarianism as it is of nationalist formation.[16]

Sectarianism and the *Mahjar*

That Lebanon's sectarian political system partly grew out of its diaspora is something widely acknowledged but less interrogated in most literature.[17] Rania Maktabi's work on the 1932 census (Lebanon's last recorded census) highlights the pivotal role that the inclusion of the mostly Christian diaspora would play in enumerating and constructing Lebanon as a majority Christian nation.[18] Fahrenthold takes this line of inquiry further back, to the French Mandatory government's initial attempts to count Lebanese émigrés in 1921. She argues that the 1921 census laid the foundations for what she terms "*mandating the mahjar,* a refraction of state authority to contain select emigrants within the strictures of citizenship."[19] Biased in favor of counting Christians within and beyond Lebanon, the policies that grew out of these initial censuses, and the attendant confessional republican system they informed, reflected the linked desire of France and the leaders of the Maronite Church to create a Lebanon that would act as a Christian stronghold.[20] The politics of including Lebanon's diaspora continues to this day; Lebanon's expatriate citizens, numbering more than a million, voted in parliamentary elections for the first time in 2018.[21] Like efforts to conduct the 1932 census, recent debates surrounding the political participation of the present-day diaspora have also centered on increasing Christian representation (as Christians continue to make up the majority of expatriate citizens, even as demographic figures have drastically changed within the country).[22]

The economic influence of the diaspora, too, has been a steady feature of this influential relationship between migrant and homeland. By World War I, nearly three hundred thousand to half a million emigrants from the eastern Mediterranean formed a diaspora abroad. This diaspora remained committed to homeland culturally, politically, and economically. On the eve of World War I, diaspora remittances accounted for nearly 40 percent of Mount Lebanon's income; today, they account for about 12.7 percent of the GDP for Lebanon as a whole.[23] According to Graham Pitts, the largely historic rural migration from Lebanon accounted for a complex demographic and economic ecology that saw a skewed impact on the country's Christian population, and had a grave impact during World War I. During the famine of that war, Mount Lebanon's population became politically and economically cut off from its diaspora, resulting in a third of Mount Lebanon's population perishing.[24] During the 1925 Syrian Revolt, Syrian-Lebanese migrants would continue to donate large sums of money for both civilians and rebel factions. This material influence entangled French imperial authorities in the affairs of the diaspora, as French consular officials would attempt to gain the support of the diaspora's key figures.[25]

Emerging scholarship on the history of the Syrian-Lebanese *mahjar* has thus rightfully acknowledged the ways in which sect has historically informed the demographic, social, and economic realities of émigré communities—and, in turn, how these dynamics have been reflected onto homeland. The political economy that emigration helped produce, skewed as it was toward Lebanon's Christians, in turn had sectarian ramifications. As Akram Khater has demonstrated, remittances and return migration produced a middle-class modernity in Mount Lebanon at the turn of the twentieth century. While it was not the focus of his study, Khater notes, "Every subsequent step toward the making of the middle class was infused with sectarian separation."[26] Disputes such as the one between *al-Huda* and *Mir'at al-Gharb* took place within a wider context of migrants working out their place in the Anglo-American and Protestant political culture of the United States, where religion—Christianity in particular—was affiliated with progress and modernity, and where whiteness was required for citizenship.[27] Such an environment produced and bolstered migration narratives that blamed emigration on Ottoman persecution of Christians. Khater remarks that Maronite emigrants renegotiated American discourses of cultural superiority "by way of justifying a separate Lebanese nation as the spearhead of 'Christian modernity' in a sea of 'Muslim backwardness.'"[28] This is evident in a 1921 letter by Mukarzil to the French Consul general, where he insisted that Lebanon be acknowledged as different from Syria. He based his appeal on an incident that had taken place in Roanoke, Virginia, complaining, "Syrians are placed in the same category as blacks; that is, they refused to sell land in a certain part of the city to blacks and Syrians." Mukarzil continued, "We are independent Lebanese, completely different than the Syrians, and we expect you [France] to protect us because you are considered one of our representatives."[29] The process of becoming Lebanese or Syrian in the *mahjar* thus evolved with sectarian articulations of community that had the potential to become all the more contentious within the racial and ethnic dynamics of American society during the 1920s. And, as Khater suggests warrants further study, in Lebanon, money from abroad—recycled and invested in the economy—reproduced diasporic notions of difference, especially between Maronites and Druze.[30]

Emerging scholarship on the history of the Syrian-Lebanese *mahjar* has thus rightfully acknowledged the ways in which sect has historically informed the demographic, social, and economic realities of émigré communities and, in turn, how these dynamics have been reflected onto homeland.[31] By contrast, in this volume, for example, Tsolin Nalbantian's chapter demonstrates how a faction of Armenian-Americans—many of whom did not hail from Lebanon—enacted sectarianism by seeking the assistance of the Armenian Church in Lebanon in response to a long-drawn-out dispute after the murder of an Armenian archbishop by Armenian nationalists in New York in 1933.[32] Both Nalbantian's chapter and this one show how émigrés leveraged sectarianism to exercise power and political preference.

Debating Nation and Sect

In October 1925, as calls for freedom and independence reverberated in southern Syria, *Mir'at al-Gharb* published an editorial titled "Treating Sectarianism." Its author described a conversation between him and a friend on the subject of Syria, of which he declared, "Immigrants have no other talk today." The conversation inevitably veered to the topic of sectarianism (*al-na'arat al-mathabiyya*), with his friend declaring: "Ah! If only these bigotries were like trees on the ground, I would uproot them until they were no more." He and his friend wished to see only one doctrine in Syria: the doctrine of nationalism. The author responded that it was a beautiful but unrealistic wish; only time could heal the "disease" of sectarianism, and it would have to be treated with the spread of free and mandatory public-school education. Future Syrian citizens who attained a modern educational background would presumably bring religious bigotry to an end, setting the Syrian nation on its path to national freedom and independence.[33] Like many around him, the author believed that a lack of standardized public education both enabled and contributed to the problem of sectarianism in Syria and Lebanon. In contrast, Nadya Sbaiti's chapter in this volume contends that private schools during the Mandate period, even when confessionally oriented, were spaces of cross-sectarian interaction and potential.[34]

Although scholarship on the Syrian Revolt of 1925–27 has emphasized the pivotal role it played in articulating a secular nationalist movement, there has been less discussion of how nationalism developed in conjunction with ongoing debates about the role of sect in communal conflict and/or solidarity.[35] As alluded to above, polemics over sectarianism picked up as the rebellion spilled into southern Lebanon; and as news of the events traveled the Atlantic, controversy only seemed to gain steam. Far removed from the battlefield, the *mahjar* press waged a war of words over the nature, aim, and outcome of the anticolonial movement. As the community's only English-language periodical, *The Syrian World*, noted, "Among Syrian immigrants who take part in home conflicts only from a distance and are not governed by feelings of actual loss . . . the effect of the controversy is more enduring and the harmful results of dissensions are more far-reaching."[36]

With keen eyes on the French Mandate, Syrian-Lebanese émigrés turned to their local Arabic-language press for updates on the rebellion. As a key institution of the diaspora, the press did more than convey the news; it also allowed émigrés to enact their sense of duty toward homeland. As community forums, diaspora periodicals ran business advertisements, solicited donations for local charitable groups, published editorials, and shared news and letters from the readers. Although not exclusively aimed for a sectarian readership, the Arabic-language periodicals of New York and beyond tended to reflect the political and sectarian leanings of their publishers. Mukarzil's *al-Huda* frequently discussed the affairs and concerns of the wider Maronite diaspora, with strong support for the French Mandate. Although more politically oriented toward Arabism and Syrianism, Diyab's *Mir'at al-Gharb* similarly acted as a place for news on the Orthodox Church. Suleiman Baddur's *al-Bayan* shared in *Mir'at*'s anti-French politics while also catering to a wider Druze and Muslim audience. Yet, to the extent that all three journals responded to one another, one can assume that the literate Syrian-Lebanese diaspora read all three. As such, the intersection of diaspora institutions and confessional community infused discussions around nationalism with greater urgency, particularly because the diasporic ethnic marker of "Syrian" collapsed and effaced the differences which in reality prevented the diaspora from being a unified political community.

Naturally, then, the press also became a battleground for the contestation of long-distance nationalism, and never more vociferously than when it debated the 1925 revolt. Regardless of their accuracy, rumors of Christian suffering at the hands of rebels in Damascus and the villages of southern Lebanon provoked debates about the rebels' aim and vision. Additionally, insofar as Greater Lebanon was considered to be a refuge for Christians, it also conjured debates about the geographic confines of the future Syrian and Lebanese states. In December 1925, for example, the Lebanese lawyer Yusuf al-Sawda penned an article in Mukarzil's *al-Huda*.[37] A Maronite, Sawda had once been leader of the Alliance Libanaise (*al-Ittihad al-Lubnani*), the first Lebanese émigré group to advocate for Ottoman reform and Lebanese autonomy from its headquarters in Cairo and Alexandria.[38] In the article, Sawda reacted to the passage of Druze rebels across the border that demarcated southern Syria from southern Lebanon. The controversial drive into towns west of Mount Hermon riled local and diasporic Lebanese Christian communities, as they found themselves recalling reprisal attacks against Christians during World War I, and even the 1860 civil war. Having lived in Alexandria several years before finally returning to Lebanon, Sawda paid special attention to the role of Lebanese migrants in the 1925 revolt:

> . . . Overseas there are hundreds of thousands of Lebanese whose mention of Lebanon shakes them, and whereupon any mention of injustice to their homes transforms their sentiments towards the Syrian cause into enmity, and who shake the opinion of the civilized world.[39]

While for Sawda, the rebels had committed an infraction against Greater Lebanon and the Lebanese, for editor Mukarzil an attack on Lebanon was also an attack on Christianity. Over the course of late 1925 and 1926, his periodical would indefatigably lodge accusations of sectarian violence against the Druze rebels. Weekly editorials referred to the Druze fighters as having veered into "barbarism" with alleged attacks on Lebanese Christians.[40] Mukarzil accused the Druze of "*ta'asub*," or sectarian fanaticism.[41] According to *al-Huda*, the Christians of Syria who were "a minority everywhere" warned foreign newspapers of an impending "religious war that would wipe out [the] Christians."[42] Given such violence, Mukarzil considered France's presence in Lebanon a necessity.[43]

Yet in the same stroke, Mukarzil's periodical also attempted to position itself as nationally minded. Concern for wider Christian suffering, regardless of sect, did not necessitate or equal a call for religiously motivated politics. In a reprint of an editorial originally published in the Beirut-based *al-Barq* (The Lightning), *al-Huda* asked its readers to ponder circulating claims that "Lebanese Christians" sought a Christian state.[44] The editorial retorted that the Christians of Lebanon were not ignorant to demand a "religious throne" in this day and age. Rather, as Lebanese hopefuls they disagreed with Syrian calls for "Islamic" unity with the Hijaz (who, the editorial added, consolidated such calls by committing crimes against the Christians in the spirit of creating chaos). The editorial concluded that, to the contrary, it was the "fanaticism" of certain Syrian factions that contributed to the idea of a separate Lebanese state based on constitutionalism.

In a similar vein, *al-Huda* printed an opinion piece by the editor of a Zahleh-based journal, *Zahleh al-Fatat* (The Young Zahleh). The author, Shukri al-Bakhash (who himself had spent some time publishing in New York during World War I), wrote a nuanced piece on Christian-Druze relations during the revolt. With the rebel reach into southern Lebanon in 1925, Bakhash feared that the country was on the verge of returning to religious war, the likes of which had afflicted Mount Lebanon in the "days when ignorance ruled the minds."[45] Bakhash decried rebel attacks on Lebanese Christians as "black pages" in history, stating that those who committed atrocities were among the ignorant who did not yet recognize that "nationalism today comes before religion in the eyes of nations."[46] Pointing to instances where Lebanese Druze came to the aid of their neighboring Christians, Bakhash hoped that such cooperation would prove that the bonds of the Lebanese nation were stronger now than the bonds of sect.

Mukarzil's descriptions of the Druze were far more colorful than those of Bakhash, yet his inclusion of such pieces as the above illustrates the transnational dialogue that fashioned national and sectarian belonging in the interwar period. On page after page, Mukarzil conflated his concern for Lebanon with his concern over Christians. In wading back and forth between the fields of nation and sect, Mukarzil's *al-Huda* demonstrates that the two intersected to produce his nationalist agency. As readers wrote in support of *al-Huda*, they also buttressed its place in the nation. One reader from Uniontown, Pennsylvania, described *al-Huda* as a periodical at the forefront of service to nation and humanity. Calling Mukarzil an exemplary "nationalist leader," the letter thanked him for his stance on the "Druze revolt," and for taking to task "those who sold their nation and hearts for a cheap price."[47]

The implied perpetrators described by the above reader could have easily been a reference to *al-Huda*'s local competition, *Mir'at al-Gharb* and *al-Bayan*. An alternative narrative emerges in the pages of these two New York journals, united in their anti-French sentiment. In them, the tables were turned, and it was Mukarzil who was guilty of propagating sectarian strife and French bias in the *mahjar*. And whereas the rebels emerged as the "barbarians" in *al-Huda*, *al-Bayan* and *Mir'at* began their critique with the French, "the barbarians of this age."[48] Mukarzil's opponents thus accused him of blindly regurgitating French tropes, lumping his periodical into a pejorative category of "Francophone" and "colonialist" newspapers of the diaspora.[49]

In response to *al-Huda*'s denunciation of "Druze Mohammedan" and Christian supporters of the revolt, the two journals poked holes in *al-Huda*'s nationalist posture. Diyab took to his periodical to directly call out Mukarzil for the war of words that had been transpiring between them, stating: "The dispute between you and us is one between two periodicals over political and national issues," and not between two sects over religious matters.[50] Diyab faulted Mukarzil for conflating political differences with sectarian ones, sarcastically calling him out for labeling anyone who disagreed with him a religious fanatic. Diyab further belied Mukarzil by stating that even among the Maronites, there was no one unified political stance. "The Maronite faith is not weak and in need of your protection," Diyab pronounced, and "not everyone who hates enslavement [a reference to the French Mandate] is against Maronites."[51] In addition to doubting Mukarzil's nationalism, Diyab also challenged Mukarzil's Christian solidarity by suggesting that Mukarzil was more concerned with Maronite interests than with the wider Christian demographic he claimed to defend.

Al-Bayan similarly questioned *al-Huda*'s nationalist and sectarian solidarities by highlighting the political diversity that existed among Maronites. While *al-Bayan* supported a wider Syrian nationalism, it nevertheless made space for the anticolonialism of Lebanese nationalists who also happened to be Maronite. In one such instance, the periodical reproduced a telegram from a "Lebanese Maronite" based in Europe who protested calls for Christians to arm themselves against Druze and Syrians.[52] Elaborating upon this sentiment, *al-Bayan* praised Maronite supporters of the revolt, some of whom, it claimed, had traveled to Syria to join revolutionary ranks. "These are the true Lebanese who love Lebanon and protect [it]," unlike those who had surrendered their ancestral lands to the colonial power, the author opined.[53] In defining the qualities of a "true" Lebanese patriot, *al-Bayan* did more than denounce the nationalism of pro-French Lebanese in the *mahjar*. In recognizing Lebanon, the editorial also responded to (and perhaps tried to allay) Lebanese concerns that the 1925 rebellion aimed to rejoin the territories of Syria and Lebanon. The implication here is that one could support the project of an independent Lebanese nation while also supporting the anticolonial aims of the Syrian rebels.

Elsewhere, *al-Bayan* returned Mukarzil's accusations of fanaticism by condemning the "colonialist periodicals" that encouraged the "Christians of Syria and the *mahjar*" to oppose the Druze and even fight them.[54] In this thinly veiled attack on *al-Huda*, the piece once again claimed that "we know that such writing offends our Christian comrades," and that "the majority of Syrians" laughed at its foolishness. Yet while *al-Bayan* denounced the divisiveness of the colonialist journal in question, it also spoke on behalf of the Druze by claiming, "We know that the Druze are better than to respond to this evil and inimical call."[55] While calling for national unity, *al-Bayan* nevertheless reified the categories of Christian and Druze, colonialist and patriot, as binary opposites. Additionally, unlike the above piece which recognized the "Lebanese" as a separate national identity, here all in question were collectively grouped as "Syrian." Moreover, national identity formation took place in relation to immigrant understandings of US American dynamics; in a debate that took place in *al-Bayan* a few years earlier, for example, the journal asserted: "We are Syrian from the same cherished region, Arab by racial origin, so if we say we are Lebanese or Hawrani or Palestinian that does not mean we are not Syrian. And if we say we are Syrian that does not mean we are not Arab." The author struck a local example for comparison: "The New Yorker doesn't call himself a New Yorker but American."[56] Channeling the overarching construct of American, the author justified the Syrian label. While this label was a common way to refer to the Arabic-speaking diaspora in the United States, the article's reference to the various labels that fell under this wider ethnic category highlights the tensions that existed at the intersection of ethnic, national, and sectarian identities.

Debates over the meaning of sectarian belonging as well as the nature of sectarianism in conjunction with the 1925 revolt illustrate the ambiguities of sectarian and national belonging in the interwar period. As the confines of Syria and Lebanon shifted in response to local challenges and events within the territories' borders, émigrés responded to these developments in kind. To demonstrate their patriotic duty and nationalist agency, Syrian-Lebanese migrants turned to fund-raising for the homeland. Disputes over the virtues of charity ensued, simultaneously (re)producing translocal, sectarian, and nationalist loyalties while highlighting the tensions therein.

Donating in the Name of the Nation

In October 1925, *Mir'at al-Gharb* wrote about Shaykh bin Salman Yusuf, describing him as a Syrian businessman in the United States who belonged to the "Druze sect" but was "a patriot above all." The paper detailed Yusuf's donation of two thousand "riyals" to help afflicted civilians back home. He was joined in this endeavor by his coreligionists in the United States, as the paper went on to mention how "the Druze associations of the *mahjar* awakened to help the victims of Jabal al-Druze."[57] In doing so, continued the author, they were motivated by the bonds of patriotism. Yet the piece also noted the "useless debates" between Christians and Druze writers, associations, and newspapers over support for France and support for the rebels. The author hoped that readers would leave behind such debates and turn their sympathies toward the nationalist revolt.

As contested as it was, the 1925 revolt provided émigrés with an opportunity to participate in nation-building even at a distance. While journalism offered one avenue for debating and defining the nation, fund-raising afforded an opportunity to practice nationalism while reinforcing sectarianism. As the fighting took its humanitarian and economic toll, Syrian-Lebanese immigrants strove to demonstrate their patriotic devotion by collecting donations for the suffering back home. Beyond this, there was mounting evidence that émigrés also collected money for the rebels, a phenomenon that focused French intelligence on the activities of the diaspora, resulting in the French counterpropaganda campaigns among diaspora supporters whom they found to have an influential impact on relatives and villages back home.[58] Channeled through various organizations, churches, and banks, these donations created a diverse landscape of charitable pathways and committees. Some, like Mukarzil's Lebanon Relief Committee, claimed to represent the nation, whereas others, like the Zahleh Relief Committee, organized around targeted village relief. Reviving World War I–era practices and debates, groups in the *mahjar* organized around party, sect, and village to collect material support for their compatriots back home. As a means of patriotic praxis, charitable donation in turn produced and reinforced sectarianism. As tensions between national representation and effective relief emerged, fund-raising for the homeland consequently encouraged the concurrent development of sectarian and nationalist identity politics.

In December 1925, *al-Huda* published an announcement of a meeting that had recently taken place at the salon of the *Nahda al-Lubnaniyya*, Mukarzil's Lebanon League of Progress.[59] It was an official gathering of the *Lajnat Mankubi Lubnan*, the Lebanon Relief Committee. The committee had decided to send one thousand dollars in donations to the Representative Council of Lebanon for the purpose of distributing it to refugees and victims of the fighting who needed it most, and, as the announcement made sure to state, without regard to their confessional background. Those on the Representative Council in charge of distributions were a religiously mixed group that included Musa Nammur, Habib al-Saʿad, Amir Fuʾad Arslan, and al-Shaykh Ibrahim Mundhir. Mukarzil wanted his critics to know that the committee "made no consideration for sect" in its distribution of funds, but was devoted to the cause of nationalism, "for the nation has no religion."[60] This common refrain of the post–World War I period summed up a consensus across the political spectrum over what a secular future should look like.

Al-Huda's editor wrote elsewhere about the sectarian dynamics of the *mahjar*'s charitable efforts. While the priest solicited donations in the name of Christians, the journal exclaimed, "The Druze extends his palms with blindness and delusion, and the Muslim does the same in the name of the Syrian people."[61] In this way, these various groups misleadingly collected money from the Americans and their own people toward their various political projects. Not only was Mukarzil shaming the sectarian landscape of donation collections, but he also implied that the Druze and Muslims more specifically were deceiving the public.[62] His paper accused the Druze of diverting fundraising money to support the rebel fighters, and *al-Mir'at* of supporting them in these efforts, writing, "There is a strange contradiction in the words and actions of *al-Mir'at*, and that it champions the Druze and Islamic committees in their collection of money to kill the Christians while it opposes *al-Huda* for working in the service of the victims (*mankubin*)." *Al-Huda* did not reserve its accusations of corruption for the Druze; it also suggested that simultaneous efforts by *Mir'at al-Gharb* to collect money for victims of the fighting in the Rif in Morocco were secretly intended for the Druze rebel fighters in Syria.[63]

In response to this patchwork backdrop, Mukarzil posited his organization as a more centralized collection effort, insisting that the Lebanon Relief Committee was the only organization that could be fully trusted.[64] To ensure its dependability, *al-Huda* printed copies of the monthly checks that were being transferred to Musa Nammur.[65] As controversy mounted over the questions of donations in the name of the (Lebanese) nation, Mukarzil hoped to demonstrate the transparency of the Lebanon Relief Committee.

Al-Huda would dwell on the question of transparency because Mukarzil's efforts were met with criticism from political opponents who dredged up the paper's institutional memory during World War I. During that war, Mukarzil's Lebanon League of Progress was instrumental in collecting money to recruit migrants for the Légion d'Orient to fight on the side of the French.[66] This, along with relief efforts, would be met with competition by migrants who did not necessarily share Mukarzil's enthusiasm for the French. As Fahrenthold has demonstrated, World War I–era relief efforts in the diaspora often blurred the lines between humanitarian work and more overtly political activity like recruitment for the US Army.[67] As the Syrian diaspora split over support for the Entente or the Ottomans, fund-raising would become so politically charged as to result in fistfights, street brawls, and even murder.[68] Mukarzil's opponents would accuse him of fraud over recruitment efforts, and this history would be frequently leveraged against his relief organization in 1925.[69]

More specifically, *Mir'at al-Gharb* questioned Mukarzil's decision to send donations to Musa Nammur, whom the paper criticized as an "officer of the French and not a Lebanese representative."[70] This was because the paper accused Nammur of bribery and of buying his votes and his seat on the Lebanese Representative Council.[71] In hazy references to World War I–era controversies over "lost" donations collected in the name of the Maronite Church, *Mir'at al-Gharb* warned the public of a potentially reoccurring "political plot against the victims, the lines of which extend across the ocean."[72] *Al-Bayan* also took aim at Mukarzil's efforts. The journal claimed that *al-Huda*'s attacks on the "national revolt"—more specifically, accusations that the rebels were attacking Christian civilians—were intended to deceive migrants in order to collect money in the name of Christian victims.[73] *Mir'at* further accused Mukarzil of purposefully advertising his charitable campaign in the name of the Orthodox victims in order to sectarianize the revolt while buttressing his nationalist credentials. Thus, while Mukarzil alleged that his organization was nonsectarian because it collected in the name of Lebanon, *Mir'at al-Gharb* and *al-Bayan* retorted that Mukarzil used sectarian strife to collect donations.

At the heart of *Mir'at*'s gripes with the Lebanon Relief Committee was tension between national representation and effective relief for the victims of the fighting. On numerous occasions the periodical would argue that Mukarzil's organization was effectively cutting off the flow of donations to more location-specific committees. According to *Mir'at*, when the "lighting of the revolt struck [, . . .] the sons of Marj'ayun, Rashaya, Damascus, Hawran and others whose villages suffered true catastrophe" rose up to organize committees to collect money in the name of the victims in those areas. Motivated by "true sincerity" and humanitarianism, these committees, argued *Mir'at*, sent their money directly to those who were suffering. In contrast, Mukarzil's committee was diverting relief away from the suffering by sending their donations to Nammur. *Mir'at* would repeatedly call upon its readers to donate to local committees, and moreover, considered it its patriotic duty to stand with them while exposing Mukarzil's "camouflage committee."[74] The periodical asserted that while contributing dollars for the homeland was a beautiful effort, "the lesson is not in [the act of] giving, but in getting the money to the areas of catastrophe and spending for the sake of the afflicted."[75] It hoped to facilitate getting money to the right places by identifying in its pages the committees that could be trusted.

Although Diyab was ardently against French colonialism, the attacks on Christians in Rashaya and surrounding villages put him on the defensive. In its persistent calls to support the relief efforts of the various local committees, Diyab's journal would continuously have to defend itself against Mukarzil's accusations that it was betraying Christians, and that it had turned into "a Druze periodical" for supporting the anti-French rebellion.[76] Diyab understood the violence against Christian civilians to be the work of "thieves and butchers who follow the rebels for [their own purposes]" and who did not understand the meaning of revolution.[77] Diyab consequently interpreted Mukarzil's sectarian reading of the revolt to be a win for the divide-and-rule tactics of the French. For Diyab, the suffering of Christian civilians in southern Lebanon tempered his commitment to the Syrian revolt while also worsening the feud between him and Mukarzil. While the ongoing conflict between the two editors reflected a personal power struggle, the sectarian discourse attached to their debates would nuance and complicate their ostensible commitments to secular nationalism. Sectarianism thereby animated ethnic and nationalist identity formation.

Letters from the readers of all three periodicals illustrate that philanthropy provided migrants with an outlet to practice their long-distance nationalism. As one reader of *al-Bayan* opined, "We look to your famous journal [to learn of] the work of generous patriots" whose donations evidenced their sincerity toward the nation.[78] Readers accordingly wrote to newspapers to document their patriotic commitments, enumerating the donations in their local cities and committees. Nevertheless, with so many committees rising to the occasion, donating in the name of the nation also had the opposite effect of creating division and discord. In advertising and centering the work of charitable committees, journal editors flexed their leadership while also complicating the work of charitable committees. As newspaper editors played out their personal feuds and accused one another of sectarianism, they called into question the sincerity of the charitable work they supported. In competing over their nationalist credentials, they brought to the fore the underlying tensions between national representation and translocal and sectarian mobilizations. In practicing their nationalism through confessionally oriented and translocal charitable committees, émigrés exerted their nationalist agency while also infusing it with sectarian dynamics.

Negotiating Sect and Nation

This chapter has posited sect and sectarianism in the *mahjar* as key frames through which the Syrian-Lebanese diaspora exercised and negotiated transnational influence vis-à-vis homeland and one another. Like many immigrant communities in the United States, the Syrian-Lebanese diaspora mobilized its many institutions around the particularist or translocal dynamics of sect and village while balancing against the racial and ethnic dynamics of the 1920s United States that prioritized and required whiteness for citizenship. Having emigrated before the dissolution of the Ottoman Empire, many of these migrants were accustomed to the fluid and diverse context of empire, adopting the overarching ethnic designation of "Syrian" as a way of situating themselves vis-à-vis "other." Yet World War I, a subsequent changing political landscape, and the realities of immigrant subjectivity produced a desire among many migrants to coalesce around the political identities attached to the emerging states of Syria and Lebanon. This not only complicated a sense of belonging to the "Syrian" identity, but also resulted in the interweaving of sectarian belonging and patriotic praxis. *Al-Huda*, *Mir'at al-Gharb*, and *al-Bayan* all agreed that "religion belongs to God, and the nation to all," and yet they also solicited support for their various political and nationalist agendas among members of their coreligionists.[79] Consequently, as migrants oriented their specific networks in the service of differing nationalist visions, they utilized the press and charitable committees to further their nationalist credentials while simultaneously engendering sectarianism as a means to discredit one another. From the nature of the Druze-led rebellion to the confines of future Syria and Lebanese states, members of the *mahjar* weighed in on the politics of the 1925 revolt with pen and pocketbook. When analyzed outside the Mandatory borders of Syria—to Lebanon, and further beyond to the *mahjar*—the 1925 Syrian Revolt thus emerges as more than an anticolonial nationalist moment: one also pivotal in the development of Mandate-era sectarianism.

5 ALONG AND BEYOND SECT?
Olfactory Aesthetics and Rum Orthodox Identity

ROXANA MARIA ARĂŞ

AMIRA AND HER FIANCÉ were eating peaches when I entered the shop where they sold Christian paraphernalia. They were talkative individuals, so the five minutes I had planned inside turned into half an hour. Since they were selling incense, I asked them how people use it in their religious practices. Detailed descriptions of Christian customs were intertwined with reserved statements on Muslim fragrance habits. This discrepancy was disrupted by a sign from Amira, who asked her fiancé to close the door. Then, in a lower voice, she confessed her dislike for what she called "the Muslim incense" (al-bakhur al-muslim). "There is something about it," she said. "I cannot explain it and I cannot stand it. When you pass by a house and there is a window open, you know that you pass by a Muslim house. It is that smell [ar-riha]."[1]

This episode from my 2016 ethnographic research is emblematic of the many diverse encounters that can be described as "sectarian" in present-day Lebanon. It also illustrates that social life has a lot to do with the senses since "sensory ways, models and metaphors inform our notions of social integration, hierarchy and identity."[2] In his appeal to decolonize the senses in the field of modern Middle Eastern studies, the historian Ziad Fahmy argues that "by being sensitive to and documenting all sensory data, and not just the visual, historians of the Middle East can only improve the depth and complexity of their historical narratives."[3] Aligning with Fahmy's call and with the aim of this volume, I explore sectarianism (ta'ifiyya) at the intersection of sensory experience, individual sensibilities, and sociocultural structures. I take a particular interest in the olfactory as social and sensorial media that permeates the mundane,[4] indexing sectarian urban aesthetics and social imaginaries that are marked by narratives of both division and coexistence. Connected directly to the limbic system as the seat of memory and emotions, olfactory stimuli can stir deep-seated feelings, influence moods, bring back long forgotten memories, and act as spatial markers.[5] From this perspective, Amira smelled more than incense. She evoked social values reflecting the constructed identity of a Muslim "other," informed by sensorial stimuli and materialized social difference.

Based on field research carried out between 2014 and 2019, I explore Rum Orthodox (*al-rum al-urthudhuks*) or Rum (*al-rum*) practices and discourses around the olfactory in present-day Beirut.[6] My ethnographic intervention engages with Orthodox religious rituals and everyday social interactions to argue for Rum identities as emergent and contingent on different sensorial stimuli, social codes, and urban materialities. My interlocutors observe the Eastern Orthodox liturgical rites and regularly partake in social activities organized by church parishes and community-based Orthodox organizations.[7] They are engaged Christians who often identify themselves and their practices by using terms like "Christian," "Rum Orthodox," or simply "Rum." I focus on both clergy and laypersons who confess, to different degrees, their allegiance to the Rum Orthodox Patriarch of Antioch and all the East, based in Damascus, and to the Metropolitan for the Rum Orthodox Archdiocese of Beirut.[8] Also, my interlocutors are what Michel de Certeau calls "the ordinary man,"[9] meaning the anonymous men and women who, more often than not, are identified through impersonal collective representations. They are ordinary individuals who live in Beirut and navigate the everyday micropolitics of sectarian networks, economic precarity, family expectations, and enduring multilayered histories of conflicts such as the 1975–90 Lebanese civil war.[10]

Recent ethnographic scholarship has offered engaging perspectives on sectarianism as processes that activate modern sociopolitical structures, perceptions, and sensibilities.[11] While aligning with this work, I also highlight the tendency to exclude or downplay the religious dimension. By focusing on practicing believers, I call back into focus the dynamic relation between religious practice and sectarian identity. This relation does not subscribe to the reductive and schematic overlap of sect (*ta'ifa*) and religion (*din*), nor does it abide by ideals of total separation between the two. For instance, symbols and materialities tied to Orthodox rituals have the potential to signify within the frame of liturgical hermeneutics and Christian canonical texts. At the same time, they can yield to narratives of sectarian, communal, and other markers of both social difference and commonality. This implies that "sect" or "sectarian" as analytical categories are not always sufficient in reflecting the complex ways in which my respondents understand and live their Rum identity. Likewise, neither is religion or confession, more specifically, a term sufficiently encompassing to reflect the historical, political, and social particularities of sectarianism in Lebanon. While I acknowledge the blurred borders of these notions in real life, I differentiate *between* them so as to underscore the dynamic relation *among* them. In this sense, I refrain from using the term "sectarian" where the focus lies on the particularities of the beliefs, rituals, symbols, and solidarities of Orthodox religious practice. Instead, I use "confessional" as a subdivision of a broader Christian community. This allows me to think of my respondents as members of an Orthodox collective that cuts across the borders of Lebanon. When these particularities become a means to underscore considerations of class, gender, ethnicity, or race in order to construe divisions, similarities, hierarchies, or prejudices within and among different sects in Lebanon, I lean toward using the term "sectarian."

With this aim in mind, I ask the following questions: How can we think of Rum Orthodox identity through sectarian narratives, religious materialities, and sensorial aesthetics? How do sensory practices and discourses contribute to the formation and re-formation of my interlocutors' identities as Rum? How do they express their identities through social interactions and communicative performances around the olfactory?

Part of the multiconfessional demographics of Beirut, Rum act as relational selves situated between individualized and collective frames.[12] Their daily social interactions within and across entangled sectarian networks reflect intra- and intercommunal exchanges, where representations of sect, class, religion, and territory reinforce each other.[13] Approaching these everyday operating modes as socio-sensory processes, I focus on olfactory aesthetics at the intersection of religious practice, daily social life, and representations of sectarian difference. This approach allows me to inquire into subtle negotiations activated by sensorial practices in the city. Here, fine aesthetic cues can take on magnified importance as they can "weaken particularisms, [but] also strengthen the narcissism of small differences."[14]

This chapter focuses on *bakhur*, roughly translated as "incense."[15] Burning incense is a ubiquitous part of the liturgical rites that define Orthodox Christianity. It is also a practice common to many religious denominations in

Lebanon, while enjoying a long-standing cultural significance in the Middle East and in the Mediterranean area.[16] As a shared commodity, it can mediate sectarian encounters, together with the narratives constructed around it, the emotions that encode it, and the objects that ground it. Through its gaseous capacity to transgress spatiotemporal borders, the diverse usage of *bakhur* hints at the permeable borders of confessional communities in Beirut. From ignorance or outspoken dislikes to friendships or intersectarian marriages, its usage is fruitful ground for exploring the variety of social interactions characteristic of everyday life in a milieu as confessionally diverse as the Lebanese one.[17]

Here, sensory codes are in a dialectical relationship with sectarian narratives, as the ephemerality of smells reinforces and is reinforced by the materiality of physical space and the production of social knowledge. At the same time, olfactory codes are part of Orthodox liturgical rituals tied to theological significations, and Orthodox ecclesiastical networks that go beyond Lebanese sectarian structures. For instance, incense can create social spaces branded as sacred through rituals in which sensorial engagement elicits communion across ontological levels. The same fragrance can transgress sacred borders, reflecting a diversity of social beliefs and practices. This diversity creates a common ground for sectarian encounters and contestations, framed within the sensorial aesthetics and urban geography of Beirut.

Why the focus on Rum Orthodox? The 1990s and the 2000s witnessed increased scholarly attention to Christian communities in the Middle East.[18] While this attention has been welcomed, it has also fostered narratives of victimization and homogeneity that overlook the diversity of practice and belief within different Christian denominations. Conversely, I consider the particularities of Arab Christians by engaging with the specificities of religious practice and the sociopolitical aspects of the region.[19] Rum Orthodox are considered the second largest Christian community in Lebanon. As a sect, they hold no seats in the highest echelons of the sectarian governmental system of Lebanon. As a community, they have steadily dwindled in numbers, as a result of civil war and emigration.[20] In this frame, my chapter yields insights into how members of this numerical minority negotiate different aspects of their sectarian identity and communal belonging.

Stories, Smells, and Sectarian Encounters

The urban topography of Beirut is characterized by complex networks of sectarian, political, and class clusters, which are replicated and maintained through a multilayered urban infrastructure and its sensoryscapes. Resurfacing memories of militarized religious and political segregation in a war-torn Beirut, together with the specter of sectarian conflicts to come, impact the ways in which Beirutis inhabit and imagine their city.[21] These memories of the future translate into everyday spatial practices that reflect the continuities and discontinuities of a mutually enforcing relation between sectarian identities and territorial representations.[22] In turn, these spatial practices intersect, overlap, and clash with neoliberal policies of fast privatization and gentrification, which uphold and deepen social and class disparities.[23]

Entangled in this dynamic urban environment, different sects activate sensory markers in order to sacralize urban space, index their presence in the city, express social difference, or define representations of Beirut. My respondents activate different notions of Rum Orthodoxy by engaging in everyday conversations and activities where urban areas and narratives are sensorially politicized. Here, the capacity of smells to communicate, evaluate, or foster contentment or discontent engenders an olfactory aesthetics in which well-being, trustworthiness, or social status can be evaluated according to fragrance.[24] Glimpses of this aesthetic emerge through stories, jokes, life lessons, and gossip. Like smoke, these narratives evade their sources, opening spaces of (mis)representation of religious ideologies, urban imaginaries, and social hierarchies that connect and disconnect people along and across sectarian lines.

In what David W. Cohen calls the "economy of debate,"[25] the competition for interpretative power and the inconsistencies of knowledge production and consumption shift the focus from sect as "text" to the processes involved in writing those "texts." This emphasis on process and potential affords situations in which different regimes of interpretation lead to contested and ambiguous significations of Rum Orthodox identity. I met Abuna Nicola when he was serving as a priest for a parish in Ras Beirut.[26] While initially reluctant to discuss any olfactory practices other than Christian ones, he eventually decided to convey some of his views through a story. In a low voice, he told me of a Rum Orthodox girl who went to a Muslim shaykh in a desperate time of need. As a solution to her problems, she received a small bag containing incense, and a piece of paper with a verse from the Qur'an. After this proved ineffective, the girl turned in desperation to Abuna Nicola. The latter described his experience of the incense in the bag: "When I smelled it. . . it was yuk. It was a great difference."[27] His face expressed his aversion to the crystals' pungent smell. The priest persuaded the girl to go to the kitchen of the church and burn the talisman. "As soon as the girl burned it, all her problems disappeared," he continued, punctuating every word to convey the moral of the story to me.

Through a narrative authenticated by the authority of the male priest, the root of the girl's problems was associated with the potential of the incense translated as a polluting agent. Its polluting character resided both in its strong essence and in its provenance. The reference to the strong essence remains ambiguous, as it can be grounded both in the materiality of incense and in social codes of sectarian difference. The *bakhur* produced in and imported from the Arabian Peninsula tends to have deep, aromatic smells. By contrast, the incense from the Mediterranean area, often used in Orthodox rituals, is characterized by earthly, flowery, sometimes choking aromas. At the same time, "the great difference" could be tied to the priest's socially educated nose, in which the pungent smell of *bakhur* indexed the intrusive presence of the Muslim "other." Here, a sectarian absence is made present through an "olfactory otherness" that is smelled with more than just a physical nose. In the words of the cultural historian Constance Classen, "The odor of the other does in fact often serve as a scapegoat for certain antipathies toward the other."[28]

Thus, sensory cues lead to sectarian antipathies that go beyond the materiality of incense, and even beyond the specificities of religious rituals. For example, several Rum with whom I interacted, including Abuna Nicola, would replicate anxious narratives on the "danger" of the presence of Muslims to the future of Rum Orthodoxy in Lebanon and Christianity in the region. This perceived existential and social danger of the encroaching Muslim "others" stems not only from aspects related to religious practice, but from issues tied to political representation, economic welfare, and urban demographics. All these coalesce in overarching discourses that project "Islamization" scenarios in the entire Middle East,[29] in which religious coexistence in Lebanon is endangered and Lebanese Christians are subjected to large-scale displacement, emigration, and persecution.

Going back to Abuna Nicola's story, the polluting potential of *bakhur* could come from the fact that it was given by a shaykh. As a consequence, it acquired a causal role by becoming the source of the girl's problems. Its burning represented the solution, as it assured purification from the polluting presence of the Muslim "other." In other words, this fragrant substance became the medium for the girl's problems and, simultaneously, the medium for their solution. Still, while reflecting a process of sectarian "othering," this story also offers insights into everyday social practices that indicate intercommunal synergies. Even though the girl was Rum Orthodox, she went first to a shaykh, rather than to an Orthodox priest. Was she advised by a friend to do so? Did the shaykh happen to live close to her house? Her reasons remain unknown, yet her course of action is reflective of a larger frame of intercommunal exchanges.

In the case of this story, it is from the ambiguity of the olfactory and its ability to signify that the sectarian "other" is encountered through religious materialities and sensorial codes. Yet the same ambiguity leaves the field open for interpretation within the Orthodox community and its olfactory practices. Sensing the potential for this story to trigger different reactions, I used it as an elicitation tool during my interviews. In his office at Notre Dame University-Louaize, I met Abuna Boulos Wehbe, who serves in an Orthodox parish in Mazra'a. A professor at a private Catholic university and a priest serving in a mixed Christian-Muslim area, Abuna Boulos's views and practices advocate for intercommunal dialogue. As I finished telling him the story of the young Orthodox girl, he readily said, "Do you know that sometimes veiled women come to my church asking me to pray over their heads? [. . .] I have many Muslim friends who come to me and say, 'Christ is risen!' [*al-masih qam!*] even though they do not believe in it."[30] After a few seconds of reflection, he continued with a story:

> Once a person came to me with a rock from Oman. And he said, "This is *bakhur* from Oman." I used it in church. I have no problem doing that. So, a person [a Christian] was saying, "Is this Muslim *bakhur*?" And I replied, "No. It is from Oman and the tree is neither Muslim nor Christian." It so happened that there was someone from Harakat Amal participating in one of the funerals. He smelled it and he was amazed. He said, "You used this smell in church?" and I replied, "Yes, they gave it to me and I liked it, so I used it in church." He replied, "This is absolutely amazing."[31]

In the case of this story, the disruptive potential of the fragrant smoke of incense led to Christian-Muslim interactions entangled in narratives of personal preference, ritual appropriateness, and sect-based social codes. Olfactory clues were mobilized as signifiers and discursive markers of sectarian difference and Orthodox liturgical propriety. These clues were attached to the smellscape of the church, which was recognized by the practiced noses of those who smelled the burnt incense from Oman. In between the material source of the incense and the perception of the observers, the fragrant smell afforded several significations. The question, "Is this Muslim *bakhur*?" was triggered by a liturgical practice that fell short of expectations. Through regular engagement in Orthodox rituals, practicing believers develop specific sensorial sensibilities and rhythms that allow them to associate the sacred space of the church with a particular smellscape. Abuna Boulos's action disrupted the expected sensation, creating a difference that triggered the question about *bakhur*. The question already included half of the answer, as the fragrant difference was coded in a Muslim-Christian frame. Whether the coding was grounded in material particularities or in sociocultural representations, Abuna Boulos challenged it by using the incense in church and dissociating the neutral raw material from the biased attempt of sectarian branding. His comparison with the reaction of the Shi'i member of Harakat Amal was meant to further emphasize intercommunal dialogue,[32] even though the member's commending reaction was also based on the exceptionality of his presence in the church and of the priest's act.

Moreover, storytelling is a discursive method of promoting Abuna Boulos's position, as he pieced these interactions together into an anecdote he told me as an argument for communal coexistence. Along the same line, he expressed his hope that "the aroma of openness will rub on other people, because being closed and constricted in a minority will herald our [Rum Orthodox] end."[33] Understanding this quote and the story requires a look into the particularities of everyday life in the Mazra'a district of Beirut, currently characterized by politico-sectarian clusters of Sunni, Shi'i, and Orthodox communities. Here, the presence of the "other" is a daily act of perception, grounded in the minutiae of ordinary life, in regulated urban mobility, and in complex representations of sect, social class, and political affiliation. Part of a numerical minority in the district, Rum Orthodox navigate a social and urban geography that is mostly defined by the sectarian politics of the Sunni Future Movement and the Shi'i Amal Movement and Hizbullah.[34] In my interactions with members of the parish where Abuna Boulos serves, they often brought up melancholic memories of "Mazra'a before the civil war," when Christians made up the majority. Invoking demographic changes triggered by war, immigration, employment-based migration, and real estate gambling in Beirut, they decried the loss of social status, while also portraying Mazra'a as an example of Christian-Muslim coexistence.[35]

Another insight into intercommunal interactions around religious materialities came from a discussion with Rita, a Rum Orthodox person working as a sort of concierge (*natur*) for the Saint George Orthodox Cathedral in downtown Beirut. As an engaging and communicative person, Rita often got bored sitting for seven hours a day (8 a.m. to 3 p.m.) in the empty cathedral. To ease her work, we saw each other two or three times a week, drank Arabic coffee or Nescafé, sang religious hymns (*taratil*), and sold icons and religious books to tourists and visitors entering the church. One day, two young women reached out to her and asked for *bakhur*. Eager to help with my research, Rita asked them how they were going to use it. "We burn it and pray to Sayyida Maryam [Lady Mary]," they replied. Rita turned toward me with a suggestive look whose meaning evaded me. After the two women left the church, she said, "They are Muslim. They used the phrase 'Sayyida Maryam,' and Christians do not call Mary like this. We call her '*al-'adhra*" [the Virgin]."[36]

As we continued discussing the topic, Rita told me that many Muslim women burn *bakhur* to the Virgin and visit Marian shrines, reputed for miraculous efficacy in fertility and childbirth. Variations on this narrative were recurrent in my interactions with Christians in Lebanon, reflecting wider cross-cultural practices of shared, contested, or appropriated religious sites and beliefs.[37] Also, this particular encounter reflects an ambiguity of signification around the Marian figure and the materiality of incense. The shared belief in the sacred efficacy of the Marian figure acts as a common ground for this intercommunal exchange. But the burning of incense also becomes meaningful at the encounter of two different semiotic configurations—the Christian one, in which Mary is "*al-'adhra*," and the Muslim one, in which Mary is "Sayyida Maryam."[38] Based on this detail of reverential language, Rita engaged in a dynamic process of both recognition of and differentiation from the Muslim "other."

This section has shown how *bakhur* and its fragrant materiality can mediate encounters where Rum activate notions of ritual practice, symbolic appropriation, and communal sensibilities to define their identity in relation to Muslim "others." These notions also hint at sectarian underpinnings of social and political differentiation as the so-called sacred olfactory becomes part of a larger urban sensory aesthetics. Thus, in between discursive formats and grounded materiality, olfactory stimuli are part of everyday sensorial encounters that construe and reproduce dynamic representations of Rumness.

Liturgical Aesthetics and Communal Sensibilities

"Religion flourishes in the in-between world that we all inhabit,"[39] where a meaningful existence is shaped by the capacity of things to signify beyond the limits of their materiality.[40] As spaces of the in-between, Orthodox liturgical rituals are predicated on a correspondence between the code of devotion (*qanun al-salawat*) and the code of faith (*qanun al-iman*).[41] Practicing believers embody canonical texts by engaging in synesthetic rituals in which objects and actions become expressions of authorized traditions negotiated, perfected, and challenged by centuries of practice. Thus, rituals are spaces of possibilities, where communion can be achieved horizontally, among Rum Orthodox as an ecclesiastical community, and vertically, between humans, saints, angels, and God.[42]

This confession-specific vision of communion intersects and cuts across representations of Rum Orthodoxy as a sect, rooted in the historical and social particularities of Lebanon. It hints at wider markers of identification dictated by particular ideas of religiosity and sensorial sensibilities, developed and maintained through Orthodox liturgical practices. These markers come to intersect with sect-based codes in varied, contextually nuanced ways. For instance, the people I interacted with would advocate for a strict separation between the political and administrative representations of the Orthodox community as sect (*ta'ifa*) and its communal representations as church (*kanisa*). At the same time, they would mobilize particularities of Orthodox rituals in arguing for sectarian and other forms of social differentiation. Thus, their Rumness was constantly shaped at the intersection of its potential significations within religious practice and within conditions of daily life. Here the olfactory, with its ability to transgress borders, reveals how sensorial sensibilities, communal representations, and symbolic materiality reflect the interconnected relation between notions of sect, religion, and ritual.

Within the synesthetic Orthodox ritual, the symbolic nature of incense is manifold and may acquire a sacrificial, reverential, or sanctifying character, depending on the moment of censing.[43] It can symbolize a prayer by reference to Psalms 141:2: "Let my prayer be set forth before thee as incense; and the lifting up of my hands as the evening sacrifice" (KJV). It can also reference the sweet-smelling "odor of Christ," in relation to Galatians 3:27: "For as many of you as have been baptized into Christ have put on Christ" (KJV). These scriptural references were taught in religious classes for laypersons,[44] and were quoted by my interlocutors as part of liturgical scripts that Orthodox Christians perform regularly. They sing them as *taratil*, smell them as fragrance, see them as icons. In this liturgical setting, "the sweetest earthly fragrance cannot be compared with the fragrance which we now feel, for we are now enveloped in the fragrance of the Holy Spirit of God. What on earth can be like it?"[45]

Moreover, the people I interacted with associated the smell of *bakhur* and the entire liturgical materiality with striving for some form of spiritual metamorphosis. Two examples that express the theological and liturgical tradition of this metamorphosis from material to immaterial and from sensorial to ethical come from two clerical voices, centuries apart:

> [...] But now, though we fill it [the church] with incense that can be perceived by the senses, yet do we not take much trouble to purge out the uncleanness of the mind, and drive it away. Where then is the use of it?[46]

> People in their religious lives have all kinds of affections and emotions [*'awatif*] but this should not be confused with spiritual experience [*tajribeh ruhiyyeh*]. You know, spiritual experience is beyond sensorial perception. The word usually used for religious experience is *anaesthetic*, so it is beyond esthesis as the sensorial faculty of man. Senses can be an entrance [*ad-dukhul*] to this experience, but the experience is not identified with the sensorial.[47]

The first quotation is part of a homily attributed to Saint John Chrysostom, the early Church father, while the second is part of a discussion I had with Abuna Porphyrios, a soft-spoken priest who teaches at the University of Balamand. What both quotes have in common is an emphasis on spiritual transformation. As believers attune their senses to the enacted liturgical script and their bodies engage in the prescribed choreography, incense dematerializes into fragrant smoke, only to materialize again into ethical sensibilities. These semiotic transformations are also aided by the intrinsic connection between olfaction and transition or category change. The evanescent physical smell of incense has a vicarious character, assuring the transition toward internal ethical transformations, which authenticate the liturgical experience.[48] However, religious practice entails a broader range of potential situations where different regimes of interpretation lead to contested and indeterminate significations. Even though practitioners are entangled in the "webs of significance" that define the Orthodox liturgical rituals,[49] practitioners get bored, rituals fail, *taratil* fall on deaf ears, incense does not smell "nice," and personal sensibilities interfere.[50] Such is the case of Najat, who is a chanter *murattil* at Saint George Orthodox Cathedral in Beirut. Every Sunday, dressed in a black robe, she stands in the *kliros*, the section in the church dedicated to chanters, and engages in the liturgical dialogue. On one occasion, as the priest was censing the altar icons, I spotted Najat out of the corner of my eye as she gently covered her nose with a scarf. Her face expressed displeasure to the point that she had to leave the church for a couple of minutes. After the liturgy, as we were sipping our habitual coffee from a café in downtown Beirut, I asked her why she left the church. Najat casually replied that she did not like the stifling smell of incense. For her, "holy matters" did not necessarily smell "nice."

The signification of *bakhur* also goes beyond institutionalized liturgical significations, where it is connected to personal sensibilities and the "circumstances and exigencies of people's lives."[51] Here the vicarious nature of smells recommends them as efficient memory triggers, with strong evocative potential.[52] From this perspective, incense can mediate embodied practices of remembering, contingent upon personal and emotionally charged experiences. This was the case of Randa, whose house altar was an eclectic collection of icons, postcards from her children in America, and memorabilia of her late husband. Pointing to the altar, I asked her if she used incense in the house and for what reasons. Though she was initially dismissive of the question, her voice gained a quavering vibrato as she remembered her late husband. Every Friday, the day of the week on which her husband had passed away, she would pray in front of the altar and burn incense in his memory. There, within the spatial particularities of her home and the temporal frame of Friday prayers, the smell of incense elicited nostalgic embodied memories. Randa's olfactory perception was tied to a performative frame of prayer that yielded to her biographical past.

Other discussions about the fragrance of *bakhur* triggered memories contingent upon collective and emotionally loaded experiences. Some of my respondents would recollect times during the civil war when Rum Orthodox in Beirut had come together to celebrate the liturgy. They understood this action as a revolt against the pollution, vicissitudes, and interdictions engendered by the politico-sectarian armed conflict. Entering the space of the church washed away the pungent smell of fear and the memories of a day-to-day war with which they did not identify. For them, the liturgy became a ritual of collective spiritual cleansing in relation to the violent conflict. Incense became an olfactory marker for a place and a joyous social event in the background of painful wartime memories. The smell of burning gunpowder was replaced by the perfume of incense, while the sound of church bells defied the debilitating noise of militarized politico-sectarian conflict.

Yet, there is more to incense than sweet-smelling stories and memories. Even though incense as scented smoke is ephemeral in form, it is always rooted in and tied to its material sources. These are the crystals that were once exudations of the *Boswellia sacra*, harvested from the oozing wounds of these shrubs and usually burned for their steaming, fragrant smoke. Once burned, the smell evades the materiality of its source, yet never fully detaches from the world of objects to which it refers. In my discussions with Rum, some would appropriate this substance as part of their "right" practice and as an instrument of sectarian "othering." By activating notions of authenticity in religious practice, they correlated the fragrance with the material origin of the crystals to be burned.

I first met Nada in an apartment in Ashrafiyya. The living room was decorated with furniture inspired by the Louis Seize style, and the voice of the singer Fairouz, coming from a new DVD player, pervaded the atmosphere. As we both reached for porcelain cups of Arabic coffee, I asked Nada to tell me about her experience as a practicing Rum in Lebanon. Her words, eyes, and hands started "talking" about her participation in the divine liturgy. "You see the thick atmosphere that veils the sacrosanct [*qadasat Allah*],"[53] she said, as she tried with her hands to convey a gesture of embrace. For Nada, as for most Rum Orthodox whom I spoke with, the liturgical smellscape is embodied as a manifestation of the sacred. Here the senses contribute to creating the possibility for an encounter between the believer and the divine. Moreover, the materiality of the entire liturgical environment enters into dialogue with sensorial perception as it attunes itself to the enacted narratives of the religious ritual. This dialogue is predicated on an aesthetic that is cultivated through the liturgy as a dazzling multisensorial event: soft light, colorful clerical garments, fragrances, omnipresent icons, and rhythmic *taratil*.

Reckoning with this aesthetic of the sacred, Nada ascribed a "special aroma" to the incense used by Christians. One source of this aroma was tied to the place and the process of production of the fragrant crystals.

For Christians, the incense has "a special aroma" [*riha khassa*]. It is not as though you take it from the shelves and use it [a reference to the practices of Muslims]. Part of it comes from the monasteries; they work it out, and they add other smells to it.[54]

Here a larger temporal and spatial network unfolds, in which the sacred efficiency of incense stems from the process of its production in an authorized sacred space. This spatial dimension is complemented by the intention of the manufacturers, who must prepare the incense with the purpose of worship in mind. Nada's attempt to authenticate religious materialities through olfactory codes fits a broader trend. In tune with the Orthodox theology of the Church as a community of faith fulfilled in the Eucharist as a liturgical expression,[55] my interlocutors often situate their identity within larger Orthodox structures. Referencing the Antiochian Patriarchate in Damascus, Orthodox monastic orders in Greece, and even pious believers in Russia, their narratives reflect interwoven relations and overlapping territories rather than just national historiographies and the geopolitical area of the Middle East. These narratives are corroborated by webs of materialities that are manufactured, distributed, and employed across a global geography of the sacred.

Consequently, particular ideas of religiosity and communion are tied to liturgical and theological significations grounded in Orthodox ecclesiastical institutions and networks that go beyond Lebanese sectarian structures. For example, being a member of the Orthodox sect as defined by personal status laws in Lebanon does not necessarily require being a religious practicant. Conversely, by being a member of Orthodoxy as a community of faith, one professes the tenets of Orthodox doctrine and is part of an eucharistic body that transcends national and temporal borders. Nada's story is a case in point. The practice of burning incense grounds her in a community of engaged believers outside Lebanon, who share common ideas of piety and proper religious practice.

Yet this does not mean that the same ideas of religiosity and their attached sensibilities cannot act as markers of sectarian difference. In my discussions with Rum, some would appropriate this substance as part of their "right" practice, and as an instrument of sectarian "othering." By activating notions of authenticity in religious practice, they correlated the fragrance with the material origin of the crystals to be burned. For instance, Nada connected the use of incense by Muslims to a discourse of aesthetics, pleasure, and commerce. Incense is trademarked as a commodity that can easily be purchased from every shop, and thus does not afford a sacred olfactory experience. This comparison is both about the materiality of *bakhur* and about objects that are part of *doings* and *not-doings*. It is about socially and morally condoned actions that establish a "us-versus-them" framework by authenticating Christian practices as sacred and Muslim practices as commodified. Even though a similar commodified dimension of incense is by no means absent in Christian commercial networks, this tactic of appropriation is part of the everyday negotiation of sensorial experiences and common cultural materialities.[56]

An example of this shared commodified dimension that complicates dichotomic narratives of "us versus them" is the censing of commercial spaces, especially boutiques and privately owned small stores. Twice a week, I took the same road to reach the Mouvement de la Jeunesse Orthodoxe (MJO) *mustawsaf*, an Orthodox social and medical center where I volunteered and did research. This center is located in the heart of Ashrafiyya, an area most Beirutis would characterize as Christian bourgeois par excellence. As I walked the streets in the morning, bursts of aromatic fragrance would linger from boutiques along the way. Hand censers sat in one corner of each store as the material sign of a morning ritual that had already happened. When I stopped to ask the reasons for censing, these varied. For some it was a prayer; for others it was done for "a good day," which sometimes meant good sales. For some it was just done out of habit; for others it was about creating a "good smell" (*riha tayybeh*) in the store. From creating sacred spaces in churches and private homes to creating a nice smell and raising sales in boutiques and stores, the fragrant practices around incense are reflective of a cultural diversity of practice and significance that cuts across the dichotomy of a Christian sacred and a Muslim commodified.

This dynamic relation between the politics of smell and the sacred sensoria is also reflected through the Orthodox liturgical approach to the core notion of spiritual communion. The connection between the liturgical materialities and the sensorial media creates social potential at the horizontal level, where the participating members can enact a spiritual community across several intertwined temporalities and spaces.[57] Thus, social relations are affirmed and agreed upon through the sensual and performative models dictated by liturgical scripts.[58]

The light of the candles is dim, casting shadows on the faces of believers and icons of saints at Deir al-Harf, a Rum Orthodox monastery in a small village above Ras al-Metn. Here, on the evening of each July 19, Rum Orthodox gather in an all-night vigil (*sahraniyya*) to celebrate the feast ('*id*) of Mar Elias. Tired faces, disciplined bodies, air infused with a strong smell of incense, and a silence broken by unpolished *taratil* and the voices of children—all part of a liturgical ritual that pushes the limits of the human body. As minutes blend into each other and time is embodied in ritual, a monk carrying a hand censer adorned with bells begins to cense. While fragrant smoke begins to rise, the voices of believers steadily attune themselves to the rhythm of the bells, engendering a gradual embodiment of the prescriptive ritual. Noise becomes sound and sound turns into voice, as incense becomes smoke and smoke turns into presence, in an attempt to reach a synchronicity that goes beyond materiality.

Incense symbolically unites in one smell individuals, saints, and souls, transforming them into "a congregation of worshippers."[59] Thus, a different sociality develops through the liturgical script, one which engenders a sense of unity across social hierarchies and emanates a "sweet savor of Christ unto God"—a liturgical reference to 2 Corinthians 2:15: "For we are unto God a sweet savor of Christ, in them that are saved, and in them that perish" (KJV).[60] This sociality is enhanced by the strong relation between materiality and the senses, as "the sensory is not only encapsulated within the body as an internal capacity or power, but is also dispersed out there on the surface of things as the latter's autonomous characteristics, which then can invade the body as perceptual experience."[61]

Nevertheless, is this the only form of sociality allowed by the olfactory in particular and the liturgy in general? One Sunday morning I arrived late for the service at Saint Mary's Orthodox Church of Dormition, in Ras Beirut. I reluctantly ended up sitting on a bench in the back, a place least convenient from which to observe the prescriptive use of incense. However, my position offered me a chance to see the unfolding of social hierarchies embodied by individuals entering the church. I could recognize the Ethiopian and Sudanese young women by their beautiful white and blue headscarves. As they entered the church, they engaged in prostrations and other forms of bodily piety. These young women usually work as cleaning ladies and babysitters for Lebanese middle-class and upper-middle-class families. They are enmeshed in a workforce market at the borders of legality, in which cheap labor is imported from Sudan and Ethiopia. As Beiruti families and their Ethiopian or Sudanese employees entered the church, they acted according to unspoken rules of social hierarchy and did not sit together.

As Orthodox, the families and their employees were equal in the body of Christ, yet unequal in the social body. Liturgical politics promoted a heavenly egalitarian community and solidarity, yet this did not preclude the preexisting social hierarchies. As the "odor of Christ" infringed on the borders of historical time, the whiff of social class, race, and ethnicity infringed on the borders of sacred space. This mutual infringement hints at Orthodoxy as a category of discourse and practice that is not homogeneous, but rather is riddled with repertoires of differentiation and exclusion, which are internally reproduced and perpetuated. It also highlights that "sect" in Lebanon is not simply congruous with "religion," but encodes ethnic and racial dimensions that operate through socioeconomic divides, power imbalances, and spatial segregation. Finally, it points to the potential of the olfactory to reflect communal unity, but also "social ordering."[62]

This section of the chapter has shown how the material and symbolic particularities of Orthodox liturgical rituals contribute to the development of particular sensorial sensibilities and narratives that are negotiated through the interplay of theological references and religious practice. They are also mobilized as social codes of difference in sectarian narratives where symbolic appropriations and standards of correctness unfold. Gaining insights into these aspects requires an approach to Rum Orthodox as a community of faith whose overarching networks transcend Lebanon, yet include Lebanese people. It is a community founded on canonical texts, yet it cannot flourish without liturgical practice—a community that intersects with political and social representations as a sect, yet does not fully identify with them.

Along and beyond Sect

Through a micro-approach to a ubiquitous detail in the social practices of Rum Orthodox in Beirut, this chapter argues for the olfactory as a methodological tool in researching how members of this Christian minority negotiate their identity in the contested urban space of Beirut. Here, *bakhur* becomes a synecdoche that signifies beyond its materiality. It hints at an Orthodox sensorial regime in which liturgical practices engender a sense of communal belonging, socializing practicing believers into an Orthodox ecclesiastical community. This communal vision intersects with sectarian practices and discourses wherein variations of Rum Orthodoxy underscore social, economic, and even racial hierarchies that are expressed through metaphors and narratives of difference. In this frame, the word "sect" functions as a verb, indicating dynamic processes negotiated through a politics of aesthetics, part of a larger spectrum of social codes mobilized by my interlocutors. As a process, it is grounded in materiality, but not fixed by it; embodied, but not naturalized.

Along these lines, I argue for Rum Orthodox identity as emergent through religious rituals and everyday life scenarios, through theological symbolism and social representations, through objects and their power to signify. It is at the intersection of all these factors where the processual dimension affords ambiguities and excess of meaning, reinterpretations, and imaginaries—all tools to explore the internal dynamic of Rum Orthodox as a Christian minority, a sect, and a spiritual community. This dynamic allows one also to think along and beyond the notion of "sectarian," by looking at the different epistemic regimes (theological, pastoral, ecclesiastical, sociopolitical) at work in defining Rumness.

Finally, as the fragrance of *bakhur* transcends and infringes on borders, it becomes a symbol for the porous borders of sects in Beirut. Here, a shared history of sectarianism engrained in memories of civil war, shifting urban geographies, and sociopolitical networks is expressed through sensorial codes that carry and contest the collective stories we tell about ourselves and others. This social salience of the olfactory is part of a larger sensoryscape of Beirut. Political posters, religious songs, streetcorner shrines of martyrs and saints, sounds of television channels and radio stations, sacred smells and smells of trash—these are all sensory stimuli contributing to the confessional, communal, and sectarian codes mobilized by Beirutis in their everyday life. Here, the minutiae and inconsistencies of social practices are fertile ground from which to gain insight into how these residents negotiate their multifaceted identities.

6 FROM MURDER IN NEW YORK TO SALVATION FROM BEIRUT

Armenian Intrasectarianism

TSOLIN NALBANTIAN

THIS CHAPTER ANALYZES THE 1933 murder of Leon Tourian, an Armenian archbishop in New York, to demonstrate how various Armenian and non-Armenian actors adapted Lebanese sectarianism in the United States, using it in an intrasectarian power struggle with political adversaries. Ideological political differences about whether to support the Armenian Soviet Socialist Republic (ASSR), an integral part of the Soviet Union, were articulated and politicized through the loyalty to a particular see: the Cilician one, headquartered in Beirut since 1930, or the Echmiadzin one, headquartered in the ASSR.

Locating sectarianism, long wedded to a Lebanese context, in the United States contests a common trope in studies of both sectarianism and Lebanon: that these two are inextricably linked and that their entanglement is responsible for violent conflict. This common reading prevents us from considering other innovative models of sectarianism that people live and practice in the everyday both in and outside of Lebanon. Rather than politicizing a *religious group*—sectarianism, classically defined—Armenians made two competing *ecclesiastical* headquarters reflections of their *political* identity, to define their own ideological boundaries in the United States. In doing so, they enacted what I will call an intrasectarian conflict in their everyday life.[1] This new national situation eventually gave the Cilician See, a religious-sectarian institution in Lebanon, the opportunity to expand its jurisdiction into the United States, pushing back against the Echmiadzin See, which, located in Armenia, had earlier been alone in formally administering the Armenian churches in the United States.[2] Meanwhile, additional actors, including the US press, which covered the events in the lead-up to and aftermath of the murder of the archbishop, also played a role in this intrasectarian conflict.

Armenian migrants to the United States before World War I hailed from many locations, including the Anatolian provinces of the Ottoman Empire as well as Mandate Lebanon, Palestine, Syria, and Transjordan.[3] Once in the United States, the members of these communities became more homogeneous; all were principally "Armenian," despite their differences. Even so, heterogeneity remained. The activity of the three main political parties, the nationalist right-wing Dashnaks and the two leftist organizations, Hnchaks and Ramgavars, marked a distinct continuity with late Ottoman times.[4] These parties modified their political platforms and adjusted them to new political theaters in and outside the United States. The leftist Hnchak and liberal Ramgavar parties had an especially direct connection to the Soviet Union, as the ASSR formed a part of the USSR. Conversely, it was of supreme importance for right-wing Armenians to criticize that connection and to reject the 1920 Sovietization of Armenia. Support or hostility toward the ASSR extended to the Echmiadzin See, and accordingly, to its appointed archbishop in the United States at the time, Leon Tourian. It likewise engaged the Echmiadzin See's rival, the Cilician See in Lebanon. The buildup and aftermath of Tourian's murder demonstrated how the supporters and opponents of these political parties used Lebanese sectarianism to enact intrasectarian difference in the United States.[5] As such, this case study pushes back against Armenian, Middle Eastern, and American historiographies that assume an internal homogeneity within the Armenian population, ignoring the fundamentally heterogeneity of a particular sect. These historiographies understand Armenians as a cohesive unit, and therefore do not consider intrasectarian power struggles that challenge Lebanese and Armenian nationalist histories.[6] In addition, they view sectarianism as an inherently "Lebanese" problem, failing to consider how it is used, produced, and moved in disparate environments and by various actors.

Sectarianism has yet to be used to describe daily interactions among members of the same sect. The religious violence in the nineteenth century that culminated in the sectarian mobilization documented by Ussama Makdisi profiles the Druze and the Maronites, and "episodes of intracommunal social violence that constituted a fundamental part of broader religious violence *across* sectarian communities."[7] Works on the Mandate period, such as Tamara Chalabi's work on the Lebanese Shi'a and their relationship to Sunni Faysalians, focus on how individual sects negotiated with the French state, or dialectically with the French and one other sect.[8] And finally, works on the National Pact emphasize the "Sunni-Maronite Entente," or what Fawwaz Traboulsi termed the "informal verbal understanding between Bishara al-Khuri and Riad al-Sulh."[9]

By contrast, the intrasectarian conflict of Armenians in the United States was not based in religious difference. Armenian nationalist ambitions, including debates over the ASSR, fundamentally drove these conflicts and transformed an ecclesiastical difference into an intrasectarian one—first in the United States, and then in the religious-sectarian institution of the Cilician See in Lebanon.[10] Armenian-Americans saw the Echmiadzin See's jurisdiction over Armenian Apostolic churches in the United States and the Cilician See's position in Lebanon as the official representative of the Armenian Apostolic sect as an opportunity to assert and practice their ideological convictions. In the lead-up and aftermath of Tourian's murder, which culminated in the invitation of the sectarian institution of the Cilician See in Lebanon *to* the United States, they transnationalized sectarianism and enrooted an intrasectarian conflict in the United States.[11] This expansion of the authoritative jurisdiction of the Cilician See in Lebanon to administer, staff, and procure dues from certain Armenian churches in the United States created a new sectarian authority there. What is more, many Armenians practicing this new intrasectarian difference were not of Lebanese descent, but hailed directly from Anatolian provinces or from Greater Syria. By showing how sectarianism traversed boundaries and was enacted by Armenian-Americans and made intrasectarian—which, to repeat, is the politicization of ecclesiastical difference—this chapter also reframes Armenians as a local rather than diasporic component of the story.

This dislodging of sectarianism as an "age-old" categorization indigenous to the Middle East, and as a process inalienable to Lebanon, likewise liberates actors from scholarly examinations that, while intending to "explain," further bind them to an analytical frame. Turning away from the more traditional readings of transnational or diasporic experiences of Armenians allows us to consider postgenocide Armenian histories, including everyday local life. This story likewise demonstrates that Armenians and sectarianism are intrinsic to community histories in the United States, be they in Chicago, New York, and

Worcester (some sites that will be discussed in this chapter). [12] By the 1940s and 1950s, these sectarian tensions collided with the Cold War, emboldening the Armenian-Americans to formally invite a Lebanese sectarian institution to the United States—not in a bid to connect to an imagined Lebanese or Armenian nation, but to (re)fashion belonging in the United States. Put together, this foray forces the consideration of Armenians and their practices within larger social and historical constructions including sectarianism, and detaches sectarianism from Lebanon.

Armenians used the US court and justice system to express what I maintain were intrasectarian positions, and to make themselves heard. The employees of the US justice system and of American media outlets, along with the general public who consumed the spectacles on the streets and in newspapers, also became actors in what was only nominally an Armenian story. A faction's unprecedented decision to invite the Cilician See, a Lebanese sectarian institution, to *settle* in the United States empowered it with additional congregants; employment positions for the priests, bishops, and archbishops educated in its seminaries; and constant funding that it received in yearly tithe. Not surprisingly, the Cilician See in Lebanon was happy to oblige. Its establishment in the United States created a new connection between a sectarian Lebanese institution in Lebanon and a group of Armenians in the United States. This connection was *not* a diasporic one, nor one connected to ancestry, nostalgia, "origin," or a perceived connected history.[13] The Tourian case therefore demonstrates the limitations of studying Armenian-Americans through the rubric of a larger Armenian diaspora, or as part of an Armenian nation.[14] In this chapter, Armenians are the local population, and in performing sectarianism they make this practice local, embedding it in the United States. The murder of the archbishop and the successful prosecution of the perpetrators had ramifications beyond Armenian institutions.[15] This innovation took place in the United States, making the story simultaneously an American one.[16]

*   *   *

The date was December 24, 1933: Christmas Eve. Crucifix in his right hand, golden pastoral staff in the left, Archbishop Leon Tourian walked down the single aisle of the Holy Cross Church on West 187th Street in Washington Heights in New York City to begin the evening mass. As he reached the fifth row in, he was surrounded and stabbed multiple times. Bleeding profusely, he lurched forward, bending his golden staff with his weight. He died minutes later. A murder weapon was found on the altar: an eight-inch butcher's knife wrapped in newspaper. Two people were arrested at the scene of the crime, and eventually nine were prosecuted. All were found guilty: two of first-degree murder, the other seven of first-degree manslaughter.

This description of the murder is from the front page of the *New York Times* on December 25, 1933.[17] The procedures surrounding the crime, investigation, trial, and sentencing required police and security detail and received extended press coverage. Demonstrating how highly charged this murder and trial was, the *New York Times* described a courtroom crowded mostly with female observers who booed the defense lawyers, and reported on the extra-heavy detail of detectives and policemen on guard at various points throughout the Criminal Courts Building to prevent "any possible disorders."[18] The police were not always successful.[19]

The Immediate Aftermath

In the days following the murder, Armenian-Americans who backed Tourian and the Echmiadzin See prevented another three hundred thousand Armenians from entering their churches for their alleged opposition to the Soviet status of Armenia. They were barred from attending weekly services, marrying, baptizing children, or having funeral rites.[20] The swiftness of the reaction and the ability to block Armenians from accessing the church and its rites throughout the United States confirmed the divisions within the Armenian-American communities. American newspapers had avidly covered the tension and violence that began to accompany Archbishop Tourian from 1932 onward.[21] Their coverage of Tourian before the animosity, however, had demonstrated just how quickly members of the community galvanized and incited others to change the nature of the discourse regarding the archbishop and what role he and the see he represented were to play vis-à-vis the Armenian community in the United States and the "Armenian nation" at large. Armenians rendered the archbishop, his rank as prelate of the Armenian Church in North and South America appointed by the Echmiadzin See, and his murder into a currency that procured power for them and used the newspaper coverage to exhibit it to their fellow Americans. At the same time, the American press revealed how the security apparatus and justice system became active agents in the story as well. By also profiling local and regional newspapers, rather than just newspapers with a national or international following, this chapter likewise acknowledges local sources of power. Locations not traditionally associated with sectarianism, intra-Armenian struggles for power, or ideological cleavages over the location of the Armenian nation and its relationship to the USSR—including Kenosha, Binghamton, Salt Lake City, and Honolulu—helped shape these discourses in the United States.

An Impressive CV

On December 8, 1931, the *Kenosha Evening News* in Wisconsin dedicated about half a page to the Archbishop Tourian's impending visit to the area.[22] The article, which included a large photograph of Tourian holding a golden staff, noted that 250,000 Armenians in North and South America fell under his jurisdiction. It detailed his credentials, so to speak, mentioning his former role as the personal secretary of the Armenian patriarch of Constantinople from 1902 to 1908, his membership in the Armenian National Assembly of Constantinople, and his position as archbishop of Smyrna (Izmir) from 1920 to 1922. The *Evening News* also mentioned that Tourian had been in Smyrna during the notorious massacres in 1922 in which 15,000 Armenians were killed.[23] Escaping through the intervention of the French, he had gone on to become archbishop of London before being appointed prelate by the Echmiadzin See. The newspaper also noted that Tourian had authored English translations of Armenian church liturgy.[24]

Other local and national newspapers covered impending visits similarly. They would first announce the visit of Archbishop Tourian to the area, identify his role as the head of the Armenian Church Diocese of North and South America under the jurisdiction of the Armenian Church in Armenia (the Echmiadzin See), inform their readership where he would be conducting mass, and then chronicle his life history and recount his numerous accolades—often including a local or regional twist. For example, the *Binghamton Press* mentioned that during his visit to Boston he had been "presented a beautifully inscribed cane by Mayor Curley," and that "Mayor O'Hara of Worcester gave him a golden key to his city."[25]

While it may not be surprising that certain biographical details were included in the newspaper articles—such as location of the archbishop's power vis-à-vis the Armenian community in the North and South America, and the respect that his position garnered from non-Armenian elected officials—it is likewise curious that the articles mentioned only "Armenia," and that both the USSR and the ASSR were absent. I stress this because just a few months later, by the summer of 1932, all articles on Archbishop Tourian included a discussion, however brief, of the political constitution of Armenia, noting its status as a Soviet republic and pointing out that the headquarters of the Armenian Church, or the Echmiadzin See, was likewise located there, and often adding the accusation that Tourian was a communist sympathizer. They also would note the anticommunist stance of Armenians who opposed Tourian, mentioning the Dashnak political party, a right-wing nationalist party that had lost power once Armenia became one of the Soviet republics.

Why the change? After all, this was not the first instance of a political matter in the press involving Archbishop Tourian. On January 4, 1932, the *Honolulu Advertiser*, located in a city and state (Hawaii) with neither a significant Armenian population nor an Armenian church, included a tiny wire article from United Press International covering the speech Tourian gave in Racine, Wisconsin, to a group of 1,500 Armenians, directing them to "become better Americans by being better Armenians."[26] This same wire article ran a little over a month later in the *Salt Lake Tribune* of Utah, another state without a sizable Armenian community or Armenian church. Were these newspapers commanding Armenians to become better citizens, or advising them how to do so? Either way, both suggested the need for Armenians to become both better Armenians and better Americans. At the same time, it could have been read as Tourian himself, using the discourse of good (American) citizenship, service to the (Armenian) nation, and the platform of the American press that often relied on wire articles to fill its newspapers, to issue his directives. After all, since he was the leader of the Armenian national church in the Americas, Armenians were to follow his example. Multiple actors used the American press in attempts to direct members of the Armenian community to expand and claim power.

Tourian dispensed advice to his flock and represented it to other Americans through these local papers, who otherwise might have never really come into contact with it. He also specifically praised US religious freedom. Perhaps this was a legacy of the Armenian genocide and the discourse of "Christian massacres" in the US media. Regardless, he seemed to have activated the common American trope of religious freedom from prosecution, stating, "This is paradise here, compared with the conditions under which we worked in Eastern countries." At the same time, he embraced an Orientalist trope: "Correspondents say the East has changed but I can't be convinced that the spirit of the Mohammedans expressed in tyranny to all Christians has been altered." It is interesting to note that the "other" here is not the communist entity of the USSR, which had been represented as antichurch, but an unnamed yet very well understood accusation against Turkey. The prelate employed sectarian language to reinforce the American belief in tolerance and freedom of religion for his own ends. After all, this would reinforce his own power as the leader of two hundred thousand Armenians, while stressing to the American reader his belief in "their" system.

Enacting Sectarianism

Armenian-Americans, through their actions against or in support of the archbishop, changed the US press's representation of both him and the Armenian community. In doing so, they simultaneously sectarianized the press and public encounters with the archbishop. From a learned figure, he was made into a communist sympathizer; from an official representative of the Echmiadzin See, he was tagged to the USSR; from one who safeguarded what he could of the Armenian community in Smyrna in the wake of genocide, he was made a traitor to the Armenian nation. The US press began to note the ideological leanings of his congregation, noting political and social discord, including the added "detail" in his biography that Armenia was a Soviet republic, or that Tourian earned his legitimacy from the Echmaidzin See, located in the ASSR. Armenian-Americans actively showcased this discord, connecting it both to the evil of communism and to an existential threat to the American way of life, in order to change the understanding of this national religious figure for their own aims.

The major event that demonstrated this took place on July 1, 1933, at the Chicago World's Fair. Numerous US newspapers had printed the fair's schedule for that dayfair: at 10:30 a.m. the "Armenian Day Program" would take place at the Century of Progress Exhibition.[27] The main speaker would be Tourian, joined by a sixty-person Armenian choir, and followed by other community leaders involved in the organization of the event.[28] What transpired, however, was described in the US press as a "battle" and "general rioting," "fomented by Communists," which broke out during the services in the court of the Hall of Science.[29] According to the *Chicago Tribune* wire service, fighting began when "some men tried to fly the Armenian flag from the speaker's platform" and the archbishop refused to speak until it was taken down, fearing that "Russians would retaliate on Armenians in the old country."[30]

It is clear that neither the *Tribune* journalists who wrote the piece nor the

New York Daily News, which ran it, were particularly familiar with Archbishop Tourian, the politicization of the Armenian-American community, or the display of sectarianism in the United States. The wire service identified Tourian as the primate and archbishop of the Greek Orthodox rather than Armenian Church, and did not clarify—as the American press would in subsequent articles—that the flag in question had been that of the short-lived independent Armenian Republic (1918–20) and *not* of the ASSR. In addition, the headline blamed the "Soviets," but the body of the article mentioned Tourian's concern about "Russian" retaliation.[31] The Associated Press, which also ran the story, correctly stated that Tourian "feared Soviet reprisals" in what it called "his homeland"—rather than the "old country," as the *Tribune* called it—if the banner were not removed.[32] It also stated that a hundred World's Fair police officers had been needed to stop skirmishes that included "swinging chairs," and that five arrests had been made, leaving two officers slightly injured.[33] The reporting included additional mistakes,[34] calling the ASSR part of "Soviet Russia," and Tourian the primate of the Armenian Church in North and South Africa.[35]

Perhaps the wire services were ill-prepared to tackle these dynamics. Perhaps they regularly conflated Russia with the USSR, and carelessly mixed up Orthodox churches. This was strange, considering that many of these same papers had often avidly followed the archbishop's visits in their local communities. Armenian-Americans manipulated this ignorance. They used this lack of sustained engagement with the goings-on in their community to claim power from one another and challenge the authority of Tourian and the Echimiadzin See, who only a few months prior had been a national Armenian hero and respected civic figure, advising Armenians on how to practice their American citizenship.

Thus, Tourian became a proxy in the struggle for power and representation in the Armenian-American community. Two months after the "riot" in Chicago, a fight erupted in Westboro, Massachusetts, whose aftermath was likened to a "battlefield" by the *Boston Globe*.[36] Citing police reports, the *Globe* reported that "trouble" had begun when a group of "1500 Armenian speaking people" were meeting in a park, and someone emerged from a car to assault Tourian while he was speaking.[37] According to the *Globe*, the violence was due to "two factions at the outing, the Worcester branch of the Armenian Revolutionary Federation and the members of the Our Saviour Church of Worcester."[38] It was so intense, the newspaper stated, that police had difficulty "rescuing some of the men involved."[39] Two men from Worcester were so badly beaten that they could not appear in court on charges of disturbing the peace and breaking up an assembly.[40]

The newspaper's labeling of those in attendance as "1500 Armenian speaking people" revealed that its reporter could not understand what was said at the meeting. This permitted the *Globe* to fashion it as a group of violent outsiders, even though they had assembled in their own community. This is evidenced also by the *Globe*'s description of the scene the following day: "When it became daylight yesterday the grove where the 1500 had been fighting until late in the night looked like a battlefield, with stones and broken glass from automobile windshields strewn around. Several automobiles were found badly disabled in the woods."[41]

It is also possible, however, that for the belligerents these representations were effective tools for their power struggles. Armenians adopted this language of "othering" in subsequent media portrayals, and used it against one another. For the *Globe* it had been a clash between two organizations: one identified as political (the Dashnak Party), the other as religious (the members of the Our Saviour Church). But for the *Hartford Courant*, which covered another clash in New Britain, Connecticut, its inclusion of divisive remarks made by Manoog Krikorian, a trustee of the local Armenian church, endorsed opposition to Archbishop Tourian.[42] Krikorian claimed that the "majority" in the church held the archbishop responsible for what the newspaper described as "the rift that has spread into the Armenian Apostolic churches throughout the country," and that they would seek Tourian's removal at the upcoming convention in New York City.[43] The *Courant* did not quote Krikorian when using the terms "rift" or "spread," but rather categorized the situation as such by itself, thus also constructing Armenians as bifurcated and intrasectarian.

By continuing to privilege the voice of Krikorian, the *Courant* also undermined the authority of Tourian and the Echmiadzin See. The newspaper profiled the voice of Krikorian, rather than that of the archbishop, to describe the situation: "The archbishop has acted several times in a manner that is not in conformance with church rules."[44] This is particularly surprising, as Krikorian was arrested for trying to open the church that Tourian had ordered closed. Local police had once again become involved, and this time they had sided with Tourian and his supporters. And yet, in response to the report that Tourian had unfrocked the local priest of the church, the *Courant* quoted Krikorian's direct challenge to the archbishop's power: "We disregard the order [made by Tourian] that our pastor conduct no services for a month."[45] Did both the presence and the absence of the Armenian flag at the Chicago World's Fair create an opportunity for Krikorian and like-minded opponents of Tourian to claim power over the community? After all, Krikorian was bold in his stance, declaring that he, along with the unidentified "majority," would seek the removal of Tourian at the upcoming convention in New York City.[46]

A few days after it covered the clash at the Armenian church in Hartford, the *Courant* reported on the outcome of the convention held in New York City. The delegates voted to unseat Tourian as primate, and notified Catholicos Khoren, head of the Echmiadzin See.[47] The newspaper did not identify Armenia as part of the USSR, but did hint at Tourian's association with the Soviet government. In referencing the flag incident in Chicago, the *Courant* included that Tourian had "refused to speak on Armenian Day until a Soviet flag was substituted for the tricolor which was used as the Armenian Republic's flag before the country was taken over by the Soviet [*sic*]."[48]

The intra-Armenian disagreement was disruptive enough to warrant the intervention of local police forces and the judicial system.[49] Aside from the arrests, the *Courant* reported that Judge W. E. Hagearty issued a court injunction against any further meetings in the church, which was then reversed. The reversal is apparently what prompted Krikorian to attempt to open the church doors, an act for which he was arrested.[50] The police, fearing "that there might be trouble," prevented the services from taking place.[51] Local law enforcement thus challenged the court's reversal of the injunction, not only indicating a dispute within the law of order but providing a space for Armenians to claim power over one another. The back-and-forth between court injunctions, meetings of "minority" and "majority" representations, police forces sent to "secure" the opening and "look after" the closing of the church, and rival conventions held in New York not only attest to an inherent chaotic or confusing atmosphere, but also demonstrate the ability of Armenians to use "order" and "procedure" to articulate power over one another.

The Specter of Communism

By early September 1933, Armenian-Americans and their local newspapers began to explicitly reference communism, the Echmiadzin See, and the USSR within the church "rift."[52] That the discourse devolved into a pro-versus-anti–Soviet flag issue also demonstrated how Armenians used tensions between the capitalist United States and the communist Soviet Union in intrasectarian struggles for power. Communist references became a simple, useful, and accessible language with which Armenians communicated to other Americans to forward their own ideological battle. The *Brooklyn Daily Eagle*, covering the convention in New York, included the claim of Tourian's "pro-Soviet bias," adding that those gathered accused the archbishop of "acting in a manner calculated to divide his people."[53]

Similar incidents between Armenians occurred in other states and were covered in local newspapers. The *Kenosha Evening News* reported on a court case between Lee Hagopian, the president-elect of the local Armenian church, and Asia Bedroosian, his predecessor. Bedroosian maintained that he was still the church's president.[54] In New York, Tourian had "issued" a declaration of Bedroosian as a "rebel," and Hagopian used it to support his claim to the presidency of the Kenosha church. Bedroosian, in turn, submitted his own documents claiming that Archbishop Tourian had been voted out of office at a convention of church delegates in September, thereby voiding his authority.[55] What must be noted is that these church board positions, while they signified community trust and prestige, did not include financial gain or mandate authority, and were completely voluntary. And yet, support or opposition to the authority of Tourian in New York connoted importance in the Kenosha community.

While the newspaper did not mention anything about communism, or whether the court had heard arguments about the political positioning of the archbishop or the Armenian Church, its use of the expression "the story goes" in recounting the World's Fair flag incident demonstrated at best an ambiguity and at worst a lack of care over the actual details of what had happened.[56] It could also be read as the newspaper doubting the archbishop's concern that the flag would "create difficulties in Armenia," where his superiors resided.[57] This reading is reinforced by the court's ruling in favor of the defendant, Bedroosian, awarding him the sum of six cents.[58] The position of church president, however, went beyond the monetary worth of the judgment. After all, these two local Wisconsinites had employed legal representatives (also named in the article), cooperated with local media sources such as the *Kenosha Evening News*, used church documents issued in New York, cited a convention of Armenian-American delegates from Armenian churches in the Midwest and the East Coast, and referenced an incident that had occurred in Chicago six months earlier—all of which indicated the value of a "voluntary" position in the church.[59]

Murder

Armenians used the US press to turn Archbishop Tourian's appointment by the Echmiadzin See in the ASSR into a public American concern. "Being sectarian" proved beneficial, as did the growing perception of an existential communist threat, which could be activated because of the existence of the ASSR. This was the case even though the archbishop's brazen murder shocked both the Armenian community and the greater American public.[60] The New York *Daily News* reported that the assassination "precipitated a riot among the 200 excited parishioners, all of whom sought to deal with the killers on the spot."[61] It also described the figure of the archbishop "clad in colorful, lace trimmed vestments of his office . . . resplendent in his gold and green robes . . . a giant of a man, weighing almost 400 pounds and more than 6 feet tall."[62] The Associated Press wire service described the scene in vivid detail too. The fifty-year-old prelate—here weighing 215 pounds—had entered the church through the center aisle, "leaning on his gold crozier," when "a man plunged a butcher knife into his abdomen . . . causing him to falter, sink into a pew, and drop his miter."[63] This was followed by a cry, and then, "for a moment, a hush fell over the congregation of 250 persons." Then, most rushed for the door.[64]

Police arrested Matos Leylegian, thirty-nine, and Nihan Sarkisian, thirty-eight, at the scene. The newspapers identified them as grocers, and reported that they were booked on charges of homicide and acting in concert with each other. The Dashnak party was also immediately identified as being involved in the murder. The AP article stated "Inspector Sullivan attributed responsibility for the slaying to 'Dashnag' or 'Tashnag,' a supposedly revolutionary society."[65] The wire service took the time and space to account for the two pronunciations of the Dashnak party, thus entering it into the media discourse. While it did not give further details on the party aside from the seemingly sarcastic description "supposedly revolutionary," it did refer to the picnic in Worcester where the archbishop had been assaulted, the melee at the Chicago World's Fair, and the convention in New York.[66] These intrasectarian incidents forced the American public to engage with Armenian power struggles, and in turn empowered the various groups engaged in the clashes. Perhaps a "supposedly revolutionary society," the Dashnak party nonetheless entered the public lexicon, making its power undeniable.[67]

Even though the murder was shocking, and though the Dashnak party and its alleged adherents were reviled in the press, both victims and perpetrators triumphed in inserting their intrasectarian conflict into the larger US political sphere. The extended coverage also normalized this power struggle. That ordinary grocers could be party adherents also suggested that the party enjoyed widespread support, while demonstrating the rootedness of Armenian intrasectarian institutions in the United States. After all, the grocers weren't the only people involved. The *Daily News* reported that twenty people were being sought for questioning, "hunted in New Jersey, Connecticut, and Pennsylvania," and also mentioned the arrest of Yervant Kelerchian, thirty-eight, a shoemaker.[68] Thus, while these reports could be read as alarming, revealing that the secret Dashnak organization had infiltrated the most everyday of spaces, they also demonstrated the party's localness. The Armenian intrasectarian conflict was very much American.

The Rule of Law

By the end of January 1934, eight men had been indicted for the murder of Archbishop Tourian. All were alleged members of the Dashnak party.[69] American newspapers followed the case as it weaved its way through the justice system. The trial was mired in delays, as the court was often unexpectedly recessed due to verbal and physical disturbances.[70] These reports demonstrated both the Armenians' deference to the rule of law and the press's celebration of it. While "an angry mob of more than 500 adherents of the Archbishop" attacked the men charged with the murder with sticks, canes, umbrellas, and fists, the police were able to quell the mob and empty the courtroom.[71] The crowd was likewise forced away from the Mott Street exit of the court. And while "women shouted and shook their fists and umbrellas, none attempted to attack the prisoners," presumably because of police presence.[72] A man who reportedly shouted "The Archbishop got what was coming to him" was taken into custody by police and charged with disorderly conduct, thus indicating the efficacy of the police force.[73]

Newspapers went on to combine Armenian intrasectarian conflict in the United States with appreciation for the rule of law. Covering an Armenian "protest meeting" held at the Mecca Temple in Manhattan, the *New York Times* reported that patrolmen were posted in the building along with "fifteen husky ushers" in the aisles and balconies.[74] They escorted and arrested a member of the audience who interrupted the speech of the chairman of the executive committee of the Friends of Soviet Armenia, which also resulted in confrontation.[75] Law enforcement was not only celebrated by the success of controlling such outbursts, however. The protest meeting also heard from

Thomas E. Dewey, a former US district attorney, who according to the *New York Times* "praised the assembly for its patience and willingness to let the law take its course instead of attempting to avenge the murder."[76] This statement revealed some astonishment at the discipline that the community sometimes exhibited.

About a month after the meeting at the Mecca Temple, the *New York Times* reported that "dozens [were] beaten as 200 reds try to break up the meeting of anti-Soviet group."[77] At this meeting, attended by another three thousand Armenians, another former district attorney spoke. Joab H. Banton counseled the imprisoned murder suspects, stating that his clients were victims of framing and perjured testimony.[78] Both groups, as it were, enlisted former US district attorneys to buttress their cause to their supporters, opponents, and American compatriots.

This particular article also marked a change in the discourse on Armenians in the press. Aside from reporting that the three thousand had gathered to hear how the "revolutionary movement was the only hope of liberating Armenia from Soviet control," the *New York Times* referred to those who opposed the Dashnaks as "reds" for the first time.[79] In describing the ensuing fracas, it also insinuated that the Dashnaks were the more mature of the two groups, and even that their opponents were cowards. It described the attackers as "raiders" who had "fled when the police arrived," offering "no resistance when the patrolmen and detectives drove them away, contenting themselves with flinging Armenian insults at the police and Tashnags."[80] These epithets, it went on to explain, "were beyond the ken of the patrolmen and the Tashnags pretended to ignore them."[81] That the epithets were unfamiliar to the patrolmen obviously was not surprising, but both this detail and the article's headline, "Five Hurt in Clash of Armenians Here," demonstrated that the American environment was adapting to the "Armenian" cleavages. The *New York Times* felt the need to state that the clashes had occurred "here." As opposed to occurring in another place? Where? Was it informing—or warning—its readership that the problem was now a "local" problem? After all, the meeting had taken place at one of the more iconic buildings of Manhattan, the Metropolitan Life Building—demonstrating that the intrasectarian conflict had found lodging in an additional home.

The Trial

In the trial, which lasted five weeks, all nine accused were found guilty. Two were sentenced to die in the electric chair, and the seven others were sent to prison for terms of ten to twenty years.[82] The day of the sentencing brought additional police protection to safeguard the rule of law. Thirty detectives and patrolmen were stationed in the courtroom, throughout the corridors, and at the entry and exit points of the criminal court.[83] While this type of "protection" was meant to guard against any disorder, which did not take place, the presence and positioning of these armed men also proved the hegemony of the American code of law. All groups engaged in the justice system. And yet, Armenians used the justice system to publicize their struggle with one another.

After the verdict was read, three spectators became involved in a confrontation in front of the district attorney's office a block away from the courthouse, on Centre Street.[84] "Justice" had already been served—so why fight? And why there? After all, the article also noted that the guilty were to be held at "the Tombs" until they would be transferred to Sing Sing Prison, north of New York City, by train, leaving from Grand Central Terminal at 2:10 p.m.[85] The confrontation between the spectators could have occurred at the court. Instead, it took place in front of a federal office and in a public space; most notably *not* in an Armenian institution or center, like the murder itself. The tension had moved, and it claimed a stake not only in the public discourse of the American media, but also in the public space of New York City sidewalks. This innovation was in contrast to the district attorney's description of the crime as something of the "old world."[86] Invoking the "old world" trope was reminiscent of how both Ottoman and European state officials categorized violence in Lebanon and Syria as "age-old" in the nineteenth century, even though it had been "rank, rather than religion" that organized the inhabitants of the region.[87]

Yet these tropes also proved useful. The district attorney stated to the *New York Times*, "I sincerely hope that the successful prosecution of these men will have a salutary effect upon those who come to us from foreign shores—a signal and unforgettable lesson, that while we believe in freedom of speech and untrammeled expression of political views, one must not trespass our laws, which condemn violence and abhor the taking of human life."[88] Armenians used these representations to reclaim power over their community from the American justice system that had been essential to articulating *their* antipathies toward one another. If the murder was indeed from the old world,

Americans did not belong. While local law officials accused Armenians of "carrying out the grudges and antipathies of the old world in America," all of the actions surrounding the murder of Tourian were distinctly new forms of articulating power struggles in the Armenian community, demonstrating the movement and life of Armenian intrasectarian life in the United States.

At the same time, Armenians continued their regular church activities. This time, however, they were reported in the local and national press. A few months after the trial, a two-day convention of the Armenian National Church took place in New York City. The convention was the first to take place since the impeachment of Archbishop Tourian in December, before his murder. Almost one hundred delegates from Armenian communities throughout the United States and Canada gathered to debate the church constitution and resolutions that called for the church to abstain from entering secular affairs and for the elimination of Soviet propaganda, among other issues.[89] What's particularly interesting about this description is that for Armenians the everyday regulations inherent in their institutions continued. New delegates were elected, meetings were held, and resolutions were debated and passed. For the American newspapers, however, this continuation was identified as "news" and was avidly covered in the press. The normal was made abnormal by the news media. After all, why cover a church convention only to let your readership know that it happened? In this case it was the newspapers that contributed to the Armenian intrasectarian conflict in the United States, by delineating these ordinary Armenian activities as extraordinary and newsworthy. American newspapers took on the role the British, French, and Ottoman imperial states had held over Mount Lebanon in the late nineteenth century. Back then, it was those states' "inability" to express their profound shock at the violence, because it was so foreign and abnormal to *them*.[90] This shock at the incomprehensible manifested in their confident support of Pasha's brutal rule of law.[91] Here, American newspapers did the same: it was the police and the American judicial and penal system that "saved" the Armenians from themselves and, in so doing, reaffirmed the supremacy of the American rule of law.

Entrenching Sectarianism

If local Armenians and American newspapers cultivated a sectarian environment in the United States, the continued prevention of the supporters of the Dashnak party from attending Armenian church—which barred them both from attending weekly mass and from being present at or receiving baptism, marriage, or funeral rites—perpetuated the situation. They were likewise blocked from going to Armenian political, cultural, and social events, as these usually took place in the same building as the church. The "ban" continued for twenty-five years while this group sought—and finally received—the assistance of the Cilician See in Lebanon. In effect, the decision of the Cilician See to "adopt" them broke the injunction. Armenian-Americans themselves used the United States and anticommunist rhetoric to encourage the intervention of the Armenian Church in Lebanon in the United States.

It was no coincidence that the Cilician See finally became involved in 1957, more than two decades after the murder of Archbishop Tourian. One year earlier, in 1956, it had elected a vocal critic of communism, the ASSR, and the USSR, Zareh I, as its new catholicos, or supreme patriarch. Zareh, in turn, accepted the request of the "outlawed" US Armenians on October 8, 1957, and sent Archbishop Khoren of Lebanon as his official representative to the United States on October 17. The agreement to "take in" Armenians in the United States served the newly elected Zareh as well. His election had been fraught, held under the "protection" of forces sent by Lebanese President Camille Chamoun. Increasing the Cilician See's membership, especially through the citizens of the United States, would strategically buttress Zareh's authority within Lebanon, across the region, and beyond.[92]

This decision also aided in the Cilician See's unprecedented geographic expansion of power. New churches that pledged loyalty to the Cilician See were built in communities that already housed Armenian churches.[93] As the churches multiplied, so did the power of the Cilician See outside Lebanon. Priests, bishops, and archbishops were brought in from seminaries in Lebanon; and the Holy Chrism, a blessed oil that was used for baptismal, marriage, funerary, and other rites, was also flown in from there. In return for this allegiance, these Armenian-Americans were able once again to practice the tenets of their religion, to receive the guidance of an Armenian religious body, and to attend Sunday mass, marry, baptize, and bury in accordance with their religious principles. In Beirut, *Aztag*, the daily newspaper of the Armenian Dashnak party, celebrated the expansion. The edition of October 18, 1957, declared, using the Cilician See's official name: "From this day forward, the American-Armenian prelacy will enjoy the great guidance of the Holy See of the Catholicosate of Cilicia."[94]

This involvement was not limited to the spiritual realm; it also included money. Armenians in the United States paid membership dues to the see under

whose jurisdiction they fell. Thus, both churches had the potential of acquir-
ing (in the case of the church in Lebanon) or losing (in the case of the church
in the ASSR) capital. These funds were integral to the ability of both sees to
function, and also helped to legitimize their sense of authority and increase
their power vis-à-vis Armenian and non-Armenian populations. Funding was
needed to cover the wages of all those employed by church institutions (sec-
retaries, deacons, priests, bishops, archbishops) and to secure the land upon
which their monasteries and divinity schools were built. Accordingly, when
Archbishop Khoren visited the United States to oversee the consecration of
the Armenian church in Watertown, Massachusetts, he also toured Armenian
communities and inspected sites for future churches in Detroit; northern New
Jersey; and Hartford, Connecticut.[95] The *Hartford Courant* called his assumption of jurisdiction "a dream held for some 37 years."[96]

The resumption of these ordinary activities and rituals challenged the authority of the Armenian Church in the ASSR and transnationalized sectarianism. The Cilician See used the assistance sought by Armenian-Americans to
contest the sovereignty of the Echmiadzin See in Soviet Armenia. The Cilician
See's new authority over US communities also demonstrated its power over
the Armenian community in Lebanon and beyond, which in effect reinforced
the Lebanese sectarian system. Claiming power over the "ejected" simultaneously brought them into the fold of the Cilician See in Lebanon. Armenian-
Americans in the United States became vehicles of Lebanese sectarianism as
the Cilician See extended its power to America. That these actions traversed
both ecclesiastic and state boundaries and took place in the United States also
reengineered the traditional Cold War struggle. Instead of the US and USSR
using proxy wars to battle one another in the Middle East, the United States
became a proxy site for a political struggle between the Armenian churches
in Lebanon and Armenia.[97] At the same time, Armenians in the United States
used the existence of the two sees—and, in particular, the location of one, in
the ASSR—to claim power over one another and practice an intrasectarian
difference.

The *New York Times* covered the arrival of Archbishop Khoren and the
Cilician See under the headline "Armenian Church Cuts Russian Link," and
referred to the assumption of authority over Armenian Apostolic Churches
in the United States as "a solution to the problem" that was also resolved by
the choice of Zareh as catholicos.[98] It referred to Soviet Armenia as "Soviet-
held," thus representing the USSR as an oppressor and Armenia as oppressed.

It also acknowledged a problem: that this meant "two separate Catholicates [*sic*] with a Catholicos at the head of each," and identified one "in the Soviet world" and the other "in the free world."[99] What must also be noted, however, is the change of language that had occurred in the twenty-five years since the murder of Archbishop Tourian. Having once cited "old-world" disagreements of a sectarian nature, in 1957 the *Times* now talked of how nationalism had survived occupation "throughout [Armenia's] history," a reference that included the Soviet status of the Armenian republic.[100] Was the *Times* suggesting that Zareh's assumption of authority over Armenian churches in the United States would aid Armenia in this latest wave of occupation? This remained unclear. The *Times* also made no mention of Tourian, marking his murder as irrelevant in 1957.

While the murder lost its relevance, the United States as a location continued to gain in significance. On October 20, 1957, the *Times* article "Armenian Cleric Assails Prelate" profiled Reverend Vartan Megherian of New York, who was under the tutelage of the Echmiadzin See in the ASSR.[101] Reacting to the struggle for power within the community, Megherian stated, "The mother church [i.e., the Echmiadzin See] will resist all efforts to subordinate religion to the political dictates of any group whatsoever."[102] Yet he also acknowledged that "the sole loyalty of the members of the true Armenian Church in America is the Government of the United States."[103] In so doing, Megherian involved the American state in this "Armenian" struggle for power, and in effect placed the Lebanese and Soviet Armenian sees under the "supra"-jurisdiction of the United States. American politicians reinforced this relationship by meeting, in their official capacities, with Archbishop Khoren and other figures under the jurisdiction of the Cilician See.

But this was not a unidirectional flow of power. With the establishment of its Armenian Prelacy in New York City, the Cilician See in Lebanon likewise became located in the United States, a short subway ride from the site of Tourian's murder. While it did not enjoy the status of "foreign soil" allocated to foreign embassies, it was the administrative headquarters of the Cilician See, and the location from which it supervised its new US congregations. It was also the meeting place between Cilician See church officials and US elected local, state, and federal officials. And while these meetings reinforced the power of American state officials who were chosen presumably because of their legitimacy with the greater American public, these meetings simultaneously acted to subvert US state power, as they in effect sanctioned the involvement of the

Cilician See in the United States. At no time was this more apparent than on October 27, 1957. After consecrating the spaces that would be used as churches in New York City until new buildings were built, Archbishop Khoren traveled to Washington and met with Vice President Richard Nixon, who saluted the archbishop's work.[104] The Hackensack, New Jersey, Record reported that Nixon said he had nothing but praise for the Armenian people, "as they had struggled to keep their Church free of the shackles of dark and sinister forces."[105] The US government essentially endorsed the erosion of its authority as it actively snubbed the Armenian Church in Echmiadzin (read: the USSR). While this could be seen as the United States using the power struggle between the two churches to passively engage in its own struggle with the USSR, it was the Cilician See that facilitated the Soviet loss of power in the United States. The Church in Lebanon exploited the Cold War to increase its own authority, in the midst of the ongoing power struggles between the United States and the Soviet Union.

The host of the Cilician See, the Lebanese government, also sanctioned this increase in authority. In addition to meeting with Nixon, Archbishop Khoren was the guest of honor for a well-attended dinner-reception given by the Lebanese ambassador to the United States, Charles Malek. Addressing the attendees, Aztag reported that Malek praised the Lebanese Armenian community and Catholicos Zareh in Lebanon, and wished Archbishop Khoren "success in his American mission."[106]

Intrasectarian Division, Continued

The church in Lebanon furthered the porousness of American state-power boundaries. This process of intrasectarian division facilitated the peculiar situation that still exists in the United States today: two separate Armenian churches operating from within each Armenian community, often only a few miles apart. Their services are almost identical, with only one variation. During the mass, one pledges loyalty to the catholicos in Armenia, and the other to the catholicos in Lebanon. The display and celebration of Soviet national symbols was once a major distinction which no longer exists today, though the split between the churches still does. Neither see sees it in their political, financial, or sectarian interest to retreat. Armenians continue to make their *ecclesiastical* headquarters reflections of their *political* identity, and define their own ideological boundaries in the United States through practicing intrasectarian difference in their everyday life.

The Cilician See operated from within multiple nation-state boundaries, actively supported by the governments of the United States and Lebanon. During the Cold War it claimed authority over American citizens and challenged the state authority of both the United States and the Soviet Union. Its penetration into the United States—invited or not by a section of that country's citizens—and its affront to the authority of the Soviet Union—by adopting the "homeless" Armenians, as they were referred to by figures of the Cilician See—inserts additional power brokers in our understandings of the Cold War. This new Lebanese/Armenian power was not located in any one city in the United States. Rather, it radiated from within cities nationwide, including New York, Philadelphia, Boston, Chicago, Detroit, Los Angeles, Fresno, San Francisco, and Washington. Since 1957 this power has only increased. As Armenian communities have grown in the United States, additional churches under the jurisdiction of the Cilician See have been built. Within the past twenty years, this power has extended far beyond the walls of the church and of "traditional" church life.

The movement of finances and the presence of "Lebanon" in the United States are often neglected in histories of the period. This is unfortunate, not merely because we miss an interesting story (and background to a dramatic murder on a Christmas Eve), but because we miss how Armenian-Americans produced and practiced an intrasectarian conflict far outside the "sectarian" state of Lebanon. In addition, Armenians both challenged and reinforced state power and the boundaries of the nation-state, adding to our understanding of the Cold War; of the relationship of particular communities with the state of Lebanon, the Soviet Union, and the United States; *and* of intra-Armenian events. After all, because Armenians and other groups are studied through the constricted idealized categories of "minority" or "sect," these power struggles too often become "merely" internal and can be ignored on account of the so-called "bigger picture." Yet it is the rich interplay within an intrasectarian conflict that sheds light on the permeation of boundaries of power by unlikely actors in unlikely places, including by a murdered archbishop on 187th Street in Washington Heights, New York.

7 INEQUALITY AND IDENTITY
Social Class, Urban Space, and Sect

JOANNE RANDA NUCHO

BOURJ HAMMOUD IS JUST outside the borders of municipal Beirut, marked by the concrete-walled Beirut river. The road stretching from Beirut's Gemmayze neighborhood to the Bourj Hammoud municipality square is officially named Armenia Street. While people rarely refer to it by that name, the streets of Gemmayze and Mar Mikhael used to be full of signs with Armenian script. Since 2010, many of these Armenian-owned businesses have rapidly given way to bars and other places of entertainment. On the other side of the bridge in Bourj Hammoud, signs in Armenian are still numerous, and the sounds of Western Armenian language and music fill the streets. Bourj Hammoud's municipality square looks similar to the main roads of other surrounding neighborhoods of east Beirut and its suburbs, with its taller commercial buildings and businesses. Apart from the main road, however, the interior streets and alleys within Bourj Hammoud are narrow, with one-way street signs that every driver ignores. These narrow streets are flanked by two- or three-story buildings built in the 1920s and 1930s to house the first wave of permanent refugee resettlement from the Armenian camps on the shores of Beirut after the systematic massacres and deportations in the former Ottoman Empire, known as the Armenian genocide.[1] Bourj Hammoud's sensorium is thick with sounds, sights, and smells. The vague smell of sewage emanating from the Beirut river mixes with the smell of bakeries selling *mana'ish* and the sound of people speaking a distinctly local dialect of Western Armenian mixed with Lebanese Arabic, Turkish, and often a little English and French, punctuated by the buzz of motorcycles and scooters whizzing around the streets.

Sometimes it seems that everything has been said about Bourj Hammoud, a city built to house the first in what would become continual waves of displacement: from within Lebanon, from Palestine, and from Syria and beyond. People have moved there for work, for economic opportunities, to flee conflict, or for a combination of all of those things. Bourj Hammoud has been at the center of these movements for a long time.[2] In what follows, inspired by recent provocations about politics, sect, and class in Lebanon, I want to further complicate a fictional but still incredibly powerful binary between class and sect as analytic categories. As Lara Deeb explains in this volume, the binary between class and sect is untenable, and is inadequate for describing how people experience relationships or definitions of community in their everyday lives. I draw on theorizations in feminist and class analysis, together with ethnographic insight from Bourj Hammoud between 2008 and 2015, to consider how sect and class are mutually constituted and always ongoing processes of differentiation, enmeshed in a broader political economy of social infrastructures.[3]

Writing this chapter from the shores of California, I only dare to say anything more about Beirut, and about Bourj Hammoud today, with full knowledge of the trajectories of movement through those places that my own Armenian and Palestinian relatives traveled in their paths of reconstitution, survival, and attempted class mobility from Cilicia and Palestine to Lebanon and then the United States. These mobilities shaped the course of my Armenian family's journeys to the United States from the refugee camps of Beirut—with me, the great-granddaughter, returning later to Bourj Hammoud as ethnographer.

Inspired by recent revolts in 2015 and 2019, within a broader moment of drawing on archives and family histories to renew the conceptual imaginary from which we write,[4] I offer some stories about Bourj Hammoud in order to ask how we might consider identities in a processual fashion,[5] co-constituted in and through urban spaces and the local sectarian social welfare institutions that shape their meaning.

How are these processes of producing sect and class irreducible to the material or the affective alone? Ethnographic sensibility and archives from the margins help us see both sect and class in processual fashion, rather than as static categories of social or political structure. By understanding class and sect as processual, not a priori to the work of actively producing community, we could then see that work as *labor*. It takes work to produce what looks like "sectarian community," and that labor did not always (and still does not) fall under the domain of the sectarian party or its institutions, or even sectarian notions of relatedness and belonging. In her prescient work, Suad Joseph argued that in Bourj Hammoud, nonhomogenous women's networks of maintenance and care were actively dismantled, and were sectarianized by political parties who more or less took over these informal networks and regarded them as threats.[6] If we think about sectarian community-making as a kind of labor rather than an innate state of being, we might then be able to reimagine the work that goes into creating and maintaining the social welfare institutions and other forms of local, neighborhood-based mutual aid networks as laying the groundwork for solidarity outside sectarian political frameworks. What I propose here is the possibility that the labor entailed in making mutual aid networks function was never completely subsumed under the aegis of sectarian political parties. That labor of "doing" collective, I argue, belongs to the people who make life, and the recognition of entangled fates between neighbors, possible in these difficult times—especially since 2019.

Sectarianization is an entangled affective material process that occurs in and through space. Social transformation will not come about by "removing" sectarianism, as though it were a superficial gloss on economic inequality or a false consciousness masking true underlying relations or essence, because these are not experienced as discrete things. Rather, attention to everyday practices, even those that exist in fields of domination and inequality, will provide resources for understanding the constitution of a nonhomogenous, nonunified, collective subject that is "constituted by socioeconomic structures and capable of subverting them."[7] Collective standpoints cannot be created by uncovering an already existing unified essence or identity from which to organize. Collectivity is a process of locating potential for transformation within everyday practices—on the street, in the workplace, and in the home. To do that, it is first important to understand how sect and class is a spatialized process with its own history.

Community-building practices are the work of "doing" collective. These practices unfold in particular urban spaces, and become associated with neighborhoods. In what follows, I describe the ways in which Bourj Hammoud provides resources for thinking about how sect and class identities are connected to urban spaces in Beirut. I then move into some histories of the building of Bourj Hammoud as a facet of a French and Armenian project in the aftermath of the 1915 genocide, in order to understand how a particular kind of working-class Beirut Armenian identity came to be associated with it.

Armenian social mobility in many cases involves physical mobility: moving out of Bourj Hammoud to elsewhere. This in turn creates ambivalence about the tension between upward mobility and authenticity around Bourj Hammoud, as feelings of belonging and nostalgia for Bourj Hammoud are complicated by a reluctance to be associated with its working-class connotation. Can this ambivalence be a productive space? Can Bourj Hammoud's "craftiness," the resourcefulness that is part of its deeply working-class connotation, be mobilized for something beyond individual class ascendance? I end with a discussion of how we might think about the October 2019 uprisings in Lebanon outsidef the binary of class versus sect, or even outside the necessity for the emergence of a new consciousness that debunks the primacy of sect for class. I ask whether the work of *doing collective*, the labor that goes into building something that looks like the Armenian community, might be what is most at stake, which can be appropriated or reclaimed from the confines of sectarian institutions.

Thinking Sect, Thinking Class in Bourj Hammoud

In Bourj Hammoud, the physical sensation of density is immediately palpable, with narrow streets barely wide enough to fit one car. Many streets are full of pedestrians. Bourj Hammoud feels distinct from more car-dominated nearby parts of Beirut, and its suburbs to the northeast. Unlike urban areas where the pedestrian has to navigate spaces designed for the driver, in Bourj Hammoud pedestrians dominate many of the narrower interior streets. Walking on narrow curbs that serve as sidewalks in some areas is impossible, as cars park onto them to create clear passage for other vehicles. During the day, the streets are full of people walking; and in some narrow streets that do not see a lot of traffic, children can take up the entire road to play. Bourj Hammoud also has an incredible density of Armenian-run social and political institutions and businesses. These institutions range from village and town associations to political clubhouses that serve a host of functions from informal security to youth recreation. Many of the primary businesses are a product of the trades that the first wave of refugees learned or brought with them and passed down generationally: shoemaking, and design and manufacture of clothing and jewelry.

That Bourj Hammoud is widely regarded as Beirut's "Armenian quarter" comes not only from its designation since the French Mandate era as a space of resettlement for Armenians, but from its vibrant daily life. It is a hub of rural to urban migration for people from elsewhere in Lebanon, and for migrants and displaced people from around the world, especially nearby Syria. Among many Armenians in Lebanon, Bourj Hammoud also functions as a kind of shorthand for being working-class, a connotation that is not only about economic status, but about an entire set of assumptions and practices tied to space. The small neighborhood contains the networks essential for small-scale shoemakers, jewelry makers, mechanics, and clothing manufacturers, as well as migrant laborers who find work and housing through connections there.

How does this provoke us to reconsider the meaning of "working-class" as rooted elsewhere than in relations of production on the factory floor? The labor of producing community via informal networks has long been the target of international development projects under structural adjustment; these programs have sought to bring the poor into the global financial market through debt, via microlending programs that have capitalized these very informal networks of the poor.[8] Of course, urban planners and municipal governments also have their own stake in manipulating the *dimughrafiyya* (demography) of Beirut and its periphery.[9] But even in more mundane ways, people understand spaces as familiar or strange based not only on accumulated experience of conflict, but in the everyday ways they procure basic services. Being a member of a sectarian "community" is often tied to specific spaces that complicate how uniform this notion of community is. The class location of the "community" matters just as much as sect, but is impossible to disentangle; most of the artisans in Bourj Hammoud I describe above are Armenian.

Within Lebanon there is no monolithic Armenianness, even within the relatively small Armenian community there.[10] Rather, being Armenian—being working-class or middle-class, being from Bourj Hammoud, Beirut or elsewhere—creates a complex web of locations from which to understand oneself as part of a "community" in ways that cannot be disentangled. Sectarian community is not an innate outcome of ethnic or religious differences and is not reducible to religion as theology,[11] though many people experience sectarian political identities in and through piety.[12] Notions of sectarian community are produced and reproduced through legal and institutional practices of differentiation,[13] as a recent modernization project developed between various actors from France to the Ottoman Empire.[14] Armenians are not exceptional to the Lebanese sectarian system, and should not be theorized as being somehow outside of it.[15]

What Bourj Hammoud helps to show is that sect as a category *and* a feeling of belonging to community is a process entangled with material and institutional forms of differentiation. This does not mean that sectarian identity is reducible to the economic or institutional. Cultural and symbolic forms carry their own very real material effects, impacts, and consequences in the world.[16] There is no sustainable opposition between "real" material, which is economic, and the "imaginary" or believed. Viewing sect ethnographically as a process of differentiation connected to channels of resources, social geography, and popular representations, rather than as just a form of religious practice or belief, helps to complicate the idea of a binary between class and sect as two distinct categories.

Sectarian identity is part of the way people navigate relationships in the world, as a process produced in and through institutions of medical care, education, and even credit and lending.[17] These institutions cannot be understood as primarily or solely cultural *or* material, and the processes of creating them, the work of making sectarian community, are absolutely related to class formation. Still, there are ways of relating to these institutions, neighbors, and neighborhoods that are not reducible to existing categories. Raymond Williams's concept of "structures of feeling" is helpful here in its reminder to be attentive to the processes that have not yet been named or formalized, but which give us the capacity to imagine change or movement over time and through emergent practices.[18] Certainly, my interlocutors often challenged the ways in which sectarian identity has been wielded by institutions that claim to act in their name; this was true even for those who worked within Armenian political, religious, or social organizations. I heard people express ambivalent feelings of pride and belonging as well as disappointment and disillusionment, particularly with the Armenian political institutions and the "Armenian community" in Lebanon as they imagined it *and* labored to produce or "maintain" it. For many of my interlocutors, community was not described as a thing that already existed without their effort. Rather, community is an *ongoing* project, something that comes into being only with collective effort. This idea of a collective effort, rather than some innate essence of being, provides grounds for thinking about processes of social transformation in the context of so much upheaval and uncertainty in Lebanon since 2019.

Here I draw on the formulations of the feminist theorist Kathi Weeks, and her provocation to resist a dichotomy between a caricatured modernist subject with the capacity and agency to self-fashion, and the subjectivity that is entirely socially determined.[19] Weeks writes:

> The project of totality—which I will try to distinguish from totalizing theory, or theories that reduce subjectivity to some functional effect of

an abstract, determinable, and monolithic system of structures—refers to an attempt to locate some of the specific connections between our everyday lives and practices and the larger framework of social structures within which they are organized. [...] For example, capitalism, patriarchy, and white supremacy are not isolated forces, but rather systems that traverse the entire social horizon and intersect at multiple points.[20]

Weeks's project is one not merely of description but of social transformation. There is no "metaphysical essence" that if brought to the surface will provide an alternative to existing social relations.[21] Rather, Weeks suggests that horizons of possibility for transformation lie in *existing practices*. By refocusing attention in this way, we might avoid the pitfalls of a rigid functionalist view of social totality while maintaining difference and contingency.[22]

Taking up the case of Bourj Hammoud as a space for both class mobility and cultural authenticity (with all the contradictions that this tension produces) allows us to consider how class and sect identities emerge from local conditions and institutions, intellectual debates among Armenians, and French imperial ambitions. To think about Lebanese Armenians is a methodological gesture toward a larger project of rethinking sectarianism outside a functionalist analysis of a unified, stable system. Armenianness and class are articulated at different points within the complex web of relations that people traverse in their everyday lives, irreducible to dichotomies of the material versus the affective. This was confirmed to me by my interlocutors, who insisted over and over that the project of producing and "maintaining" Armenianness was a process, rather than an unshakable, taken-for-granted essence, because the Armenian community did not just exist. The history of genocidal annihilation and the fear of erasure helped make this Armenianization process even more urgent and its lack of "essence" ever more clear. It is not taken for granted that everyone is always already "authentically" Armenian.

In the next section of this chapter, I explain how Bourj Hammoud provides resources for thinking about class and sect as a dynamic process. First I turn to its history as conceptualized by French Mandate officials and Armenian political actors, and how that project is remembered by some of my Armenian interlocutors today. I show how popular memories of the refugee camps and ideas about progress and development animate the way people understand Bourj Hammoud as a contradictory project, a place to maintain as a locus of

Armenian authenticity and territorial integrity within a sectarian imaginary of urban governance, *and* as something to surpass as part of a narrative of progress and class mobility. I then provide an account of how sect and class can be better understood as shifting locations within the context of everyday social relations, geographies, and institutional arrangements. I end with some examples of how forms of identification and belonging, entangled with systems of domination as well as modes of care and mutual aid, could provide resources for thinking about new ways of *doing* collective.

Elsewhere in the world, architects of structural adjustment have already identified informal networks as a valuable resource.[23] In Lebanon, these networks of aid and care in Bourj Hammoud were taken over and dismantled in the 1970s by sectarian political parties that found intersectarian cooperation to be threatening to their consolidation of power in the area.[24] But can these networks, produced as they are by people laboring to make community, be reclaimed as part of a project of transformation? Could those informal networks of care, the "infrastructures of poor peoples' social practices," which are a kind of "commons," provide resources for thinking about a transformation of social relations that is not locked into the "privatized" channels of sectarian political parties, but is instead a public good?[25] To unpack these questions, I first present a tentative methodology of thinking about class and sect in Lebanon without reducing either one to a narrative of false consciousness, and of imagining a way to analyze the material and symbolic as inseparable. Because class and sect are deeply spatialized processes, I also turn to histories of how these categories of belonging were produced historically and in some cases intentionally, though the outcomes of the intentional projects remain unfixed.

Building Bourj Hammoud, Producing Sect and Class

What the history of Bourj Hammoud helps to show is that notions of class, upward mobility, material accumulation, spatial politics, and sectarian identities are produced in and through relationships across geographical scales over time. As Fawwaz Traboulsi writes, "Two major functions of sects are often neglected: first, their role as enlarged clientelist networks designed to resist the inequalities of the market, and compete for its benefits and for the appropriation of social wealth and services of the state; second, their long-standing habit of enlisting outside help in their struggle for power or for sheer survival."[26] The implication of communities within broad global networks of aid is part of the history of how ideas about sect and class are produced in

Lebanon in the context of the fall of the Ottoman Empire, the influence of competing quasi-imperial powers and global relationships, and the rise of a modern capitalist nation-state with privatized forms of social welfare routed through sect-affiliated channels. These processes are also urban and spatial, as municipalities and the political parties that tend to dominate them see the demographic makeup of neighborhoods as a means of consolidating political influence in space, particularly in the context of heightened fears around security and the potential for conflict to occur again in the "postwar" era.[27]

In Lebanon, sect and class are processes that shift in and through historical and ongoing relationships with imperial actors like France, or through migration experiences within the region and across the world. Migrations to West Africa, France, Canada, or the Persian Gulf shape ideas about class and sect, both through the fact of moving between these different contexts and through the forms of accumulation that these trajectories enable. While I want to avoid essentializing the impact of these routes on the identities of people who traverse them, there are existing associations with each of these migrations, owing to linguistic, sect, and class differences in Lebanon. A French-Lebanese Armenian dual citizen told me that she feels "more Lebanese than Armenian" because she always attended mixed elite Francophone Lebanese schools with Lebanese elites of various sects. Migrations and relationships that stretch from particular neighborhoods to thousands of miles away are symbolic and material processes that shape these identities and identifications. Similarly, making the "local" of Bourj Hammoud appear as something locally authentic was in fact a long process that unfolded across different geographical scales of influence, from local Armenian political parties to the French Mandate officials who saw their role as one of creating new, eventually independent nation-states out of the former Ottoman Empire that would remain in their sphere of influence.

Today's Bourj Hammoud is evidence of an accumulation of histories of dispossession and resettlement, starting with the resettlement of Armenians in the early twentieth century. It is a hub for migration within Lebanon, as well as one for migrants and displaced people from the region and around the world who seek work and affordable housing. It is a city of mechanic's shops, ateliers that manufacture clothing and shoes, and workshops that do all manner of repairs. Aside from its reputation as Beirut's "Armenian quarter," it is a shopping center for clothing, textiles, shoes, furniture coverings, hardware, stationery, printing materials, and various services. Bourj Hammoud's "crafty" reputation for being a place where you can find or fix anything is touted by many of its inhabitants, who are proud of their ability to make something out of nothing. "You could even find bird's milk in Bourj Hammoud," my friend Seta loved to say whenever I was looking for something, anything, whether it be real licorice sticks, a book, or a particular kind of tool.

The "craftiness" of Bourj Hammoud, and the density of Armenian-run institutions, residences, and businesses, is partly the outcome of a project during France's Mandate in the 1930s, in which land in Bourj Hammoud, then an agricultural area, was transformed into a neighborhood of houses and shops to permanently resettle Armenians. As the historian Keith Watenpaugh writes, the Mandate's policies "were intended to integrate the Armenians by providing them with property, a trade or a profession in a way that intensified their linkage with the French state."[28] These projects were based on the creation of urban spaces and trades that would encourage Armenian ascendance into a "respectable lower middle class."[29]

One of my Armenian interlocutors, whose grandfather was part of the Mandate-era intellectual and political elite (though, interestingly, not part of the Armenian economic elite), narrated his version of this history. For some Armenian political actors, he recalled, the resettlement was driven by concerns different from those of the French. The Armenian political and intellectual project of building the "Armenian quarter" was one of educating the working classes and tradespeople in Armenian language and culture, and of cultivating authentic Armenianness. The refugees from the genocide were not a monolithic or homogenous group; many of them spoke Turkish or other regional dialects, not standardized Western Armenian.

Building the Armenian neighborhood of Bourj Hammoud was, from the beginning, part of a project that made class and sect: specifically, an Armenian (or more importantly, for French officials, Christian) middle-class society. The creation of these geographies was also an Armenian intellectual and political project.[30] As Tsolin Nalbantian shows, Armenian political parties intentionally cultivated and spatialized their spheres of influence geographically in different neighborhoods in Lebanon, and particularly in Beirut.[31] The building of Bourj Hammoud may have unfolded as a pair of overlapping French and Armenian political projects—though I avoid collapsing the two, since they came from radically unequal positions of power. Keith Watenpaugh's contribution to the intellectual history of middle-class modernity in the eastern Mediterranean is helpful here, as he cautions that middle-class modernity did not lead to a disidentification with sect.[32] He writes, "A majority of the middle class who sought to articulate a substantive role for themselves in the politics of their society came from the region's large commercial middle class; as a class dominated by religious minorities, their exclusion and activism added an inescapable dimension to the form of conflict and change."[33]

My own family and many other members of the new Armenian middle classes are part of the outcome of this process of class mobility through permanent settlement in Bourj Hammoud and elsewhere (like the nearby Beirut neighborhood of Nor Hadjin), and through the Armenian political project as a spatial, educational and affective one in Lebanon. For many people of the Armenian middle class, there is a connection to Bourj Hammoud, or to the refugee camps; and, as I will describe later, the story of class ascendance often coincides with leaving the neighborhood.

After the 1930s, Bourj Hammoud continued to be a hub for migration, particularly for working-class people of different sects from around the world. The migration grew after many Armenians left Lebanon as part of the "repatriation" movement to Soviet Armenia in 1946.[34] During that period and in subsequent decades, other migrants—particularly displaced Palestinians, Shi'i Muslims from the south of Lebanon, and Syrians—came to Bourj Hammoud because of its proximity to Beirut, its affordable housing, and the availability of work in its many ateliers and workshops. In the 1970s it was a highly diverse working-class urban area inhabited by Maronite Christians, Shi'i Muslims, Palestinians, and migrant workers from Syria and elsewhere. During the 1975–90 Lebanese civil war, ethnic cleansing and violent displacement of Shi'i Muslims and Palestinians by Christian right-wing militias changed the demographic makeup of Bourj Hammoud again. During the war, many Armenian institutions in Beirut moved to Bourj Hammoud, like the headquarters of the Armenian Apostolic church in Lebanon, and the Armenian-owned gold and jewelry markets. By the 1990s and 2000s, many Shi'i property owners were able to reclaim their properties. Some moved back to Bourj Hammoud, though others rented or sold their properties. Today, Bourj Hammoud is again demographically quite diverse, not just in terms of members of different Lebanese sectarian groups, but with transnational migrant workers from countries all over the world, including Sri Lanka, Ethiopia, and Syria. Since 2011, the conflict in Syria has driven people from that country, including Kurds and Armenians, to Bourj Hammoud.

Bourj Hammoud is at the center of a contradiction around the classed and sectarian identities its architects aimed to produce in the 1930s. Among Armenians, the popular discourse is that their "cleverness" and "industriousness" is praised even when their neighborhood's "working-class" connotation is mildly derided. With the praise comes a popular idea that these skills should result in upward mobility. Among many of my Armenian interlocutors of the professional class, notions of "development" or progress mean leaving Bourj Hammoud and moving to wealthier suburbs to the northeast.

There is a middle-class ambivalence about Bourj Hammoud: a hope for upward mobility, and a simultaneous desire to keep the neighborhood intact as an "Armenian quarter." So far, the gentrification in nearby Mar Mikhael—on Armenia Street, no less—has not occurred in Bourj Hammoud. Nor does Bourj Hammoud have an analogue to the Shi'i middle-class gentrification of Dahiya, described by Deeb and Harb in their ethnography *Leisurely Islam*.[35] There have been recent evictions and attempts at high-end development in Bourj Hammoud, like the destruction of the informal Sanjak camp, which was razed to build Saint Jacques, a large mixed-use residential and commercial building. Still, Bourj Hammoud remains largely working-class. The contradictions in Bourj Hammoud provide one way of understanding the entanglement of sect, class, and labor that shapes notions of community in Lebanon today.

Contradictions of Class Mobility and Authenticity

In everyday conversation even outside Lebanon and throughout the Lebanese Armenian diaspora, Bourj Hammoud is often used as a shorthand term for "working-class Armenian." It has a complicated and contradictory reputation among those whom I have been calling "middle-class" or professional Armenian interlocutors. By "middle-class," I refer not merely or exclusively to economic circumstances, but to a social position connected to notions of modernity, class mobility, professionalization, and education—all usually associated with material and economic circumstances, but not reducible to them.

One middle-class Armenian interlocutor with family connections to Bourj Hammoud noted a vacillation between a certain playful derision about the lower-class status of Bourj Hammoud, and a nostalgic attachment to the neighborhood as a place of origin or even authenticity. I was surprised, however, to find that the idea of it as a source of authenticity rather than an ongoing project of developing Armenianness is also somewhat recent and contradictory. Another interlocutor, a middle-class Armenian professional in his fifties who grew up in Beirut but has since immigrated to the United States, remembers a number of official projects launched as late as the 1970s and 1980s to make working-class Armenians *more* Armenian. Specifically, he recalled a public campaign, promoted through posters all over Bourj Hammoud, encouraging people to stop speaking Turkish and switch to Western Armenian. According to him, there was a popular assumption that Bourj Hammoud Armenians were more likely to intermarry across sects, and that this was associated with being working-class—and, from the perspective of Armenian religious and political institutions, a thing to be discouraged. Suad Joseph's research in the 1970s revealed the ways in which women's cross-sectarian networks in Bourj Hammoud were perceived as threats to the dominance of Christian political actors, and described the actions those actors took to dismantle the networks (1983).[36] Today, these discourses about Bourj Hammoud's authenticity have shifted. While Armenian political actors in the 1970s and 1980s tried to make Bourj Hammoud more "authentically" Armenian, the neighborhood is regarded today as a source of authenticity in need of preservation.

Some of my middle-class Armenian interlocutors with relatives in Bourj Hammoud or experience working there can describe very well the contradictions in their understanding of the neighborhood and of working-class Armenians in Lebanon. One evening in 2010, I was invited to dinner at an Armenian middle-class interlocutor's home. She was in her early sixties and lived in the East Beirut neighborhood of Ashrafiyya. I met the other guests, whom I would describe as Armenian professionals. All had spent time abroad for education and work, and all traveled frequently. Throughout our conversation, the contradictions within popular ideas about Bourj Hammoud became clear, and they too were aware of them. They viewed the neighborhood as an important cultural and historical home for Armenian intellectual life, and a living space where at least one very local version of the Western Armenian language could be heard and spoken daily. Yet they admitted that many middle-class Armenians want to distance themselves from being associated with it. The historical connection between Bourj Hammoud and the refugee camps, one interlocutor said, made some people view association with the neighborhood as something a middle-class Armenian was supposed to have "escaped." The Sanjak camp, the last remaining Armenian refugee camp in the neighborhood, was then in the process of being demolished and its inhabitants evicted.[37] The dinner guests expressed much compassion for the residents of Sanjak, and an acute sense that they were being betrayed by the Armenian leadership, who were not being transparent about plans for resettlement or recompense.

In other instances, some of my middle-class interlocutors, even some of those working in Armenian social welfare organizations, thought that the Armenian parties were doing their constituents a disservice by trying to keep them in Bourj Hammoud. One interlocutor who worked in an NGO, and who since the 1970s had witnessed various projects to move residents of Armenian camps into apartment buildings, was more definitive in his ideas about social mobility and Bourj Hammoud. He said that anyone who could escape would do so, and that it was in fact natural, even desirable, that people leave Bourj Hammoud and move out to more affluent suburbs. He went on to suggest that the drive to keep Armenians in Bourj Hammoud was mainly a project of politicians who sought to maintain their own interests by keeping their constituents in place.

Still, many middle-class Armenians hope for the preservation of Bourj Hammoud. Their feelings cannot be explained merely as the political machinations of the dominant Armenian political party. As one of my interlocutors said, "Historic preservation of the old neighborhood is important, so that all of Bourj Hammoud doesn't become a parking lot." For some, it is important to keep the neighborhood intact as a means not only of remembering history, but of supporting the continuation of the Armenian social world that the neighborhood helped to produce—physically, with its institutions, as well as materially and affectively, as a nationalist project in exile. Despite obvious parallels with the Palestinian camps in Lebanon, one important distinction here is the axis of citizenship, which the vast majority of Palestinians have not been granted. Armenian political organizations are deeply integrated into Lebanon's formal political establishment, and operate to consolidate their power through urban planning.

Developing Bourj Hammoud was in many ways the modernist urban planning project par excellence; trying to make people "more modern" through spatial interventions of urban planning is as old as the profession itself. It is not uncommon for working-class neighborhoods elsewhere in the world to be labeled as somehow "not modern," and for urban development projects to be leveraged precisely to "modernize" people and their practices. For example, Farha Ghannam analyzes the Egyptian state's discourses of modernization via spatial hegemony in its project to relocate its urban poor from the centers of towns to housing at the periphery.[38] While Bourj Hammoud offers quite different circumstances, we can also understand it as a modern project of producing "authentic" Armenianness while simultaneously promoting social mobility and permanent settlement. As a modernizing project it has a number of contradictions, namely between notions of authenticity and progress, Armenianness and social mobility, both within Lebanon and elsewhere. Those contradictions animate the way in which many middle-class Armenians view the people who live there, who are by and large of lower socioeconomic status.

Even though many middle-class Armenians work to maintain the Armenian schools, clinics, and religious and political institutions in Bourj Hammoud, most Armenians with the means to move out of the neighborhood do so. Bourj Hammoud is valuable not only as a locus of authenticity, but for the sheer density of its Armenian institutions. People who live there and those who only do business there may experience the space and its nexus of institutions differently, and may have different reasons for their attachment to the place that cannot be divided by to a binary distinction between affective and material. Space, class, and sect are not static categories, but processes that are all part of how a person can navigate institutional channels or, all too often, be excluded from them. Those frequent exclusions, when people cannot connect to resources in circulation, are what I turn to next.

Density, Access, and Exclusion

One of the first things one might notice about Bourj Hammoud, as I have mentioned, is the feeling of sheer density—of bodies, sounds, residential buildings, workshops, stores, schools, churches, and clinics. The proximity to Beirut and its rich density of institutions and markets makes Bourj Hammoud valuable to many middle-class Armenians as a place of work and socialization—even if it has become a less desirable place to live, owing to the pollution of the nearby Beirut River, the crumbling infrastructure and old residential buildings, and the area's propensity to flood during the rainy winter season. Working-class Armenians also value the proximity to Armenian schools, and to centers that provide social services and medical care. Many of these centers, both those operated by Armenians and those run by other religious organizations, provide medical services to anyone in need, regardless of sect. And of course the many workshops and businesses in Bourj Hammoud are not run, staffed, or patronized solely by Armenians.

Many of my interlocutors mentioned this density as one reason why Bourj Hammoud is an important place even if they do not reside there. An Armenian jeweler explained to me why the gold markets remained in the area even after the civil war, after many of their owners had moved to more affluent suburbs. He said, "Bourj Hammoud is a base for this, artisanal crafts. [. . .] It's good to set up shop here, because you can find all the raw materials here."

But despite Bourj Hammoud's association with its commercial sector, it is also dense with churches, social and political clubs, cafes, bakeries, and places to socialize and organize. But not everyone has equal access to the essential servicesprovided by this density of institutions, manufacturing, and commerce.[39]

Living in Bourj Hammoud gives its residents more points of contact with the political party, the church, and other Armenian institutions. As they do elsewhere in Beirut and its peripheries, political parties dominant in Bourj Hammoud manipulate urban planning to secure their dominance amid anxieties about *dimughrafiyya* (demography) or changing demographics in certain neighborhoods that are understood to be potential sites of future conflict.[40] In the context of that overall spatial anxiety, the *agoomps*,[41] or political clubhouses, have a prominent role as centers of activity and security in each neighborhood under a particular club's spatial jurisdiction. These *agoomps* function as neighborhood gatekeepers and provide services including social welfare distribution, recreation, and children's educational activities, socialization, and celebrations. *Agoomps* are frequently called upon to resolve disputes and are viewed as a kind of informal security connected to other Armenian organizations, including the church—at least for Armenian residents. There is a strong public perception that the *agoomps*, as well as other Armenian social organizations, have jurisdiction over Armenians living in Bourj Hammoud, even if that is not the case in every situation.

The unfortunate case of someone I will call Tamar illustrates the limits of sectarian affiliation for working-class people without material resources, particularly in obtaining legal assistance.[42] Tamar and her siblings, who had been born in Lebanon to Lebanese-Armenian parents, lacked any kind of legal identification papers. For some reason, their parents' births had never been registered on their grandparents' family identity document, a necessary step to being issued a personal identity document. After both her parents died, Tamar, who was still a teenager, could not secure the necessary legal assistance to sort out the matter. While she was able to access local aid networks to find work and get basic forms of assistance, including a fund-raising appeal made on her family's behalf on the local Armenian radio station, she lacked the money to hire a lawyer.

A social worker I knew tried to access legal aid for Tamar via another nonprofit organization that specialized in legal assistance for women sorting out identity issues, particularly unmarried mothers who needed identity documents for their children. In Lebanon, citizenship is inherited only via male

Lebanese citizens. Unmarried women must jump many hurdles to obtain papers for their children, and it is impossible for Lebanese women married to noncitizens to pass on citizenship to their children. That particular organization did not feel it could take up Tamar's case, stating that she needed to go through Armenian organizations and resources—her own "community."

The social worker who was trying to help Tamar noted that the problem was twofold. Since the dominant Armenian political party had clearly delineated its jurisdiction over all Armenians in Bourj Hammoud, especially those who were poor, without much recourse for institutional or legal representation outside Armenian organizations, other organizations tended not to "interfere" in what they viewed as "Armenian issues." The second problem was that it was exceedingly difficult to register a grown adult onto a family document in Lebanon, partially because of all the sensitivity around "demography" and sectarian balance; the issue of "demography" is the reason why no official census has been conducted there since 1932. Even an appeal to the United Nations High Commissioner for Refugees (UNHCR) for legal assistance was not helpful, because Armenians were no longer considered refugees; it suggested that Tamar appeal to an international Catholic aid organization, which she was hesitant to do because she was not Catholic and wondered whether they would be willing or even able to help. For Tamar and the social worker, it was completely out of the question to go to the Lebanese General Security office, knowing they would never offer help unless approached by some kind of proper intermediary—possibly a well-connected lawyer, or an organization with the right contacts, but no one in the Armenian community really knew.

The difficulty Tamar faced in getting identity documents is another example of how class and sect are deeply implicated in how people can relate to institutions within Bourj Hammoud and to the Lebanese state's bureaucratic apparatus. Even as sectarian political actors and organizations create boundaries and barriers, social workers and informal mutual aid networks provide resources for thinking and working across categories to possible futures. Maintaining the "community" is arguably the focus of their labor, as they provide working-class Armenians in Bourj Hammoud with medical care, educational scholarships for children, and even food coupons. However, the contents of that notion of collective and community are not static; they are subject to change. A focus on these practices might be a way out of an essentializing argument about sectarian identity as ideological cover for material inequality, or a functionalist argument that sees sect and class as two identities that contribute to a total closed system that is destined only to reproduce itself. Neither direction captures the ambivalence people feel. As they work within and outside these organizations in ways that do not always narrowly align with their aims, their practices can actively make and remake their lifeworlds. I believe these practices should matter to any speculative project about the future.

Practices and Potentials

Many Armenian social welfare organizations in Bourj Hammoud have a stated mandate to serve Armenian clients, but they also provide services to non-Armenians—particularly medical services, but also other forms of aid. By providing these services, the social workers, teachers, and volunteers working in these organizations help to produce whatever the community is. The criteria for "belonging" to the Armenian community are not consistent or reducible to essential features, and can change over time. What ethnography can show is that people can and do often mobilize resources and institutions across boundaries set by "higher-ups" in the organizations. In many situations at different institutions and in everyday conversations, I witnessed the willingness of people to cooperate, build viable networks, and even organize in ways that intentionally defy or stretch the narrow mandate to serve "Armenians." This "know-how"—the resourcefulness people have developed through waves of displacement, violent conflict, and economic crisis—is the property not of the sectarian organizations, but of the people who do the work. Can this "craftiness," so much a part of Bourj Hammoud's popular reputation, be mobilized not only for individualized forms of class ascendance, but also for something collective? In some ways, it already has been.

Even as I have seen *agoomps* and Armenian organizations mobilized in ways that exclude, I have also met social workers in Armenian clinics and the women's auxiliaries of the political clubs who understand that part of their task is caring for longtime neighbors. They redistribute food coupons, help people get medical care, and make house calls to check on the sick. I have attended informal rotating credit association meetings with women, Armenian and non-Armenian, who pool resources and build viable networks, not only for collecting money but for the distribution of information: where to get medicines, how to get clean water for cheap, where to go for work.

These everyday practices are rooted not in essential knowledges, but in practices of doing community. They are maintained partly through what I have been calling the dense spaces of Bourj Hammoud, spaces that in some instances are slowly disappearing. Take the case of the Sanjak camp, for example. While one of my middle-class interlocutors understood social mobility to mean movement out of the camps, and indeed out of Bourj Hammoud itself, in the years when Sanjak was slowly being demolished, several of its residents described to me why they had fought so hard to stay. While many were holding out for an equitable settlement, others explained that they really did not want to leave, mainly because Sanjak had become a close-knit community of people who really knew each other. Despite the difficulties of life there, including the fact that it was subject to flooding and was a highly polluted space right near the *autostrade* (highway), they would feel a great sense of loss if their community was torn apart and resettled in distant apartments. It is the "doing" of community that they would miss, and that is both a material and an affective process, not really reducible to being working-class, or being Armenian.

The sectarian political parties may try to steer or harness the "doing" of community in various ways. All evidence shows that they are quite intentional in mobilizing social welfare to consolidate political relationships,[43] and, historically, to politicize sectarian identities in particular ways.[44] However, the practices are not solely their domain. In this chapter I have put forward a necessarily incomplete and tentative line of questioning, not only as a challenge to the reduction of class and sect as two separate and static identities, but also toward a methodology that comes from the openness and willingness to learn by doing that comes from ethnography. There are resources that exist for thinking about how to *do* collective. Certainly we saw this in the streets of Lebanon in the summer of 2015, and again in the months following the uprising of October 2019. In both years, people organized on the streets of Beirut and beyond, calling explicitly for accountability of *all* Lebanese politicians, the entire government, rather than any specific political party or faction. Neither protest could be claimed by a political party or leader. These events were enactments of a vision of solidarity and urban citizenship that many political actors have tried, unsuccessfully for the most part, to actively dismantle and contain within narrow sectarian frameworks.[45] These practices of "doing collective" did not emerge out of nowhere.

8 WHEN EXPOSURE IS NOT ENOUGH

Sectarianism as a Response to Mixed Marriage

LARA DEEB

IN ONE OF THE demonstrations that comprised the uprising in Lebanon that began on October 17, 2019, women living along the fault line of a former civil war evoked a wedding. A video of this event, circulating on social media, begins with a woman saying, "When the barricades went up, we stepped on them, and we came together, and we built a family." Women of all ages, some marked by their dress as Muslim or Christian and others unidentifiable, carry white roses as they walk their streets. Their voices claim the streets for all, and refuse violence and sectarianism. The slogan "No to sectarianism, we want national unity" dominates the soundscape until it is broken by loud *zaghroutas*, a celebratory ululation. A man smoking on a balcony tosses rice down upon the marchers. And two women, likely of different religious backgrounds, lift a single white rose to the sky together.

This demonstration directly addressed brief clashes that had recently taken place between young men along the former Green Line that divided Beirut during the 1975–90 civil war. The video's title, *From Ain El-Rummaneh to Chiyah, You* [feminine plural: *antunna*] *Are the Revolution*, explicitly linked two neighborhoods in antisectarian unity and called upon women to confront sectarian violence—past, present, and future—and embody the revolution. The white roses, the *zaghroutas*, the flung rice, all evoke wedding processions and craft the demonstration itself as a wedding linking both these neighborhoods and their diverse residents together. Marriage here is configured as a path to interreligious and antisectarian national unity. Another response to those clashes also evoked marriage as a solution to the problem of sectarianism. On November 27, 2019, the Lebanese actress Maguy Bou Ghosn posted on Twitter: "I am Christian and proud of it. My husband is Muslim and I am proud of that. My mother-in-law lives in Chiyah. If anyone [any barriers, *ayy 'a'iq byimna'ni*] tried to block me from visiting her to kiss her hand [a sign of respect], I would mess them up [pluck them out, tear them up into little pieces, *bintifkun tantif*]." The ensuing comments on Ghosn's tweet ranged from support to criticism of her mixed marriage to accusations that her statement itself reproduced sectarian identities.

While not the primary discourse of the revolution, the variety of ways in which marriage, and mixed marriage in particular, emerged as a theme suggest something about both the salience of desiring kinship that crosses religious boundaries and the strength of the taboo against crossing those boundaries. Put simply, if mixed marriage were socially irrelevant, people would not be talking about it. It hovers in the background, as it has done for decades in Lebanon, only to materialize in unexpected places and times. Most concretely, mixed marriage has long served as one driver behind efforts to push a civil marriage law through Lebanon's Parliament. Intermarriage has also served for some couples as a symbol or evidence of their antisectarian commitments, made real through their affective, intimate, and kinship ties. Whether abstract or concrete, one of the many hopes carried by the revolution was that it would lead to the dismantling of sectarianism in Lebanon, including sectarianism in relation to kinship.

Indeed, during fall 2019 and in the period of uncertainty that continues as this book goes to press, sectarianism itself has been on the table for discussion, debate, dismantling, and reassembly. Some scholars, reporters, pundits, and observers have been quick to diagnose the revolution as evidence that Lebanese society is not sectarian. Such claims carry the important goal of highlighting that sectarianism is a political, economic, and social structure rather than an inherent or essential characteristic of Lebanese, Arab, or Middle Eastern societies. Scholars have thoroughly established these ideas, showing that sect, like other communal identities, is socially and historically constructed and that political sectarianism in Lebanon is not the inevitable outcome of age-old divisions.[1] Yet with few exceptions, including the chapters by Nucho and Araş in this volume,[2] this critical scholarship mainly addresses sectarianism in the political, institutional, or legal registers rather than its social or interpersonal meanings—thus missing the material and affective impact of such structures. In this chapter, I take up the latter, and explore sectarian social difference as expressed in personal bias or discrimination. My interest lies in analyzing sectarianism as a form of discrimination in what is perhaps the most intransigent arena of life when it comes to embracing difference: kinship. I do so by showing how the discourses threading through stories of family opposition to mixed marriage produce sectarianism in the first place.[3] Within my larger project, this chapter specifically investigates the impact of exposure to diversity within Lebanon on the practice of sectarian bias, and looks to mixed couples as potential exemplars for living antisectarianism.

Intermarriage and Sectarianism

Why marriage? Sect is one of the key ways in which social difference is understood in Lebanon, and kin relations are a key arena where such understandings of social difference are produced.[4] Endogamy and sectarianism serve here as a chicken-egg problem, each leading to the other. The commonality of marriage within religious or sectarian groups "reinforces people's belief in the myth of sectarianism."[5] Furthermore, despite my underlying premise (and that of this volume) that society is not essentially sectarian but has been constructed as such through political and institutional structures over time, the interpersonal continues to matter. Dismantling structures of oppression does not necessarily lead to the disappearance of social discriminations or biases. In an imagined future where political sectarianism is dismantled, where the structural inequalities that persist via institutions are eliminated, and where civil marriage laws exist, sectarianism will not vanish. An imperfect analogy comes to mind: the dismantling of Jim Crow laws in the United States. As the Black Lives Matter movement highlights, Jim Crow practices continue to exist despite the loss of many of the legal legs on which they have stood.[6] We need only recall feminist and antiracist scholars' arguments that discrimination based on constructed differences has material and affective consequences.[7] Social constructs and discursive formations have power. And even if all structural and institutional practices are eliminated, discrimination on an interpersonal level persists.

Hints of interpersonal change were an accomplishment of the 2019 revolution. In a February 2020 "Featured Analysis" on the Lebanese Center for Policy Studies website,[8] Bassel Salloukh added his voice to those suggesting that "no matter the short-term outcome . . . something [had] changed irreversibly in Lebanon" since the October 17 uprising. While focusing on shifts in political and economic power, Salloukh pointed to the affective achievements of the revolution—what he called "an introspective interrogation"—and noted that sectarianism no longer had "the monopoly it used to have over peoples' modes of mobilization *and identification*." Although this chapter is based on research conducted prior to the revolution, it takes up the slow tides of social change, as the seeds for that introspective interrogation have long been sown and are particularly resistant to growth when it comes to mixed marriage. Kinship is among the stickier realms where change is slow. My interviews help us to understand what it means to see different possibilities while remaining entrenched in sectarian ways of thinking about one another. In other words, to understand how to move beyond sectarianism, we must understand how it seeps into intimate and familial interactions, decision making, assumptions, and conflicts. We must acknowledge that people act in what can be considered "sectarian" ways, meaning that they align with those of the same sect and act in a discriminatory manner against people of different sects. This chapter and the larger project it represents are an exercise in thinking about how people, through their practices, continually create discourses about sect, identity, and difference that fill the gamut between antisectarian and sectarian. To understand how sect emerges in the social and interpersonal is to know better how to work against it in this imagined future where structural and institutional sectarianism no longer shape life to the same extent.

Most Lebanese take it for granted that intermarriage is difficult—if not for the couple, then for all but the most open-minded parents.[9] But why is it so difficult? Many of the parents who oppose these marriages are not especially pious. Many don't practice their religion; some call themselves "secularists" (*'ilmaniyyin*), and a few say they don't even believe in God. All of them have friends, colleagues, or business associates from other sects. So why have they rejected future sons- or daughters-in-law because of religious or sectarian difference? At first glance the answer may seem obvious: That people ought to marry someone from within their own religious community is a presumed social norm. Family conflicts around intermarriage have occurred in Lebanon for generations, ebbing and flowing with migration, political violence, and changing university structures, among other factors.[10] As Barbara Drieskens notes, "Transgressing these rules of marriage within the confession usually leads to some form of social exclusion: from the community . . . from the family."[11] But allowing the answer to appear obvious in this way requires a number of assumptions about both sect (that sectarian identity is more important than other forms of identity in Lebanon) and kinship (that endogamy is somehow natural).

The sheer variety of family responses belie these assumptions. Despite expectations of opposition to intermarriage, whether a specific family will react negatively or immediately embrace a new member from a different religion or sect is always an open and sometimes unpredictable question. Factors that matter include the historical moment when the couple met, their ages (especially for the female partner) and financial status,[12] the reactions of siblings or extended family, the degree of closeness each member of the couple feels to their parents, and the personalities involved. The presence or lack of characteristics, in addition to religious or sectarian endogamy, of a normative desirable spouse—such as wealth, status, education, reputation, residence, and age difference[13]—also matter. Most of my interlocutors' stories include some degree of opposition to the marriage, ranging from tears, pleas, and feigned health emergencies to the deployment of family or clerical pressure, or even disownment. With time, ranging from a few months to a decade, parents usually came around. There are stories of perfect unflappable family harmony, and stories of dramatic cross-continent elopements. This variety challenges any easy assumptions about sectarianism or endogamy as natural. Instead of being a site that supports their essential or natural character, marriage emerges as a prime site for *creating* the importance of their discourses and practices.

Three elements are common across parental responses. Parents desire the well-being of their children. They believe that such well-being is contingent upon a harmonious marriage. And they assume that such harmony has something to do with affinity or similarity. However, parents define this similarity or affinity in various ways. For those who understand sect as the key form of difference in Lebanon, similarity is harder to see in mixed marriages. For others, class is the more important factor, echoing the processual imbrication of sect and class that Joanne Nucho has described in the preceding chapter of this book.[14] For still others, similarity is constructed over time, sometimes deliberately, by the couple in question. Discourses of parental acceptance, whether immediate or eventual, often invoke similarity: "Oh, he is actually just like us." In other words, the pattern in parental responses is a desire for similarity or shared social characteristics. This is neither surprising nor in any way unique to Lebanon.

Ghassan Hage's analysis of how racist imaginations work is helpful for understanding sectarian and other forms of discrimination in relation to kinship.[15] Hage proposes thinking through the lens of what he calls "generalized domestication," a way of shaping one's home or space—*where kin, community, and nation can all be understood in these terms*—through forms of control. That control rests on hierarchies of domination, which in turn rest on difference. Racists (or, in my case, "sectarians") thus do things they think will protect their sense of "being at home" by polarizing difference, "evacuat[ing] each element of what makes it similar to the other."[16] Once difference has been polarized, the racist (sectarian) works to manage their space (family, community) through forms of exclusion, elimination, or control of the other. What is therefore at stake when a child wants to marry someone viewed as "outside" the community is the objecting parents' control over their sense of home, of belonging, of comfort. Parents who act in sectarian ways can thus be understood as working, through practices of exclusion, to preserve a notion of comfort and well-being in their home, family, and community. Once again, this raises the question of how "home" or community is itself understood by these parents. What characterizes a sense of similarity, identification, comfort? What makes a potential child-in-law an insider or an outsider?

Elsewhere I have answered this question through a focus on the relationship between sect and class—as always interrelated categories of social difference in Lebanon—and the relationship of sect and class to different and ever-shifting measures of status and social hierarchy in Lebanon.[17] Here I take up the thread of geography or neighborhood as a key source of anxiety about sectarian difference (always imbricated with sect, class, and status) and consider "exposure" to a variety of people and places in Lebanon as a factor that may influence the expression or suppression of sectarian bias. I argue that, although exposure captures a key mechanism through which sect, class, and geography intersect, it does not necessarily lead to a positive outcome.[18] Complicating assumptions about exposure disrupts the erroneous idea that people of higher socioeconomic status, who may claim to be more cosmopolitan than people of lower socioeconomic status, are also more open-minded when it comes to sect. It also disrupts the notion that people in rural areas are always more closed-minded than those in urban ones. Exposure can lead to greater open-mindedness about mixed marriage or to greater adherence to endogamy, depending on how the exposure takes place and its consequences. Exposure to the other in a context of violence—for example, in May 2008, when armed conflict between political parties erupted in Beirut, can solidify sectarian lines between communities. Exposure to the other as comrade students can lead to greater acceptance of or participation in mixed marriage. I suggest that exposure alone is not sufficient for reducing sectarian bias; it must be accompanied by a sense of commonality, what Hage describes as "home," and I have described elsewhere as shared *bi'a*, meaning environment or milieu.[19]

Exposure

The concept of exposure came up in many of my interviews, occasionally in English (e.g., "They were never exposed to . . ." or "The problem was their lack of exposure"). But more frequently, it was expressed in either English or Arabic through phrases like "They have never seen [people of another sect] . . . ," or "They don't know anyone [from another sect]," or "They have never been to [neighborhood or area associated with another sect] . . . ." Interlocutors consistently invoked exposure as a source of positive multisectarian harmony, and a lack of exposure as an explanation for opposition to intermarriage or general bias against others. Considering how topographically small Lebanon is, the idea that people have not traversed its spaces or do not know anyone of a different sect or religion may at first seem surprising—until one considers that many cities and spaces across the world are also segregated in these ways. Take Los Angeles County, which takes up about the same amount of geographic area as Lebanon. Most residents of Los Angeles have ideas about neighborhoods they will or won't frequent—assessments based on assumptions about "danger" which in turn are based on stereotypes about the people who live in those neighborhoods.

At the same time, Lebanon's small scale reminds us that, despite my interlocutors' absolutist terms, exposure to difference is not a binary question. One is not either exposed or unexposed, but has experienced some degree of exposure to some range of social difference. Exposure as a spectrum applies equally to larger sites. Residents of Los Angeles may imagine themselves as maintaining strict lines between neighborhoods, but rarely do their lived experiences line up with those demarcations. Of course, the specific associations or differences along which these segregation practices adhere vary. In the United States, stereotypes about particular areas hinge on the intersection of race and class. In other words, racist and classist biases combine into new forms to produce fears of specific places in the city. In Lebanon, it is the intersection of sect and class; sectarian and classist biases compound to produce new biases in this way.

Such fears operate both countrywide and among Beirut's neighborhoods. Stereotypes abound about Lebanon's various regions, highlighting not only assumptions about differences between rural areas or villages and urban areas, but also assumptions about different parts of the country, linked to ideas about who lives in those places, and their sects, social status, morals, and values. A popular Wael Kfoury song from 1994 captures this in its chorus:

> Tell your mom to, please, stop explaining her roots [aslha] to me.
> Just because your uncles [her brothers] are from Beirut, don't think that
>   you're better than me.
> My roots are from the Beqa' and Zahle, I'm from the Beqa' and my roots are
>   in Zahle.[20]

In Beirut, many neighborhoods became segregated by sect through processes of violence and displacement during the 1975–90 civil war.[21] Hiba Bou Akar describes how in the twenty-first century, fears of violence and of people of different sects have had a continued impact on ideas about residency, property sales, neighborhoods, and safety.[22] Writing about Southern California, Wendy Cheng theorizes how "everyday landscapes" can be "crucial terrains through which racial hierarchies are learned, instantiated, and transformed." In other words, space itself leads to racial or sectarian identity formation.[23] Cheng calls this process "regional racial formation"—defined as "place-specific processes of racial formation, in which locally accepted racial orders and hierarchies complicate and sometimes challenge hegemonic ideologies and facile notions of race."[24] Thinking in these terms highlights a focus on the small scale, the neighborhood, and how multiple identities and aspects of identity can sediment into that space over time, via a variety of processes. In Lebanon's case, these processes include violence and war as well as both the material and the affective. As Roxana Arãş shows in this volume, the affective incorporates sensorial practices and experiences. How it feels to live in a particular neighborhood matters, and affects the identities of those living there.

Linking "exposure" to Hage's notion of "home" allows us to develop an understanding of the relationship between place and identity that hinges on a sense of comfort. Since at least the late 1990s, some Lebanese have expressed this sense of neighborhood-based identity and comfort using the term *bi'a*. *Bi'a* translates most literally to "environment"—though, to better capture the layering of political, social, and religious meaning into space and identity, I translated this term in my 2006 book as "milieu." Some people have used *bi'a* in the loose way that some people in the United States will use "culture" to ascribe similarity and difference. Most commonly, my interlocutors used the word to explain why they felt comfortable or uncomfortable in certain parts of Beirut and Lebanon.[25] One's *bi'a* can be understood as one's home; both terms convey the comfort of being with people whom you deem to be of your world. And both terms are infused with meanings related to identity, including sect, class, and notions of morality, all of which are projected onto geographic spaces and neighborhoods.

More exposure to a multisectarian *bi'a*, by this logic, should engender greater comfort in multisectarian spaces, the breaking down of sectarian biases and stereotypes, and the possibility of embracing a multisectarian home or family. Less exposure should lead to new or increased discriminations and biases, enabled by segregated spaces or milieus. Indeed, one of the hopeful observations about the effects of the revolution on sectarianism has been that, as Maya El Helou put it on a panel at the 2019 annual meeting of the Middle East Studies Association, "the hypothetical sectarian walls between regions of the country that have been built are collapsing"—new exposures potentially leading to a less sectarian future. My interviews show, however, that while exposure may be a condition of intermarriage, it does not necessarily correlate with family acceptance of such marriages, despite my interlocutors' assumptions.

Exposure as Pride, Exposure as Pragmatic

Many of my interlocutors in mixed marriages highlighted their own exposure and cross-sectarian friendships and relationships with pride. Some claimed to be "sect-blind," saying, "I don't see sect." Some related how they couldn't tell the background of their future spouse on the basis of any of the usual cues (name, place of origin), and continued, "I didn't think to ask." Their lack of curiosity served as a marker of their secularism and antisectarianism. Some couples cited their marriages as explicit disavowals of sectarianism, while others simply acted as though their relationships fit the norm, refusing to acknowledge it as a matter of interest unless pressed. Many held staunch antisectarian political views and saw their shared political outlook as a key source of their compatibility. In some cases, this led to an "us against Lebanese society" perspective that did not acknowledge historical antecedents to their political perspectives.[26]

This view was most common among people who came of age in the "golden Nineties," the post–civil war era of rebuilding in Beirut, which came to an end with Prime Minister Rafiq Hariri's assassination in 2005, and the 2006 Israeli war on Lebanon. As one person explained to me:

> All the people I know around me, in my network, who married from different religions or sects, they had the same history somehow, the same history on a different level. Either on the level of school, where you have mixed environments that help you to actually jump over the borders and limits made by society, or the next level, in university when you have more platforms to act, more freedom, where you have opportunities to be involved and integrated with different mindsets, different environments. . . . And this is where young people actually start to revolt against their families . . . where they start building their own personality. And I think what helped us back then, like my generation, . . . was the mixed secular political environment that helped us, actually. It's not like now. These days you find people going back to religion, and going back to being more closed-minded. . . . Also, during our time, we had a lot of causes to work on. . . . After the war, Beirut was divided into two pieces; so for us, we were, like, the generation who worked on building these bridges. . . . But unfortunately the new generation does not have the same background. They are more fractured.

Outside this "golden Nineties" generation, too, many people attributed their mixed marriages to their nonsectarian upbringing, or to meeting other people with open minds as young adults in university. But this was not always the case. Quite a few of my interlocutors grew up in monolithic social circles, attended religious schools or public schools in segregated areas, and met their partners of different religions at work or through friends later in life. Other couples met because they resided in mixed neighborhoods or villages; or met at school; or met through family members, often siblings who unintentionally facilitated their intersectarian romantic encounters.

There is a pragmatic dimension to the idea that exposure correlates with intermarriage. When neighborhoods are segregated and people do not move between them in their daily lives, how can a person meet potential friends and partners from different groups? Shared school, college, or work environments play a crucial role. Most of my interlocutors met through common friends, at university or in the workplace, or through a common activity like volunteering at the same NGO or charitable organization. In these instances, by virtue of participating in a shared network, commonality has been established, taking the experience beyond being one of mere exposure. This is one reason why the fate of the public Lebanese University during the civil war was described by one interlocutor as "tragic." For the generation that came of age just before the war, in the 1960s and early 1970s, Lebanese University, with its then unified campus, provided a space of intersectarian, interreligious, and geographic mixing for students of a wide range of class backgrounds from around Lebanon. As the sole public and affordable university option in the country, this was especially important for middle- and lower-middle-class students, working-class students, and first-generation college students. This generation represents the second largest cluster of my interviewees. During the war, Lebanese University splintered into many branches, each located in a different part of the country, and each offering only certain majors and specializations. In addition to limiting career and educational options for students who could not or did not want to travel far from home, this splintering meant that the public university campus could no longer serve as a multisectarian meeting place for youth. Today, the universities that serve this purpose—the American University of Beirut (AUB), the Lebanese American University (LAU), and Université Saint-Joseph (USJ)—are all elite, private institutions. Two of these, AUB and LAU, are in an area of the capital known as Ras Beirut.

Ras Beirut as Center of Exposure

Ras Beirut is an area of the city that many of my interviewees, whether or not they lived there, lauded as "mixed" in ways that other parts of the city did not seem to them. About 25 percent of the couples in my sample resided in this area at the time of our interviews, and others had met their spouses there. To a certain extent, this high percentage results from snowball sampling. However, interlocutors who were raised or who lived outside Ras Beirut—whether in rural areas or villages, other working-class suburbs of Beirut, or in diaspora— still described the area as a multisectarian haven. They assumed that their relationships would be more readily accepted there. Others had chosen to relocate to Ras Beirut if they could afford to do so, and spoke about their new neighborhood as a space where "the *bi'a* is mixed." What is striking about these ideas of the multisectarian character of Ras Beirut is that the official sectarian makeup of its population is actually predominantly Sunni Muslim, with a persistent mostly Orthodox Christian minority. It is also a part of the city that has grown denser over time, has seen significant population shifts with violence and regional wars, and has more recently been utterly devastated by Lebanon's economic collapse. (Since we spoke, some people have moved out of Ras Beirut, seeking quieter suburbs, while others have emigrated.)

Jana, who still lives there, explained it like this:

> I'm still convinced that Ras Beirut is the most open place. . . . Yesterday, my friend was telling me that her cousin is studying medicine at AUB; he's lived his whole life in Hazmiyya [a Christian suburb], and he was a student in Jumhour [a Christian private school in a Christian town]. And she told me—and he is maybe very Frenchie, and his parents are very Maronite—she told me that he used to come to T-Marbouta [a café in Ras Beirut] all the time, and he lived in Hamra [a central part of Ras Beirut]. And she told me that he told her he discovered that in Hamra he feels very comfortable, like people are accepting. And I believe that. Actually now people, for example, why are there beggars in Hamra and not Ashrafiyya, for example? This is because it's a place that's really open. It's a place where homosexuals can come out also. Like anyone can find a place in this area. And this is what's nice about it, with all the advantages and disadvantages of this openness.

Ziad, who grew up in Ras Beirut, was less convinced that the area was unique:

> You can describe the mix any way you want; there are many places that have a mix, so what? But the atmosphere here is predominantly Islam. The atmosphere we grew up in was like fireworks and Muslim holidays, and that kind of stuff. Now of course there was a secular aspect; like everyone celebrates Christmas for some reason. Schools and even the neighbors put up Christmas trees, and there are buildings in Beirut that put Christmas trees in hallways; I don't know where that [practice] came from. And even Easter too, you know? And there are even Muslims who don't just put up Christmas trees, but also put up wreaths.

When I asked Ziad to elaborate, he continued, "There are a lot of Orthodox in this area, especially in Hamra, and they are easier than Maronites because they are secular by nature and live with us. They are Arab too." Here Ziad is reproducing multiple stereotypes about the various Christian sects in Lebanon. Most important for my purposes is his equation of Ras Beirut and Hamra with what he calls secularism (*'ilmaniyyeh*), which for him includes speaking English and Arabic but not French, celebrating all the holidays with meals and decorations, and only going to mosque or church on holidays but never for weekly prayers or services. His statement that Orthodox are "easier" because they "live with us" again alludes to exposure as a mechanism for multisectarian harmony.

Ziad's spouse, Mona, grew up in a Christian suburb of Beirut, and today describes Ras Beirut as "home." "I feel a very strong sense of belonging to this area, and a source of pride," she told me. "I feel very comfortable here and I'm very happy in this space." Mona and Ziad, as well as Jana, are all speaking about certain parts of Ras Beirut—primarily the area encompassing AUB and LAU, and between them and the sea. This area is not representative of all of Ras Beirut, and is certainly not representative of all of Beirut proper, let alone the Greater Beirut area.

Ras Beirut is also expensive. As couples marry and seek spaces to live and raise their families, they are often forced to move to the suburbs to establish their households. Those who could afford to do so tried to live in places like Badaro, chosen again because it is an area perceived as being more open-minded about mixed couples and more secular than other options, in part because of the concentration of progressive NGOs with offices there. Mixed couples face an additional layer to the housing struggles common in Lebanon. A few told me stories about not being able to find an apartment to rent because landlords stopped returning their calls when they realized that one partner was Muslim.[27] Others related being the only person of their religious group in their building, with doormen or neighbors referring to them as "the Christian/Druze/Muslim" or "the one married to the Christian/Druze/Muslim." Many mixed couples linked their desires about where to live to the idea of exposure, assuming that a mixed environment would be better for them. Rami explained it succinctly: "I don't like to live in the areas that are Christian, and I don't like to live in the Muslim areas. I can't, I feel like I'm suffocating. I don't like seeing religious symbols anywhere, cluttering your face. I hate it." Rami continued into a ten-minute exposition of a wide variety of problems he saw in Lebanese society, all of it coming back in the end to sectarianism, which he linked unequivocally to segregation and "lack of exposure." While

Rami, along with many of my interlocutors—especially but not only those who had some connection to Ras Beirut via school, work, leisure, friends, or residence—believed that exposure led to greater intersectarian acceptance and harmony, that belief was sometimes shattered by the failure of this process for their parents.

Exposure and Responses to Mixed Marriage

Most of my interlocutors expected responses from their parents that correlated with the degree of their parents' exposure to people of other groups. People whose parents lived in mixed areas or had friends and business associates from other sects generally expected any resistance to their marriage to be relatively mild and short-lived. Many Lebanese with whom I have discussed this problem imagine that the more "cosmopolitan" and "connected" a family is, the more "open-minded" they will be about mixed marriage. Even on a small scale, people suggested that exposure leads to open-mindedness. For example, one of my interviewees was musing about why her father, who had spent his entire life in a small Christian town, had been relatively accepting of her marriage to a Muslim. She attributed his openness in part to his level of education, and in part to the fact that "he has one very good Muslim friend. He accepted in his life a friend from a different religion." Others also explained acceptance in parents they wouldn't have expected to be open-minded as being due to the influence of "one friend" of a different religion.

Another woman told me that as soon as she met her fiancé's father, who had lived his entire life in a village, she knew all would be "smooth," because he "had exposure." She explained,

> To tell you the truth, when I met his dad, I felt that he was open-minded, and very educated compared to the usual person who comes from a village and lives a rural life. Instead he's so open and exposed to people and to different religions. . . . I don't think he has a degree, so he is more like, you call it self-educated; he is a guy who is educated through books, through exposure.

Yet my interlocutors' expectations about how parents would react were just as likely to be upended as fulfilled, and many described their surprise or "shock" at the vehemence or duration of parental anger.[28] There are just as many parents with high exposure who disown their children for years, and just as many parents who have never interacted much outside segregated communities or don't have that "one friend" who accepts a mixed marriage relatively quickly, as there are those who fit the assumption that exposure leads to open-mindedness.

One interviewee described his mother, who he had initially hoped would be open-minded about his marriage to a non-Muslim woman but had fought with him about it for more than a year, as "living in Ras Beirut, but really living in the Beqaʿ. It's the same thing; almost everyone she talks to is from [village in the Beqaʿ Valley]." Another, who had been raised in Ras Beirut to embrace a secular and antisectarian political outlook by parents who espoused the same, lamented to me that when she decided to marry a Christian, her parents were enraged and did not speak to her for a year. To this day—despite resumed, though damaged, relations—she still doesn't understand why they were angry.

There are also quite a few cases in which people I interviewed had assumed that their parents would be closed-minded or intolerant because of their segregated lives, only to have those assumptions upended when their marriages were accepted relatively easily. Sometimes this acceptance has to do with a perception that the marriage will lead to class mobility. And sometimes, contrary to expectations held by many of my secular interlocutors that religious people would be less likely to accept a mixed marriage, a parent's faith served as a source of comfort or security in their decision to accept the marriage.

A pious Shiʿi Muslim mother, who supported her daughter's decision to marry a Christian, explained her perspective to me:

> First of all, this is her own personal decision, this is her life. And I also consulted with an important religious authority: Sayyid Mohammad Hussein Fadlallah. . . . Now, he was deceased, so I called his office, and I told the shaykh my story, that my daughter wants to marry and that they want to do a civil marriage. Now, I am absolutely for civil marriage because it is a one hundred percent valid marriage. Because for us in Islam, marriage is a declaration and consent between two people; when there is consent and declaration in marriage it becomes valid. And yes, there should be a judge or a religious cleric to make the contract, and in Cyprus there was a judge and witnesses and family—*yaʿni*, OK. So I asked the office of Sayyid Mohammad Hussein Fadlallah at the time. I told [the shaykh], "As a mother I want to feel reassured that from a religious perspective, that civil marriage is sound and valid." And the shaykh said, "It is one hundred percent sound and valid." Now we

were still discussing civil marriage; I didn't get into the issue of religion yet. Then I told him, "Now, she wants to marry a Christian." He asked, "How old is she?" I said, "She is thirty-five years old." He said, "In principle, in our religion there is no problem if a man marries from another religion, but there is a problem for a woman [to marry someone from another religion]." I said, "What's the problem?" He said, "The problem is if he [the groom] forces her away from her religion." I told him, "In civil marriage every person remains in their religion and does not influence the other." I told him, "As a mom, what am I supposed to do, *ya'ni?*" He said, "You're not responsible for anything. She is thirty-five years old, and you don't have any—what do they say—you don't have any religious responsibility or anything. She is thirty-five years old, she is a grownup. I mean, she makes her own decisions and so on. So I felt very encouraged.

In this case, the mother was set at ease because of her belief, confirmed by the shaykh, that a civil marriage is religiously valid, and because the shaykh essentially absolved her of any responsibility toward God if her daughter had in fact made a mistake by marrying a Christian. The mother's piety and fear for her own soul were the crucial factors here, outweighing issues like social considerations. Another pious mother, this time a Maronite Christian, told me her story as well. "Christine came to me and said, 'Mama, I have a plan.' And I reacted badly at the beginning, very negatively. I said no, I told her no, and she became sad and said, 'I can't do anything if you are not with me.' And that was all for a while." After a brief interruption, this mother continued, "I am a believer, and I said, 'Oh God, I don't know. I put this situation to you for guidance.'" She explained that she prayed constantly for two days, and then,

> My heart softened, and I became as if I were another person, someone else, who could accept the situation. . . . It was like this: When I went to church I said, 'Oh Lord, I am putting this relationship on your altar.' And just like that, I left it in the hands of our Lord, and I felt that there was something at work within me, changing me. . . . And when I met [the groom], I knew that this was right, because, I can even say that he helped me to see that our Lord came for all people. I don't accept that Christ came only for Christians. I know that our Lord came for all people. . . . I saw common sides. And I saw that [the groom] is a person who searches for God too and that he loves in Christine her faith.

This mother's faith allowed her to pass the burden of her daughter's desire to marry a Muslim to God, and her prayer opened her up to a strong sense of common humanity which included her future son-in-law. Importantly, it is this sense of commonality, fostered by her faith, that eased her discomfort with adding a Muslim to her family. Indeed, common humanity, and in this case the notion of a shared relationship with God and a shared love for her daughter, were the elements that moved this mother past "mere exposure" to acceptance and even embrace of the other.

The importance, for parents and family members, of such a sense of commonality—of the potential to maintain a shared community, or "home" in Hage's terms—frequently emerges in comments, often snide, made to or about an in-law. Mona and Ziad grew up in very different environments; her family are practicing Maronites who live in a Christian suburb of Beirut, while his are, in his terms, "secular Sunnis" living in Ras Beirut who fast during Ramadan, rarely pray, and put up a Christmas tree in their house, and who sent their children to a local Christian school. During our conversation they initially described their story as one of minimal struggles with their parents—a situation they (and I, concurring) attributed to the fact that by the time they decided to get married, they were both in their early thirties and financially independent. But as our interview continued, they began recalling incidents when people in Mona's social or family circles had made discriminatory remarks to Ziad:

Ziad: Like, her aunt used to say to me, "You know, you look just like us." And I would look at her, and say like, "As opposed to the Muslims who have tails, like what, what?"

Mona: It's like you're the good one.

Ziad: Yeah, exactly.

Mona: "You look like us"—yeah, like, they have this idea . . . and he sounds and looks and, you know, listens to music, like . . .

Ziad: . . . I'm Westernized.

Mona: It's completely . . .

Ziad: I think it's also that there's an urban issue, like . . .

Mona: It's exposure for—sorry [for interrupting]—Ziad, for us. I think for my side of the family it is a matter of exposure.

Ziad: Exposure, yeah.

Mona: They're not exposed to Muslims very much. They're not exposed to people from different sects. I mean, even this area [Hamra]: they don't really know how to get here.

Ziad: They don't come to it. Your family doesn't come to west Beirut, and if they do, it's like each one needs a visa to come here, and they are very conscious of being here. But my family, they will go anywhere.

Mona: That's true.

Ziad: Even trying to get them to come to Gemmayze [another Christian neighborhood near Ras Beirut] is a struggle.

Mona: And I think that's where it comes from, this sense of similarity: "Ahhh, you're like us." It's because of lack of exposure, they actually have an idea of something different, and the more they see it, the more they're like, "Ohhhh." . . . Like when they first met . . .

Ziad: Yeah, like I broke that down actively; in my mind, I worked on it consciously. Like, first I drink [alcohol]; second, I . . .

Mona: But sometimes he makes—sorry, Ziad, but sometimes you made it a very big point, I think unconsciously, to display the similarities to the extent where . . .

Ziad: No, they always have asked me, "Don't you want to drink?" It's like I have to drink alcohol to prove to you that I'm not Muslim, or I don't hate Christians, you know?

Mona: But, I'm not so sure this was actually happening. . . .

Ziad: No, no, no, it's actually happening. Come on.

Mona: No, no, I'm not saying—sorry, I'm not saying that it's not, but I'm saying . . .

Ziad: It is. It is more conscious than you think it is.

In this interview excerpt, Ziad and Mona connect her family's bias against their new Muslim family member to their low degree of exposure to other places and people. Mona assumes that the more they "see" Muslims, the more they will realize how similar they all are, and that such similarity is the solution to family tensions. Ziad experiences this as having to prove that he is just like them, specifically through drinking alcohol,[29] while Mona suggests that Ziad is reading too much sectarian social pressure into the situation and is overcompensating as a result. No matter which interpretation of the situation one holds, the importance of constructed and demonstrated similarity remains, as do the ways in which discrimination can emerge through small comments (*taltish*) like, "You know, you look just like us."

It is telling that Ziad and Mona mention Gemmayze, a Christian neighborhood in Beirut known for its pubs and restaurants. Why wouldn't Mona's family happily meet them there? Perhaps their resistance signals their knowledge that, while Gemmayze's residents may be primarily Christian, its nightlife establishments draw a mixed crowd from around Beirut and Lebanon. Perhaps they are uncomfortable in spaces they see as urban, assuming such spaces engender greater exposure to the other? Or perhaps their unfamiliarity with Beirut—their lack of knowledge of the city, including its Christian-majority areas—has magnified their fear.

Knowability

In addition to the possibility of shared community in kinship, acceptance by one's parents and the sense of comfort on which their "home" is based may hinge on knowability. It is important to have a known social world, and this knowability knits geography, sect, class, status, and kinship together. "My son's teacher is from [village]," Rana says, naming the village her mother is from. Without being asked, her mother, who is sitting with us and has never met the teacher or their family, begins explaining who the teacher is: where their house is located, who their parents are, who they married, where their spouse is from, and what relationship they may or may not have with anyone else they might know in that social world. People are narrated by others through their relationships. They are placed on a mental map that is constructed using kinship, place, sect, and class. Doing that work of narration or placement allows the narrator to then understand where she herself also belongs on that social map. One's circle of knowledge may be narrower, like a village or neighborhood, or wider, like a vaguely constructed and usually class-based social circle. There is a generational component to this practice; media technologies and migration have changed the boundaries and possibilities of social mapping. But many of my interlocutors in their twenties and thirties continued to place people in these ways, despite sometimes using social media and other tools to do so. Knowledge here, being able to place a person on one's social map, creates comfort. Maintaining this social map is part of the work of domestication; the map and the knowledge it contains *create* the social world in which people live, the social world that they are trying to protect.

For some parents, mixed marriages challenge their ability to place a new family member onto their social map, because the person is more likely to be unknown. New people can be integrated, but some form of mappable knowledge of them is required to do so. One of my interviewees described her mother's refrain during several years of arguing about her choice of groom: "She kept saying, 'Who's this nobody?'—like she didn't mean 'nobody,' but like 'we don't know him.' Like, they don't know anything about him, they don't know who his family is. Like he just doesn't belong to the society they know."

When a person is known, conflict over marriage often resolves itself more quickly. A Maronite woman I interviewed told me that in the mid-twentieth century, when she was a teenager, she fell in love with her Sunni neighbor in their mixed-sect village. Her father refused them permission to marry, so they eloped by walking to the mosque and doing a *katab kitab* (getting married with a Muslim marriage contract). A day later, all was well, and the families resumed their neighborly relations—if anything, strengthened by this new marital bond. Theirs was neither the first nor the last mixed marriage in this village. As long as the relationships between the families were otherwise good, such marriages were a relatively rare but not particularly dramatic occurrence. They usually followed the same pattern: a formal proposal, a refusal, and elopement (perhaps expected), followed by a quick resumption of relationships all around. An interlocutor who married in this way in the 1950s told me that today, more parents are willing to give their blessing to such matches if the groom is from the village and is known to them.

Occasionally, despite a lesser degree of exposure on the part of the family, investigating a potential child-in-law so as to map them solved the problem. For example, Olivia, raised in a Rum Orthodox family in the northern village from which both her parents hailed, told her family that she wanted to marry Farid, a Druze man she had met at work in Beirut. Her parents initially panicked. Then her father took a taxi from his village to Farid's village, three hours away, and began asking around about Farid and his parents to determine what kind of family they were. "When he made sure that they are a good family, he said that he was fine with [the marriage]," Olivia told me. In this case, it was not knowability alone but the discovery of commonality that aided in resolving the situation: both families shared the same political outlook, one that was deliberately secular and embraced a pan-Syrian Arab identity at its core. Such shared politics, even shared communist or *qawmi suri* (a pan-Syrian nationalist party) politics, do not always smooth things over; but in this case they were instrumental for both families. Most Druze families do not accept mixed marriages as readily as Farid's did. For his parents, the factors that mattered were that shared political outlook, Farid's older age and financial status in the family (which gave him decision-making power), and a prior mixed marriage in the family. In this situation, less exposure to others led not to opposition to the marriage but to a push toward knowability, and the discovery of a shared sense of home.

Had that commonality not been discovered, would the new exposure have been enough? Other stories suggest not. Another mixed couple who fell in love in the mid-twentieth century had a very different experience. They were not from the same village, but their maternal grandmothers were. The young woman's paternal line was from a different village and a different religion. The couple's maternal grandmothers not only knew one another but were good friends, and multiple cousins had married across the two family lines. Despite this knowledge of the family and evidence of positive relationships, the groom's family objected strongly to the marriage. Today all is well, but it took years to repair the damage done by the family's opposition. I heard several similar stories involving families who were well known to one another in Ras Beirut, sometimes even with overlapping social circles. And yet these preexisting social connections did nothing to alleviate the drama that ensued on one or both sides when their children decided to get married. Exposure and knowledge are not always enough.

Living Antisectarianism; or, Exposure Is Not Enough

Despite the beliefs of many of my interlocutors—and indeed, of many Lebanese with whom I have discussed this project over the past two decades—that exposure to others is a key indicator of open-mindedness when it comes to mixed marriage, mere exposure is rarely sufficient. To understand why exposure does not necessarily lead to parental acceptance of a mixed marriage, I return to Hage's notion of "domestication." This concept turns comfort into a *practice*, "a mode of relating to the world that, in the process of relating, creates the very world it is relating to."[30] Hage goes on to explain that this process of creating comfort in the world "is also a mode of domination, control, extraction, and exploitation."[31] With this explanation applied to the parents and families of mixed couples, we can understand how a threat to expected comfort—the prospect that one's child will marry someone dissimilar to oneself—can prompt parents with high levels of exposure to others to mount campaigns to try to stop a marriage, whether through tears and argument or through more drastic measures like cutting off communication or financial support.

My data suggests that middle-class or upper-middle-class "cosmopolitan" parents are just as likely to oppose a mixed marriage as are parents who have lived and worked in segregated communities all their lives. The only class in Lebanon among whom mixed marriages are relatively unremarkable is the long-standing political-economic elite, who have long married among themselves.[32] Why might this be? Exposure may provide an answer for some families, especially in cases where we see the gradual acceptance of a child-in-law accompanied by a "We learned that they are just like us" narrative. But many of my interviews with people from middle- and upper-middle-class families who live in mixed neighborhoods, or who have multiple friends and colleagues from other sects, reveal stories of dramatic opposition to mixed marriage. One explanation is the deep concern with social status that some middle-class parents feel, and their fear that a mixed marriage will damage it. In this context, where status is not necessarily a reflection of socioeconomic status and is always linked to sect, parents react in response to anxieties about what they will tell people and how they will be viewed if their child marries an outsider. For some parents, sect may even disrupt the status that comes with wealth, especially if the potential child-in-law is viewed as "nouveau riche"—an accusation frequently levied at Shiʻi Muslim families who have generated wealth through emigration to West Africa, for example.[33] Social anxieties about mixed marriage reveal the instability of status among middle-class families, and work to reinforce the relationship between sect and status. Parental responses here have the effect of reinforcing discourses of both sectarianism and endogamy through efforts, not always successful, to keep the child within the community fold.

For exposure to work as a solution to sectarian discrimination in relation to mixed marriages, it must be linked to a belief in commonality, a shared humanity, and a sense of "home," *biʾa*, and social status. What constitutes that commonality—the similarity that parents believe is necessary to a harmonious marriage—must not hinge on sect. In other words, for parents and families to accept mixed marriages more easily, they need to be able to map people of different sects onto their own social maps in ways that include them in a shared community. This requires expanding or modifying the ways in which community boundaries are understood in the first place.

Mixed couples also want the well-being and harmonious marriages that their parents want for them. And they often agree with their parents that similarity or affinity is key to that household harmony. The difference lies in the way they define a new kind of commonality or similarity. Might this be a space for practicing antisectarianism? Many of my interviewees imagine or hope that it is. Yet the extent to which this potential is fulfilled rests on how the couples define the affinities in their relationships, and that is never perfect. Ideally, couples find commonality in their mutual refusal to relate sectarian difference to social hierarchy. There are couples who erase sect by prioritizing their shared Lebanese identity, flirting with the slippery descent of nationalism into chauvinism. There are those who uphold legal and patriarchal norms by prioritizing the husband's traditions and practices. There are couples who treasure their differences, each maintaining their own faith as they raise children embedded in both communities. There are those who imagine the erasure of difference—in their relationships, in their families, and in Lebanon overall—and adopt a "sect-blind" approach. They usually insist on their mutual secularism. For some of them, this secularism hides an unmarked Christian sensibility.[34]

Most people I interviewed draw on more than one of these strategies as their relationships with one another, their families, and their communities change over time. And some of them strive, with varying degrees of success, to embrace multiple traditions and identities in merged and hybrid family formations. Perhaps we can view mixed couples as taking a step toward fulfilling Joanne Randa Nucho's proposal, in this volume, to reimagine the labor of "doing collective" to create cross-sect solidarities, forms of community that render sect irrelevant. If the current time of uncertainty in Lebanon is one that creates opportunities to transcend sectarianism in all its guises, including the interpersonal, my interlocutors have shown us one way to do that in practice, through their lived experiences and their kinship choices.

NOTES

Introduction

1. Several "thematic conversations" held at the annual meeting of the Middle East Studies Association during this time addressed sectarianism, including one in 2017 that highlighted its everyday forms, organized by then-graduate students Jenna Rice Rahaim and Yasemin Ipek.

2. For a discussion of the consequences of this semantic muddle for scholarship, see Fanar Haddad, "Sectarianism and Its Discontents in the Study of the Middle East," *Middle East Journal* 71, no. 3 (2017): 363–82.

3. In Lebanon, there are fifteen personal status laws for the eighteen sects.

4. Maya Mikdashi, *Sextarianism: Sovereignty, Secularism and the State in Lebanon* (Stanford, CA: Stanford University Press, 2022).

5. Suad Joseph, "Pensée 2: Sectarianism as Imagined Sociological Concept and as Imagined Social Formation," *International Journal of Middle East Studies* 40, no. 4 (November 2008): 553.

6. Ussama Makdisi, *The Culture of Sectarianism: Community, History, and Violence in Nineteenth-Century Ottoman Lebanon* (Berkeley: University of California Press, 2000).

7. A nonexhaustive list includes Caesar E. Farah, *The Politics of Interventionism in Ottoman Lebanon: 1830–1861* (London: I. B. Tauris, 2000); Caroleen Marji Sayej, *Patriotic Ayatollahs: Nationalism in Post-Saddam Iraq* (Ithaca, NY: Cornell University Press, 2018); Fawwaz Traboulsi, *A History of Modern Lebanon* (New York: Pluto Press, 2007); Max Weiss, *The Shadow of Sectarianism: Law, Shi'ism, and the Making of Modern Lebanon* (Cambridge, MA: Harvard University Press, 2010); Karen Kern,

Imperial Citizen: Marriage and Citizenship in the Ottoman Frontier Provinces of Iraq (Syracuse, NY: Syracuse University Press, 2011).

8. Suad Joseph, "The Politicization of Religious Sects in Borj Hammoud, Lebanon," (PhD dissertation, Columbia University, 1975). Iliya Harik, *Politics and Change in a Traditional Society, Lebanon 1711–1845* (Princeton, NJ: Princeton University Press, 1968); Ahmad Beydoun, *Al-Jumhuriyya al-Mutaqati'a: Masa'ir al-Sigha al-Lubnaniyya ba'd Itifaq al-Ta'if* (Beirut: Dar al-Nahar, 1999); Mas'oud Daher, *Al-Judhur al-Tarikhiyya li-l-Mas'ala al-Ta'ifiyya al-Lubnaniyya, 1697–1861* (Beirut: Ma'had al-Inma' al-'Arabi, 1981); Fouad Shahine, *Al-Ta'ifiyya fi Lubnan: Hadirha wa Judhurha al-Tarikhiyya al-Ijtima'iyya* (Beirut: Dar al-Hadatha, 1986); Mohammad Tarhini, *Al-Usus al-Tarikhiyya li-Nizam Lubnan al-Ta'ifi, Dirasa Muqarina* (Beirut: Dar al-Afaq, 1981).

9. This literature includes Suad Joseph, ed., *Gender and Citizenship in the Middle East* (Syracuse, NY: Syracuse University Press, 2000); Paul Kingston, *Reproducing Sectarianism: Advocacy Networks and the Politics of Civil Society in Postwar Lebanon* (Albany, NY: SUNY Press, 2013); Janine Clark and Bassel Salloukh, "Elite Strategies, Civil Society, and Sectarian Identities in Postwar Lebanon," *International Journal of Middle East Studies* 45, no. 4 (2013): 731–49; Lara Deeb and Mona Harb, *Leisurely Islam: Negotiating Geography and Morality in South Beirut* (Princeton, NJ: Princeton University Press, 2013); Melani Cammett, *Compassionate Communalism: Welfare and Sectarianism in Lebanon* (Ithaca, NY: Cornell University Press, 2014); Bassel Salloukh et al., *The Politics of Sectarianism in Postwar Lebanon* (London: Pluto Press, 2015); Joanne Nucho, *Everyday Sectarianism in Urban Lebanon: Infrastructures, Public Services, and Power* (Princeton, NJ: Princeton University Press, 2016); Kristin Monroe, *The Insecure City: Space, Power, and Mobility in Beirut* (New Brunswick, NJ: Rutgers University Press, 2016); Hiba Bou Akar, *For the War Yet to Come: Planning Beirut's Frontiers* (Stanford, CA: Stanford University Press, 2018); Maya Mikdashi, *Sectarianism;* Max Weiss, "The Historiography of Sectarianism in Lebanon." *History Compass* 7, no. 1 (2009): 141–54.

10. Elizabeth Shakman Hurd, "Politics of Sectarianism: Rethinking Religion and Politics in the Middle East," *Middle East Law and Governance* 7 (2015): 63.

11. Hamid Alkifaey, *The Failure of Democracy in Iraq: Religion, Ideology and Sectarianism* (New York: Routledge, 2020); Toby Matthiesen, *Sectarian Gulf: Bahrain, Saudi Arabia, and the Arab Spring That Wasn't* (Stanford, CA: Stanford University Press, 2013). Geneive Abdo, *The New Sectarianism: The Arab Uprisings and the Rebirth of the Shi'a-Sunni Divide* (Oxford, UK: Oxford University Press, 2017).

12. Mona Damluji, "'Securing Democracy in Iraq:' Sectarian Politics and Segregation in Baghdad, 2003–2007," *Traditional Dwellings and Settlements Review* 21, no. 2 (Spring 2010): 71–87; Haider Ali Hamoudi, *Negotiating in Civil Conflict: Constitutional Construction and Imperfect Bargaining in Iraq* (Chicago: University of Chicago Press, 2014); Elisheva Machlis, *Shi'i Sectarianism in the Middle East: Modernisation and the Quest for Islamic Universalism* (London: I. B. Tauris, 2014); Joel Rayburn, *Iraq after America: Strongmen, Sectarians, Resistance* (Stanford, CA: Hoover Institution Press, 2014); Frederic M. Wehrey, *Sectarian Politics in the Gulf: From the Iraq War to the Arab*

Uprisings (New York: Columbia University Press, 2016); International Crisis Group, *The Central Sahel: The Perfect Sandstorm* (Brussels: International Crisis Group, 2015). There are, of course, some exceptions that take a more nuanced view, including Fanar Haddad, *Sectarianism in Iraq: Antagonistic Visions of Unity* (Oxford, UK: Oxford University Press, 2014), Sayej, *Patriotic Ayatollahs*; and Omar AlShehabi, *Contested Modernity, Sectarianism, Nationalism, and Colonialism in Bahrain* (London: Oneworld, 2019).

13. Hurd, "Politics of Sectarianism."

14. Fanar Haddad, *Sectarianism in Iraq*, 2. Caroleen Marji Sayej, in her study on senior Shi'i clerics in Iraq after 2003, similarly demonstrates how "rather than co-opting the state, as the clergy serving the majority, or encouraging sectarian violence, they were central in keeping the state-building project on track." *Patriotic Ayatollahs*, 4.

15. AlShehabi, *Contested Modernity*, 10.

16. In contrast to these over-idealizations, for an excellent recent study of the complexity of this coexistence, see Ussama Makdisi's *Age of Coexistence: The Ecumenical Frame and the Making of the Modern Arab World* (Oakland: University of California Press, 2019), which highlights the possibilities for pluralism rather than sectarianism in the multireligious Levant.

17. For example, John Eibner's edited volume *The Future of Religious Minorities in the Middle East* (Lanham, MD: Lexington Books, 2017) approaches sectarianism as a phenomenon that requires a scholar-as-outsider to warn people of its dangers, presumably because people living within that environment cannot understand, or refuse to understand, their apparently dire circumstances.

18. See Laure Guirguis, *Copts and the Security State* (Stanford, CA: Stanford University Press, 2016).

19. Nader Hashemi and Danny Postel's edited volume *Sectarianization: Mapping the New Politics of the Middle East* (Oxford, UK: Oxford University Press, 2017) is a good example—it includes nuanced chapters, but the overall framing of the volume has the effect of getting in its own way.

20. Salloukh et al, *Politics of Sectarianism*.

21. Cammett, *Compassionate Communalism*; Kingston, *Reproducing Sectarianism*.

22. Our volume thus joins a growing body of scholarship that has thus far been primarily ethnographic, including Bou Akar, *For the War Yet to Come*; Deeb and Harb, *Leisurely Islam*; Sami Hermez, *War Is Coming: Between Past and Future Violence in Lebanon* (Philadelphia: University of Pennsylvania Press, 2017); Mikdashi, *Sextarianism*; and Nucho, *Everyday Sectarianism*.

23. Black feminist scholars have long made this argument about race and racism. For example, see Faye Harrison, "The Persistent Power of 'Race' in the Cultural and Political Economy of Racism," *Annual Review of Anthropology* 24 (1995): 47–74.

24. Elizabeth Thompson, *Colonial Citizens: Republican Rights, Paternal Privilege, and Gender in French Syria and Lebanon* (New York: Columbia University Press, 2000).

25. See, for example, Cyrus Schayegh and Andrew Arsan, eds. *The Routledge Handbook of the History of the Middle East Mandates* (New York: Routledge, 2015).

26. Lara Deeb and Jessica Winegar, "Anthropologies of Arab-Majority Societies," *Annual Review of Anthropology* 41 (2012): 537–58.

27. For clarity: We do not use "confessional" and "sectarian" as synonyms, but hold "confessional" as the term for divisions within transnational religious communities, and "sectarian" as the specific politicized form these divisions have taken in the context of Lebanon and its diasporas. For more, see Arāṣ, chapter 5 in this volume.

28. See Makdisi, *Culture of Sectarianism*, for the best elucidation of these processes.

29. See Carol Hakim, *The Origins of the Lebanese National Idea, 1840–1920* (Berkeley: University of California Press, 2013), 10.

30. One can convert to another sect, and people do so all the time, to change the personal status law that will apply for matters like inheritance or divorce. But the feasibility of such a move depends on one's resources, and upon the two sects between which one is moving. For example, it is relatively simple for a Christian to become a different kind of Christian in order to be able to divorce, or for a Muslim to become a different kind of Muslim to facilitate an inheritance. Switching between religions is more complicated (becoming Christian in particular often takes time), but is still quite doable for many Lebanese.

31. Tsolin Nalbantian, "Going beyond Overlooked Populations in Lebanese Historiography: The Armenian Case," *History Compass* 11, no. 10 (2013): 821–32.

32. See Rima Majed on how transformations in protest politics created new alignments that affect the shape of sectarian differences. "In Defense of Intra-Sectarian Divide: Street Mobilization, Coalition Formation, and Rapid Realignments of Sectarian Boundaries in Lebanon," *Social Forces* 1 (2020): 1–26.

33. Ussama Makdisi's *Culture of Sectarianism* and *Age of Coexistence* both discuss sectarianism in relation to modern political systems outside Lebanon., Makdisi lays out this research agenda clearly in "Corrupting the Sublime Sultanate: The Revolt of Tanyus Shahin in Nineteenth-Century Ottoman Lebanon," *Comparative Studies in Society and History* 42, no. 1 (2000): 181–82.

34. Eli J. Finkel et al., "Political Sectarianism in America," *Science* 370, no. 6516 (2020): 533–36.

35. There are, of course, scholars who rail against this. See, for example, Radhika Gupta, who argues that the lack of looking at "sectarian relations and their salience in everyday life due to the attention paid to the study of communal relations and critical events marked by violence reinforces the ghetto effect by homogenizing and reifying Muslims into a singular, undifferentiated category." Radhika Gupta, "There Must Be Some Way Out of Here: Beyond a Spatial Conception of Muslim Ghettoization in Mumbai?" *Ethnography* 16, no. 3 (September 2015): 367–68. See also Nosheen Ali, "Sectarian Imaginaries: The Micropolitics of Sectarianism and State-Making in Northern Pakistan," *Current Sociology* 58, no. 5 (September 2010): 738–54.

Chapter 1

1. By archive, I mean the texts and the meaning the texts elicit—not only the extractive spaces of research. but the knowledge produced. In this reading, archive is an interactive space for both validating and refuting knowledge.

2. See for example, Mas'ud Dahir, *Tarikh Lubnan al-Ijtima'i, 1914–1926* (Beirut, 1981), and *Lubnan, al-Istiqlal al-Sigha wa al-Mithaq, 1918–1946*, 2nd ed. (Beirut: Dar al-Matbu'at, 1984); Kais Firro, *Inventing Lebanon* (London: I. B. Tauris, 2003); Max Weiss, *In the Shadow of Sectarianism* (Cambridge, MA: Harvard University Press, 2010).

3. See Nadya Sbaiti, "'If the Devil Taught French': Strategies of Language and Learning in French Mandate Beirut," in *Trajectories of Education in the Arab World*, ed. Osama Abi-Mershed (London: Routledge, 2010), 59–83.

4. A. L. Tibawi, *Islamic Education: Its Traditions and Modernization into the Arab National Systems* (New York: Crane, Russak & Company, 1972), and the section on Lebanon in Roderic D. Matthews and Matta Akrawi, *Education in Arab Countries of the Near East* (Washington: American Council on Education, 1949); Munir Bashshur, *Education and the Secular/Religious Divide: The Case of Lebanon* (Los Angeles: G. E. von Grunebaum Center, 1992); Mirna Lattouf, *Women, Education, and Socialization in Modern Lebanon* (Lanham, MD: University Press of America, 2004); Mark Farha, "The Historical Legacy and Political Implications of State and Sectarian Schools in Lebanon," in Maha Shuayb, ed., *Rethinking Education for Social Cohesion: International Case Studies* (London: Palgrave McMillan, 2012), 64–85; Susanna Ferguson, "A Fever for an Education: Pedagogical Thought and Social Transformation in Beirut and Mount Lebanon, 1861–1914," *Arab Studies Journal* (2018): 58–83.

5. Alice Conklin, *A Mission to Civilize: The Republican Idea of Empire in France and West Africa, 1895–1930* (Stanford: Stanford University Press, 1997).

6. See Marie-Paule Ha, "From 'Nos Ancêtres, Les Gaulois' to 'Leur Culture Ancestrale,'" *French Colonial History* 3 (2003): 101–17.

7. *Al-mahfuthat al wataniyya al-lubnaniyya* (Lebanese National Archives; hereafter LNA), Haut commissariat de la République Française en Syrie et au Liban, arrête no. 86.

8. Centre des Archives diplomatiques de Nantes (hereafter CADN), Fonds Beyrouth, Série instruction publique, box 16. "Rapport de Prise de Service," March 17, 1922.

9. It also included several remaining *katatib*, primary-level Qur'anic schools that also taught basic Arabic language and grammar. CADN, *Rapport* (1929), 33. The French authorities did not recognize these as official schools, however, until 1938. CADN, Fonds Beyrouth, Série instruction publique, box 144, "Liste nominative des écoles officielles. . . ." 1938.

10. The Mission laïque française (MLF) schools served as spaces of more secularized education (meaning there was no religion class) and were intended to function parallel to the religious French schools. See Randi Deguilhem, "Impérialisme, colonisation intellectuelle et politique culturelle de la Mission laïque française en Syrie sous mandat," in *The British and French Mandates in Comparative Perspectives*, ed. Nadine Méouchy and Peter Sluglett (Leiden, Netherlands: Brill, 2004), 321–44.

11. See Jens Hanssen, *Fin de Siècle Beirut* (London: Oxford, 2005); Ilham Khuri-Makdisi, "The Conceptualization of the Social in Late Nineteenth- and Early Twentieth-Century Arabic Thought and Language," in *Global Conceptual History: A Reader*, ed. Margrit Pernau and Dominic Sachsenmeier (London: Bloomsbury, 2016), 259–287; Uta Zeuge-Buberl, *The Mission of the American Board in Syria*, trans. Elizabeth Janik (Stuttgart, Germany: Franz Steiner Verlag, 2017).

12. See, for example, Nicola Cooper, "Making Indo-China French: Promoting the Empire through Education," in *Empire and Culture: The French Experience 1830–1940*, ed. Martin Evans (New York: Palgrave Macmillan, 2004), 131–47; Suresh Chandra Ghosh, *The History of Education in Modern India* (London: Orient Longman, 1995); Rodric Matthews and Matta Akrawi, *Education in Arab Countries of the Near East* (American Council on Education, 1949); Farzin Vejdani, *Making History in Iran: Education, Nationalism and Print Culture* (Stanford, CA: Stanford University Press, 2015); Talal al-Rashoud, "Modern Education and Arab Nationalism in Kuwait, 1911–1961" (PhD thesis, SOAS, University of London, 2017); Timothy Mitchell, *Colonising Egypt* (Berkeley: University of California Press, 1988); Sam Kaplan, *The Pedagogical State: Education and the Politics of National Culture in Post-1980 Turkey* (Stanford, CA: Stanford University Press, 2006); and Antoine Léon, *Colonisation, Enseignement, et Education* (Paris: L'Harmattan, 1991).

13. The French Mandate charter promulgated on July 24, 1922, contained two articles that specifically impacted education. Article 8 stated that the right of each community to maintain its own schools for the instruction and education of its own members in its own language, "while conforming to such educational requirements of a general nature as the administration may impose, shall not be denied or impaired." Article 10 of the charter also declared that the Mandate's supervision of foreign missions in Syria and Lebanon would "be limited to the maintenance of public order and good government; the activities of these religious missions shall in no way be restricted nor shall their members be subjected to restrictive measures on the grounds of nationality, provided that their activities are confined to the domains of religion." See "French Mandate for Syria and the Lebanon," *American Journal of International Law* 17, no. 3 (supplement: official documents, July 1923): 177–82. The 1926 Lebanese Constitution later adopted very similar language.

14. CADN, Fonds Beyrouth, Série instruction publique, box 21, dossier 3. Quoted in the *Rapport de mission: L'Enseignement Français en Orient* (June 1924): 55.

15. CADN, box 144, report to the high commissioner, January 21, 1938. They educated 18,000 students, including 5,288 girls. A. L. Tibawi concurs on the number of 18,000. See Tibawi, *Islamic Education*, 134. Among the students educated in private schools were some 21,095 girls. Also see Report of French Mandate to the League of Nations, 1938.

16. Christoph Schumann, "'The Generation of Broad Expectations': Nationalism, Education and Autobiography in Syria and Lebanon 1930–1958," *Die Welt des Islams* 41, no. 2 (July 2001): 189.

17. Her father, Salim Kassab, was a Damascene who had been active with the British Syrian Schools in the mid-nineteenth century with British missionary Elizabeth

Bowen Thompson. A. L. Tibawi, *American Interests in Syria*, 157; Selim Kassab, *Our Inspector's Story* (Gloucester, UK: John Bellows, n.d.); and Wadad Makdisi Cortas, *A World I Loved* (New York: Nation Books, 2009), 30.

18. CADN, Fonds Beyrouth, Série instruction publique, box 21, *Barnamaj al-Madrasa al-Suriyya al-Ahliyya li-Sanat 1920–1921* (Beirut: al-Matbaʻa al-Adabiyya, 1922), 5. Italics added.

19. See, for example, "Kalimat al-Shaykh Munthir fi al-Majlis al-Niyabi," *al-Marʾa al-Jadida* (January 1926).

20. Cortas, *A World I Loved*, 34–35, 37–40.

21. Anissa Rawda Najjar, interview with the author, June 2006.

22. When Mary Kassab petitioned for a tariff exemption for some school materials, the French SIP granted it on the condition that two French teachers, Mlles Lay and Hivert, be placed there. The mandate authorities sent French women to teach French language, geography, history, mathematics, and home economics all in French, and paid their salaries. CADN, Fonds Beyrouth, Série instruction publique. box 21, dossier "École Nationale Syrienne." Letter of December 21, 1923, from Mlle Lay to Conseiller de l'instruction publique. See also Cortas, *A World I Loved*, 81.

23. Widad Makdisi Cortas, *Dhikrayat: 1917–1977* (Beirut: Muʾassassat al-Abhath al-ʻArabiyya, 1982).

24. Ahliyya School Archive, annual reports.

25. Nidal Ashqar and Samia Bakhʻazi, interviews with the author, June 2006.

26. Norma Musa, interview with the author, October 2006. Ahliyya School Archive, enrollment records, 1937, 1941, 1948.

27. Donald Cioeta, "Islamic Benevolent Societies and Public Education in Ottoman Syria, 1875–1882." *Islamic Quarterly* 26 (1982): 40–55; Juhayna al-Ayyubi, "Jamʻiyyat al-Maqasid al-Khayriyya al-Islamiyya fi Bayrut" (MA thesis, American University of Beirut, 1966), 39. For more information on the social and political positions of some of these men, see Jens Hanssen, *Fin de Siècle Beirut*, 64–65, 71, and 146–47.

28. Archive of the Maqasid Islamic Benevolent Society, Maqasid Annual Report, 1920–21, 3.

29. See Maqasid Annual Reports, 1918–38, and Cioeta, "Islamic Benevolent Societies," 43–45.

30. Maqasid Annual Reports 1927–35. Even after the Shiʻi ʻAmiliyya Society of Beirut was established in 1928 for a small growing Shiʻi bourgeoisie, the Maqasid would continue to have relatively steady Shiʻi student enrollments.

31. Linda Schatkowski, "The Islamic Maqasid of Beirut: A Case Study of Modernization in Lebanon." (MA thesis, American University of Beirut, 1969).

32. CADN, Fonds Beyrouth, Série instruction publique, box 144, "Enseignement officiel Libanais," 1938; box 144, "Confessionalisme," January 21, 1938, 3; and Schatkowski, "Maqasid Islamic Society," 148.

33. LNA, Zaki Naqqash, and ʻUmar Farrukh, *Tarikh Suriya wa Lubnan al-Musawwar: Al-Juzʾ al-Awwal* (Beirut: Dar al-Kashafa, 1933), and *Tarikh Suriya wa Lubnan al-Musawwar: Al-Juzʾ al-Thani* (Beirut: Dar al-Kashafa, 1936).

34. Wadad Makdisi Cortas, *A World I Loved*.

35. See Hala Dimechkie, "Julia Tu'mi Dimashqiyi and *al-Mar'a al-Jadida*, 1883–1954." (MA thesis, American University of Beirut, 1998). For a mapping of how class was maintained through familial and marital connections, see Maria Bashur Abunnasr, "The Making of Ras Beirut: A Landscape of Memory for Narratives of Exceptionalism, 1870–1975." (PhD dissertation, University of Massachusetts at Amherst, 2013), 286.

36. Ahliyya School Archive, *Bayan Madrasat al-Banat al-Ahliyya*, 1932; and also *Al-Jalsa al-Thaniya li Umana' Madrasat al-Ahliyya*, 1927.

37. The Secondary Schools Principals' Association's *Education Report*, authored by Cortas in 1957, elaborated plans to expand secondary school education in Lebanon including public schools. The mandate had not opened a single public secondary school during the entire mandate era; the first was opened in 1951.

38. See for example, CADN, Fonds Beyrouth, Série instruction publique, box 16; CADN, Fonds Beyrouth, Série instruction publique, box 119; CADN, Fonds Beyrouth, Série instruction publique, box 163; CADN, Fonds Beyrouth; Série instruction publique, box 161; and see Maria Bashshur Abunnasr, "*We Are in This Together*": *An Oral History of Ras Beirut* (Beirut: AUB Press, forthcoming).

39. Ahliyya School Archive, internal correspondence; author interviews with V. Corm, Norma Mousa, and Najla Hamadeh, as well as MAE Nantes; and Jennifer Dueck, *Claims of Culture at Empire's End* (Oxford, UK: Oxford University Press, 2010).

40. CADN, Fonds Beyrouth, Série instruction publique, box 101, classement: "écoles normales." See Cortas, *A World I Loved*, 53–59.

41. CADN, Fonds Beyrouth, Série instruction publique, box 119.

42. Virginie Corm, Samia Corm, and May Seikaly, interviews with the author, June 2006. See also Najla Hamadeh. "Bayna Dumu' al-'Ajz wa al-Muwatiniyya al-Fa'ila: Muqarana bayna Madrasatayn." In *Al-Muwatiniyya bayna al-Rajul wa-al-Mar'a*, ed. Najla Hamadeh, Jean Said Makdisi, and Su'ad Joseph (Beirut: Dar al-Jadid, 2000), 381–96.

43. CADN, Fonds Beyrouth; Série instruction publique, box 161, classement: incidents scolaires. Letter titled "Confession," July 11, 1940.

Chapter 2

1. *Al-mahkama al-shar'iyya al-ja'fariyya fi Bayrut*, case 107 (November 18, 1937). The names from the court records are either altered or removed to protect the identities of the individuals who came before the court.

2. The majority of Shi'i Muslims in Lebanon are Twelver Shi'i Muslims who believe in the twelve Imams. However, all other denominations of Shi'a adhere to the Ja'fari shari'a courts and their jurisprudence.

3. French High Commissioner Henri de Jouvenel issued decree 3503, recognizing the Shi'a as a legal and political sect. This will be discussed later in this chapter.

4. Courts examined were in Beirut, Sidon, Tyre, Ba'albek, Marja'yun, and Bint Jbeil.

5. Scholars have shown how personal status issues are always much more than

familial matters, and are engulfed in social, political, and legal concerns. Maya Mikdashi, "Sex and Sectarianism: The Legal Architecture of Lebanese Citizenship," *Comparative Studies of South Asia, Africa and the Middle East* 34, no. 2 (2014): 279–93; Judith Tucker, *In the House of the Law: Gender and Islamic Law in Ottoman Syria and Palestine* (Berkeley: University of California Press, 1998); Leslie Peirce, *Morality Tales: Law and Gender in the Ottoman Court of Aintab* (Berkeley and Los Angeles: University of California Press, 2003).

6. Suad Joseph, "The Public/Private: The Imagined Boundary in the Imagined Nation/State/Community: The Lebanese Case." *Feminist Review* 57 (1997): 73–92. Tucker, *In the House of the Law*, 1–36.

7. Maya Mikdashi, "Sex and Sectarianism," 282.

8. For the institutional making of the Ja'fari shari'a courts, see Max Weiss, *In the Shadow of Sectarianism: Law, Shi'ism and the Making of Modern Lebanon* (Cambridge, MA: Harvard University Press, 2010).

9. Cases of Shi'i Muslims appear in the Tyre court, dating from before its establishment of separate Ja'fari courts in 1926. It is believed that the Ottomans had already appointed Shi'i *qadis* and religious courts that functioned within the Hanafi shari'a court system by the late nineteenth century. As Rula Jurdi Abisaab and Malek Abisaab argue, the establishment of the Ja'fari shari'a courts by the French on January 27, 1926, was "simply reinforcing an earlier Ottoman arrangement." Abisaab and Abisaab, *The Shi'ites of Lebanon: Modernism, Communism and Hizbullah's Islamists* (Syracuse, NY: Syracuse University Press, 2014), 13.

10. Like the French republic, the Lebanese government was based on a unitary semipresidential republic or parliamentary democracy. Both are voted in by Parliament as representatives of their constituents. Stephan Longrigg, *Syria and the French Mandate* (Oxford, UK: Oxford University Press, 1958). Kais Firro, *Metamorphosis of the Nation (al-Umma): The Rise of Arabism and Minorities in Syria and Lebanon, 1850–1940* (Portland, UK: Sussex Academic Press, 2009), 94.

11. Talal Asad, *Formations of the Secular: Christianity, Islam, Modernity* (Stanford, CA: Stanford University Press, 2003), 227. Bernard Cohn, *Colonialism and Its Forms of Knowledge: The British in India* (Princeton, CA: Princeton University Press, 1996), 3. Asad also argued this element of the "documentation" in judicial procedure. Asad, *Formations of the Secular*, 211.

12. Wael Hallaq, *Shari'a: Theory, Practice, Transformations.* (Cambridge, UK: Cambridge University Press, 2010).

13. Thompson, *Colonial Citizens and Makdisi, the Culture of Sectarianism: Community, History, and Violence in Nineteenth-Century Ottoman Lebanon* (Berkeley and Los Angeles: University of California Press, 2000).

14. Asad, *Formations of the Secular*, 230–31.

15. The staff of the Ja'fari shari'a court was initially hired and salaried by the French Mandatory state.

16. Weiss, *In the Shadow of Sectarianism*; and Chalabi, *The Shi'is of Jabal 'Amil and the New Lebanon.*

17. Asad, *Formations of the Secular*, 230–31.

18. Rogers Brubaker, *Nationalism Reframed: Nationhood and National Question in the New Europe.* (Cambridge, UK: Cambridge University Press, 1996); and Lisa Wedeen, *Peripheral Visions: Publics, Power and Performance in Yemen* (Chicago: University of Chicago Press, 2008).

19. Etienne Balibar, "The Nation Form: History and Ideology," in *Race, Nation, Class: Ambiguous Identities*, ed. Etienne Balibar and Immanuel Wallerstein (London: Verso, 1991), 86–106.

20. Makdisi, *The Culture of Sectarianism.*

21. Mikdashi, "Sex and Sectarianism," 282. The anglicized term *madhhabs* will be used, as opposed to the Arabic plural, *madhahib.*

22. A *marjaʿ al-taqlid* or *marjaʿ* is considered the highest authority on shariʿa law among Twelver (Jaʿfari) Shiʿa.

23. This is a claim further articulated by Max Weiss, as he sees the institutional underpinning of the court as one enforced by the French authorities and pushed for by leading Shiʿi notables.

24. *Al-mahkama al-sharʿiyya al-jaʿfariyya fi Bayrut*, Muhammad Hussein vs. Badiʿa, case 40 (June 13, 1937). For the most part, pseudonyms or the litigants' last names have been changed due to requests made by the court deputies in Beirut not to reveal the exact names of the people who appeared before it.

25. Munir ʿUsayran reiterates Arrêté 3503, confirming the court's authority over the case as decreed by the French High Commission.

26. The second appearance of Muhammad appeared in case 221. *Al-mahkama al-sharʿiyya al-jaʿfariyya fi Bayrut*, July 17, 1937.

27. *Al-mahkama al-sharʿiyya al-jaʿfariyya fi Bayrut*, July 17, 1937. Muhammad actually traced his lineage to the town of ʿAynatha while the case revealed that Badiʿa was from the town of Nabatiyya in Jabal ʿAmil. Her claim was not that she did not hail from Lebanon, but rather that she has been living in Palestine for more than seven years, and considered it her home and place of residence.

28. *Al-mahkama al-sharʿiyya al-jaʿfariyya fi Bayrut*, July 17, 1937.

29. Maya Mikdashi, "Sectarianism: Notes on Studying the Lebanese State," in *The Oxford Handbook of Contemporary Middle Eastern and North African History* (Oxford, UK: Oxford University Press, 2020).

30. This is pushing back against claims that assume that sectarianism and sect have always existed in the case of Lebanon.

31. Asifa Quraishi and Frank E. Vogel, *The Islamic Marriage Contract: Case Studies in Islamic Family Law* (Cambridge, MA: Harvard University Press, 2008).

32. This porosity is particular to the Mandate period, in which national boundaries and the institutions that define them were newly formed and authorized.

33. Mounira Charrad, *States and Women's Rights: The Making of Postcolonial Tunisia, Algeria, and Morocco* (Berkeley: University of California Press, 2001); Iris Agmon, *Family and Court: Legal Culture and Modernity in Late Ottoman Palestine* (Syracuse, NY: Syracuse University Press, 2006).

34. As a modern apparatus of the state, the written word came to hold authority over and supersede the oral tradition of shariʿa practices in premodern society.

35. Rania Maktabi, "The Lebanese Census of 1932 Revisited: Who Are the Lebanese?" *British Journal of Middle Eastern Studies* 26, no. 2 (1999): 219–41.

36. The 1921 census was the first census taken by the French for administrative purposes.

37. Maktabi, "The Lebanese Census of 1932 Revisited," 225.

38. The Paulet-Newcombe Agreement of February 3, 1922, resulted in the annexation of seven villages that were presumably part of Greater Lebanon in 1920. The inhabitants of these villages were predominantly Shiʿa and fought for Lebanese citizenship on that basis. The creation of the state of Israel in 1948 only complicated their legal status. George Karam, *al-Jinsiyya al-Lubnaniyya bayna al-qanun wal-waqiʿ* (Beirut: Maṭhaʿat Joseph al Hājj, 1993).

39. Elizabeth Brownson, *Palestinian Women and Muslim Family Law in Mandate Period* (Syracuse, NY: Syracuse University Press: 2019), 125–46; Guy Burak, *The Second Formation of Islamic Law: The Hanafi School in the Early Modern Ottoman Empire* (Cambridge, UK: Cambridge University Press, 2015), 163–207.

40. The case first appeared in the records of *Al-mahkama al-sharʿiyya al-jaʿfariyya fi Bayrut*, Watʿa vs. Musa, case 68 (April 5, 1938). The case reappeared on Musa's accord in *Al-mahkama al-sharʿiyya al-jaʿfariyya fi Bayrut*, Musa Ahmad vs. Watʿa, case 146 (May 17, 1938).

41. However, this is not noted in the records of the Jaʿfari shariʿa court of Beirut, when the rebuttal decree came from the Damascus court. No mention of the religious orientation of the decree is made. *Al-mahkama al-sharʿiyya al-jaʿfariyya fi Baʿalbek*, Watʿa vs. Musa, case 68 (April 5, 1938).

42. In Fatima's case, she could have mobilized the Jaʿfari personal status courts. But this was not true in Watʿa's case, as Damascus did not have separate personal status courts.

43. Joseph, "The Public/Private," 82.

44. Guy Burak, *The Second Formation of Islamic Law: The Hanafi School in the Early Modern Ottoman Empire* (Cambridge, UK: Cambridge University Press, 2015), 163–207.

45. *Al-mahkama al-sharʿiyya al-jaʿfariyya fi Bayrut*, case 164, no. 68 (March 7, 1938).

46. *Al-mahkama al-sharʿiyya al-jaʿfariyya fi Bayrut*, case 164, no. 68 (March 7, 1938). Another case of this nature appeared on November 15, 1934, in case 4. Mustafa Ibrahim came before the court to confirm that the amount of *nafaqa* ordered in the Hanafi court was legitimate in the Jaʿfari court. Mustafa was able to get the amount of alimony verified in the Jaʿfari court for his wife Hasma, as noted in other cases. Many cases of this nature appeared where *thabat al-zawaj* was requested. Refer to Hussein vs. Fatima, case 18 (December 17, 1938); Muhammad vs. Sikina, case 6 (December 6, 1937); and Ahmad vs. Lamya, case 257 (November 19, 1929), all in *Al-mahkama al-sharʿiyya al-jaʿfariyya fi Bayrut*.

47. *Al-mahkama al-sharʿiyya al-jaʿfariyya fi Bayrut,* case 269 (December 10, 1932).

48. This was only based on Zahra's written text and claim. There was no effort made by the Ja'fari court to extract the history of this case from the Hanafi court. This point should be further investigated. What was the degree of intercourt communication and debate during this period? Was there a conscious effort not to sanction other shari'a courts of different denominations in their designated legal domain? Is this only the situation during the Mandate period? This aspect has changed over time with the creation of *al-Hay'a al 'Amma Li-Mahkamat al Tamyiz*, the Court of Cassation's Council of General Oversight, which intervenes in juridical disputes between different shari'a courts.

49. Wedeen, *Peripheral Visions*, 150–85.

50. In his discussion of the state, Timothy Mitchell argued that "one can trace it to methods of organization, arrangement, and representation that operate within the social practices they govern, yet create the effect of an enduring structure apparently external to those practices." Timothy Mitchell, "Society, Economy, and the State Effect," in *The Anthropology of the State: A Reader.* ed. Aradhana Sharma and Akhil Gupta (Oxford, UK: Blackwell Publishing, 2006), 180.

51. Sharma and Gupta, *Anthropology of the State*, 181.

52. Thompson, *Colonial Citizens*, 1–2.

53. Timothy Mitchell, *Colonising Egypt* (Berkeley: University of California Press, 1991), xi. See also Sbaiti, this volume.

Chapter 3

1. The archivists at the Court of Cassation are clerks for their respective courts; they ferry papers, request documents, and act as liaisons between judges, lawyers and the bureaucracy of the courts. In addition, they are in charge of the court archive and of access to it. My use of the word "archivist" is a recognition that their work, even as clerks, revolves around the maintenance, curation, indexing, and organization of documents, both as they circulate in the temporality of an active court case and in their capacity as archival files. The Arabic word *qalam* traverses the boundaries between what might be called "clerk" "scribe" and "archivist" in English.

2. In *A Thousand Plateaus*, Deleuze and Guattari conceptualize *lines of flight* as movements or propulsions of thought that may illuminate (if only for a second) or foreclose alternative paths, histories, and futures. Crucially, *lines of flight* are realized and unrealized when they enmesh with the creative forces of others. They represent the possibility (and only the possibility) of thinking and doing otherwise, even when it may be impossible to do so.

3. It is important to note here the generous funding that enabled me to dwell for years in this archival space. My research was supported by external grants, as well as research funds from Columbia University and Rutgers University. The generosity of this funding, coupled with my Lebanese and American citizenships, allowed me to conduct two and a half years of uninterrupted PhD research, more than five subsequent months-long research trips, and, later, more than a year of sabbatical research and writing. The material conditions of our research directly impress on the research

itself. If research and writing take time, we only have the time we are literally afforded. I offer myself as an example of the need to be transparent about the political economy of academic research, particularly as research funds, sabbaticals, PhD funding, tenure stream jobs, and *time* are diminishing goods in the US academy.

4. Ann Cvetkovich, *Archive of Feelings*, vol. 2008 (Durham, NC: Duke University Press, 2003).

5. See Maya Mikdashi, *Sextarianism: Sovereignty, Secularism, and the State in Lebanon* (Stanford, CA: Stanford University Press, 2022).

6. Examples include Elie Hobeika (assassinated), Dany Chamoun (assassinated), George Hawi (assassinated), Nabih Berri (speaker of Parliament), Walid Joumblatt (MP, former minister), Michel Aoun (president), Amin Gemeyel (former president), and Bashir Gemeyel (assassinated, president-elect).

7. Ian Hacking, *Rewriting the Soul: Multiple Personality and the Sciences of Memory* (Princeton, NJ: Princeton University Press, 1998); Wittgenstein, *The Blue and Brown Books*.

8. Trouillot, *Silencing the Past*.

9. I am grateful to conversations with Anjali Arondekar for helping to sharpen this point.

10. Bruno Latour, *The Making of Law: An Ethnography of the Conseil d'État* (Polity, 2010). See also Achille Mbembe, "The Power of the Archive and Its Limits." In *Refiguring the Archive* (Dordrecht, Netherlands: Springer, 2002), 19–27.

11. Instead of looking for holes, gaps or ruptures in the archive of Lebanon's highest court, I trace bureaucratic and legal logics, practices and continuities. I attend to the amplifications, repetitions, and narrations of state power during both war and "peace." I heed Ann Stoler's warning that "the search for 'dramatic reversal,' 'usurpation' and successful 'appropriation' can hide 'events' that are more muted in their consequences, less bellicose in their seizures, less spectacular in how and what they reframe." Stoler, *Along the Archival Grain*, 51.

12. "Failing to Deal with the Past: What Cost to Lebanon?" (International Center for Transitional Justice, 2014).

13. For more on law and its multiple relationships to violence and history, see Renisa Mawani, "Law's archive," *Annual Review of Law and Social Science* 8 (2012): 337–65.

14. Jacques Derrida, *Archive Fever: A Freudian Impression* (Chicago: University of Chicago Press, 1996); Carolyn Steedman, *Dust: The Archive and Cultural History* (New Brunswick, NJ: Rutgers University Press, 2002); Avery F. Gordon, *Ghostly Matters: Haunting and the Sociological Imagination* (Minneapolis: University of Minnesota Press, 2008); Saadiya Hartman, *Lose Your Mother: A Journey along the Atlantic Slave Route* (Macmillan, 2008); Michel Foucault, *The History of Sexuality: An Introduction* (New York: Vintage, 1990); Anjali Arondekar, *For the Record: On Sexuality and the Colonial Archive in India* (Durham, NC: Duke University Press, 2009).

15. For the inseparability of archival spaces and archival documents, see Achille Mbembe, "The Power of the Archive and its Limits," in *Refiguring the Archive* (Dordrecht, Netherlands: Springer, 2002), 19–27.

16. Sune Haugbolle, *War and Memory in Lebanon*, vol. 34 (Cambridge, UK: Cambridge University Press, 2010).

17. Omnia El Shakry, "'History without Documents': The Vexed Archives of Decolonization in the Middle East," *American Historical Review* 120, no. 3 (2015): 920–34.

18. Sherene Seikaly, "How I Met My Great-Grandfather: Archives and the Writing of History," *Comparative Studies of South Asia, Africa and the Middle East* 38, no. 1 (2018): 6–20, esp. 7.

19. See Marisa J. Fuentes, *Dispossessed Lives: Enslaved Women, Violence, and the Archive* (Philadelphia: University of Pennsylvania Press, 2016); Michel-Rolph Trouillot, *Silencing the Past: Power and the Production of History* (Boston: Beacon Press, 1995); Saidiya Hartman, *Wayward Lives, Beautiful Experiments: Intimate Histories of Social Upheaval* (New York: W W Norton, 2019).

20. Ann Laura Stoler, "Colonial Archives and the Arts of Governance," *Archival Science* 2, no. 1–2 (2002): 87–109.

21. Anjali Arondekar. "In the Absence of Reliable Ghosts: Sexuality, Historiography, South Asia," *Differences* 25, no. 3 (2014): 98–122.

22. Kirsten Weld. *Paper Cadavers: The Archives of Dictatorship in Guatemala* (Durham, NC: Duke University Press, 2014).

23. Arondekar, *For the Record*.

24. In *Along the Archival Grain*, Anne Stoler writes that "the ethnographic space of the archive resides in the disjuncture between prescription and practice, between state mandates and the maneuvers people made in response to them, between rules and how people actually lived their lives."

25. Todd Shepard, "'Of Sovereignty': Disputed Archives, 'Wholly Modern' Archives, and the Post-Decolonization French and Algerian Republics, 1962–2012," *American Historical Review* 120, no. 3 (2015): 869–83.

26. Elizabeth Freeman, *Time Binds: Queer Temporalities, Queer Histories* (Durham, NC: Duke University Press, 2010).

27. Mezna Qato, "Forms of Retrieval: Social Scale, Citation, and the Archive on the Palestinian Left," *International Journal of Middle East Studies* 51, no. 2 (2019): 312–15.

28. United Press International, "Rocket Strikes Beirut Justice Palace, Destroys Files." *Los Angeles Times*, 1985.

29. United Press International, "Rocket Strikes Beirut Justice Palace."

30. There is a common misconception that militia leaders became state officials and politicians after the civil war. In fact, politicians and statesmen became militia leaders, and militia leaders sometimes became politicians and statesmen. The line between militia leaders and political leaders has always been a blur, rather than a diagnostic between the pre- and post–civil war eras.

31. Rosemary Sayigh, *Too Many Enemies: The Palestinian Experience in Lebanon* (Al-Mashriq, 2015).

32. The Taif Accord lays out a process through which the practice of sectarian quotas in the civil service is to be ended. More than thirty years after its signing and incorporation into the Constitution, the accord remains unrealized.

33. UN Economic and Social Commission for Western Asia, press release, "ESCWA Warns: Three-Quarters of Lebanon's Residents Plunge into Poverty."

34. Indeed, a news wire bulletin described it this way at the time: "The Palace of Justice, on the Christian eastern side of the city, was hit twice during militia combat last week. Monday's incident was believed to be the work of Muslim militiamen firing Soviet-made Grad rockets."

35. There is another formulation of "us" today in Lebanon: everyone who was in the country when the largest nonnuclear explosion in human history occurred at the Beirut port.

36. US Office of the Inspector General, "Audit of USAID/Lebanon's Rule of Law Program," https://oig.usaid.gov/sites/default/files/2018-06/6-268-10-006-p.pdf.

37. Mona was also concerned that my research was funded by US government money, and she was adamant in her belief that legal reform should not arrive on the wings of imperial power. This encounter was only six years after the US invasion of Iraq, and three years after the US-supported Israel-Lebanon war.

38. Haugbolle, *War and Memory*; Arondekar, "In the Absence"; Tsing, *Friction*.

39. Messick, *Shari'a Scripts*.

40. The transformation from "active" to "passive" files and readers is similar to Ilana Feldman's ruminations on the distinction between archives of governance and archives of history, but with a crucial difference: the legal case files themselves will never be open to the public or housed in a national archive, though court decisions might be.

41. Middle East Studies Association Committee on Academic Freedom, "Digitization of State Archives Could Affect Access to Archival Material," April 2016.

42. Members of the Lebanese Forces, the Phalange (Kata'ib), and the South Lebanon Army have all been implicated. Bayan Nuwayhed al-Hout, *Sabra and Shatila: September 1982* (London: Pluto Press, 2004).

43. Brubaker, *Citizenship and Nationhood in France and Germany* and *Nationalism Reframed*; Isin, *Citizens without Frontiers*; Isin and Nielsen, *Acts of Citizenship*.

44. Hirschkind, *The Ethical Soundscape*, 29.

45. I am thinking here of Iraq, Yemen, Syria, and Palestine.

46. See Sayigh, *Too Many Enemies*, and Sherene Seikaly, "The Matter of Time," *American Historical Review* 124, no. 5 (2019): 1681–88.

47. As Carolyn Steedman writes, "Nothing starts in the Archive, nothing, ever at all, though things certainly end up there. You find nothing in the Archive but stories caught half way through: the middle of things; discontinuities." Steedman, *Dust*, 28.

48. Hull, *Government*; Derrida, "Force of Law."

49. Author interview with ex-Phalangist militia member in Beirut, 2013.

50. "Why They Died: Civilian Casualties in Lebanon during the 2006 War," Human Rights Watch, 2007.

51. Human Rights Watch, *World Report 2009*.

52. Andrew Arsan, *Lebanon: A Country in Fragments* (London: Hurst & Company, 2018).

53. Foucault wrote of how the specter of war is always already present in domi-

nant understandings of peace: "This does not mean, however, that society, the law, or the state are like armistices that put an end to wars, or that they are the product of definitive victories. Law is not pacification, for beneath the law, war continues to rage in all the mechanism of power, even in the most regular. War is the motor behind institutions and order. In the smallest of its cogs, peace is waging a secret war—peace itself is a coded war." Michel Foucault and François Ewald,*"Society Must Be Defended": Lectures at the Collège de France, 1975–1976* (New York: Macmillan, 2003), 50–51.

54. Maya Mikdashi, "The Magic of Mutual Coexistence: The Taif Accord at Thirty." *Jadaliyya*, October 2019.

55. Hiba Bou Akar, *For the War Yet to Come: Planning Beirut's Frontiers* (Stanford, CA: Stanford University Press, 2018).

56. Hacking, *Rewriting the Soul.*

57. Arondekar, "In the Absence."

58. Hana Sleiman has written persuasively about the multiple archives possible within any collection of documents and material objects. In ruminating on the history of the PLO archive and the different curations of it by Israel, the Palestine Authority, and researchers, she writes, "Here lies the crux of the matter: archives do not perpetually serve the narrative of their creator. Rather they come to serve the narrative of their captor. Hana Sleiman, "The Paper Trail of a Liberation Movement," *Arab Studies Journal* 24, no. 1 (2016): 42–67, esp. 49.

59. He was not physically there at the massacre, and has denied responsibility for it. But he has neither denounced nor taken responsibility for the role played by the militia he co-led in the massacre.

60. A few years later, my choice was rendered irrelevant when a large portion of the case file was leaked online.

61. Hacking, *Rewriting the Soul*, 238.

62. Ariella Azoulay, *Potential History* (Verso, 2019).

63. https://www.thenation.com/article/society/gig-academy-meritocracy-trap-universities-crisis/.

64. See Matt Brimm, *Poor Queer Studies: Confronting Elitism in the University* (Durham, NC: Duke University Press, 2020).

65. I take the phrase "living together and apart" from Sherene Seikaly, "Return to the Present," in Elizabeth Weber, ed., *Living Together: Jacques Derrida's Communities of Violence and Peace* (New York: Fordham University Press, 2012), 227–24.

Chapter 4

1. "Liman tajma' al-Huda al-amwal?" *Mir'at al-Gharb,* January 14, 1926.

2. For more on the fighting in Rashaya and surrounding areas, see Phillip Khoury, *Syria and the French Mandate: The Politics of Arab Nationalism, 1920–1945* (Princeton, NJ: Princeton University Press, 1987), 181; Meir Zamir, *Lebanon's Quest: The Road to Statehood, 1926–1939* (London: I. B. Tauris, 1997), 9; Reem Bailony, "From Mandate Borders to the Diaspora: Rashaya's Transnational Suffering and the Making of Lebanon in 1925," *Arab Studies Journal* 26, no. 2 (2018): 44–73.

3. Rashaya today is primarily Druze, although it remains an important site for Greek Orthodox and Eastern Catholic adherents.

4. *Mahjar* literally translates to "place of immigration," but it conceptually takes on the meaning of "diaspora." Immigrants hailing from Ottoman *bilad al-sham,* or from Greater Syria, referred to themselves and have been traditionally discussed in the literature as broadly "Syrian," representing people from today's Syria, Lebanon, Palestine, and Jordan. However, with the dissolution of the Ottoman Empire, debates over the future of the region transpired transnationally, making salient the political identities of this diaspora. The debate over the 1925 revolt largely took place among the Syrian-Lebanese subset of this population, and since the distinction between the two was becoming ever more important during the 1925 moment, I will henceforth refer to this immigrant population as Syrian-Lebanese. The two identities become increasingly distinct for the diaspora after World War II and independence.

5. While the civilian victims were primarily Christian, the destruction of the town took place in large part due to French aerial bombardment.

6. For a discussion on the development of various nationalist strains in the region, see Kais Firro, "Lebanese Nationalism versus Arabism: From Bulus Nujaym to Michel Chiha," *Middle Eastern Studies* 40, no. 5 (2004): 1–27.

7. See Bailony, "From Mandate Borders to the Diaspora."

8. Writing about this population in 1924, the scholar Philip Hitti opined that this made "the Syrian the man without a country par excellence," whose patriotism had "no political aspects." Philip Hitti, *The Syrians in America* (New York: Doran Company, 1924), 24.

9. This was done in order to distance themselves from the broader classification of "Turk"—often read as "Muslim"—for those originating from the Ottoman Empire. See Sarah Gualtieri, *Between Arab and White: Race and Ethnicity in the Early Syrian American Diaspora* (Berkeley: University of California Press, 2009). For more on the use of identity markers, see Akram Khater, "Phoenician or Arab, Lebanese or Syrian— Who Were the Early Immigrants to America?" *Khayrallah Center for Lebanese Diaspora Studies Blog,* September 20, 2017, https://lebanesestudies.news.chass.ncsu.edu /2017/09/20/phoenician-or-arab/. Khater notes: "Thus, by the dawn of the 20th century, when the majority of Levantine immigrants arrived in the US, 'Syrian' as an ethnic and national origin was reasonable enough to accept even if they were not quite sure what it meant. As community organizations and publications proliferated and gave ethnic substance to these migratory individuals and families, the term 'Syrian' became more common."

10. I use the term "translocal" rather than "transnational" to describe particularist subjectivities linked to kinship, village, and sect. Moreover, while I use the term "transnational" to describe mobilizations that transcended borders, I refer to cross-border nationalism using Benedict Anderson's term "long-distance nationalism." Because Syrian-Lebanese migrants were working for and not surpassing the nation, it more accurately describes their political mobilizations. See David Conradson and Deirdre McKay, "Translocal Subjectivities: Mobility, Connection, Emotion," *Mobili-*

ties 2, no. 2 (2007): 167–74; and Roger Waldinger and David Fitzgerald, "Transnationalism in Question," *American Journal of Sociology* 109, no. 5 (2004): 1177–95.

11. Rogers Brubaker, "Migration, Membership, and the Modern Nation-State: Internal and External Dimensions of the Politics of Belonging," *Journal of Interdisciplinary History* 41 (2010): 66.

12. For a discussion on the identitarian politics of the diaspora, see Stacy Fahrenthold, *Between the Ottomans and the Entente: The First World War in the Syrian and Lebanese Diaspora, 1908–1925* (New York: Oxford University Press, 2019); Sarah Gualtieri, *Between Arab and White: Race and Ethnicity in the Early Syrian American Diaspora* (Berkeley: University of California Press, 2009); and Camila Pastor, *The Mexican Mahjar: Transnational Maronites, Jews, and Arabs under the French Mandate* (Austin: University of Texas Press, 2017).

13. Fruma Zachs has argued how American Presbyterian interactions with Christians in *bilad al-sham* helped "define and promote a concept of 'Syria' in which Arab Christian intellectuals then grounded their aspirations and ideals of Syrian patriotism (*wataniyya*)." Fruma Zachs, "Toward a Proto-Nationalist Concept of Syria? Revisiting the American Presbyterian Missionaries in the Nineteenth-Century Levant," *Die Welt des Islams* 41, no. 2 (2001): 146. Also see the works of Adel Beshara, ed., *The Origins of Syrian Nationhood: Histories, Pioneers and Identity* (London: Routledge, 2011); Christoph Schumann, "Nationalism, Diaspora and 'Civilisational Mission': The Case of Syrian Nationalism in Latin America between World War I and World War II," *Nations and Nationalism* 10, no. 4 (2004): 599–617; Keith David Watenpaugh, *Being Modern in the Middle East: Revolution, Nationalism, Colonialism and the Arab Middle Class* (Princeton, NJ: Princeton University Press, 2012); and Deanna Ferree Womack, "Syrian Christians and Arab-Islamic Identity: Expressions of Belonging in the Ottoman Empire and America," *Studies in World Christianity* 25, no. 1 (2019): 29.

14. Stacy Fahrenthold, "Transnational Modes and Media: The Syrian Press in the Mahjar and Emigrant Activism during World War I," *Mashriq & Mahjar: Journal of Middle East and North African Migration Studies* 1, no. 1 (2013): 30–54.

15. James Gelvin, "'Arab Nationalism': Has a New Framework Emerged? Pensée 1: 'Arab Nationalism' Meets Social Theory," *International Journal of Middle East Studies* 41, no. 1 (February 2009): 10.

16. Michael Provence's work on the Syrian Revolt demonstrates how, despite French attempts at divide-and-conquer, rebels maintained a secular, anticolonial, and Syrian nationalist message. Michael Provence, *The Great Syrian Revolt and the Rise of Arab Nationalism* (Austin: University of Texas Press, 2005).

17. In this volume, Tsolin Nalbantian argues that it was not even Lebanon's diaspora that facilitated Lebanon's sectarian system, but that Armenians from different countries enhanced diasporic sectarianization by inviting the Armenian church of Lebanon to the United States.

18. Rania Maktabi, "The Lebanese Census of 1932 Revisited. Who Are the Lebanese?" *British Journal of Middle Eastern Studies* 26, no. 2 (1999): 219–41.

19. Fahrenthold, *Between the Ottomans and the Entente*, 139.

20. On the subject of Lebanon's creation, see Meir Zamir, *The Formation of Modern Lebanon* (Ithaca, NY: Cornell University Press, 1988); Kais Firro, *Inventing Lebanon: Nationalism and the State under the Mandate* (London: I. B. Tauris, 2002); and Asher Kaufman, *Reviving Phoenicia: The Search for Identity in Lebanon* (London: I. B. Tauris, 2004).

21. This is an increase from the 2009 elections, which witnessed political parties subsidizing trips for expatriates to travel to Lebanon and vote in the highly contested general election. See Wendy Pearlman, "Competing for Lebanon's Diaspora: Transnationalism and Domestic Struggles in a Weak State," *International Migration Review* 48, no. 1 (2014): 34–75.

22. "Lebanon Expats Prepare for Voting First," *France 24,* April 27, 2018, https://www.france24.com/en/20180427-lebanon-expats-prepare-voting-first.

23. See Graham Auman Pitts, "The Ecology of Migration: Remittances in World War I Mount Lebanon," *Arab Studies Journal* 26, no. 2 (2018): 102–29.

24. Pitts, "The Ecology of Migration," 102–29.

25. For more on this, see the works of Lily Balloffet, Reem Bailony, Stacy Fahrenthold, and Camila Pastor on the transnational dimensions of French Mandatory politics.

26. See note 2 of the epilogue in Akram Khater, *Inventing Home: Emigration, Gender, and the Middle Class in Lebanon, 1870–1920* (Berkeley: University of California Press, 2001), 232 n2.

27. For more on whiteness, see Gualtieri, *Between Arab and White.*

28. Gualtieri, *Between Arab and White.*

29. Archives de Ministère des Affaires Étrangères (henceforth MAE-La Courneuve) Syrie-Lebanon, vol. 120, carton 313, Letter from Mukarzil to the French consul general, New York, September 7, 1921.

30. Akram Khater, *Inventing Home,* 232.

31. See for example, Andrew Arsan, *Interlopers of Empire: The Lebanese Diaspora in Colonial French West Africa* (Oxford, UK: Oxford University Press, 2014); Lily Balloffet, "From the Pampas to the Mashriq: Arab-Argentine Philanthropy Networks," *Mashriq & Mahjar: Journal of Middle East and North African Migration Studies* 4, no. 1 (2017): 4–28; Hani J. Bawardi, *The Making of Arab Americans: From Syrian Nationalism to U.S. Citizenship* (Austin: University of Texas Press, 2014); Gualtieri, *Between Arab and White*; Randa Kayyali, "Race, Religion and Identity: Arab Christians in the United States," *Culture and Religion* 19, no. 1 (2018): 1–19; Akram Khater, *Inventing Home: Emigration, Gender, and the Middle Class in Lebanon, 1870–1920* (Berkeley: University of California Press, 2001); Pastor, *The Mexican Mahjar.*

32. See Tsolin Nalbantian, this volume.

33. "'Ilaj al-ta'ifiyya," *Mir'at al-Gharb,* (October 6, 1925).

34. See Nadya Sbaiti, this volume.

35. See Provence, *The Great Syrian Revolt.*

36. Sallum Mukarzil, "Echoes of the Syrian Revolution in America," *Syrian World,* February 1927, 25–29.

37. Yusuf al-Sawda, "Junun al-Harb al-Ahliyya," *al-Huda,* December 14, 1925.

38. Stacy Fahrenthold, "Transnational Modes and Media," 37.

39. Sawda, "Junun al-Harb al-Ahliyya."

40. "Dam yalum wa hibr yaloom," *al-Huda,* January 26, 1926.

41. "Suriyya al-miskina bayn al-naʿra wal maslaha," *al-Huda,* December 21, 1925.

42. "Suriyya al-miskina bayn al-naʿra wal maslaha," *al-Huda,* December 21, 1925..

43. "Al-rifq al-fransawi," *al-Huda,* January 25, 1926.

44. "Lubnan lan yakun watan masihi," reprinted in *al-Huda,* January 25, 1926.

45. "Al-watan li-l-jamiʿ: Lubnan ya ʿaba hurub al-diniyya," *al-Huda,* December 22, 1925.

46. "Al-watan li-l-jamiʿ: Lubnan ya ʿaba hurub al-diniyya," *al-Huda,* December 22, 1925.

47. "Al-Shawaʿir al insaniyya al-wataniyya," *al-Huda,* January 26, 1926.

48. "Baraba hatha al-zaman," *Mirʾat al-Gharb,* October 10, 1925.

49. "Ma araq tilk al-qulub," *Mirʾat al-Gharb,* September 11, 1925; "Makhluf safil yuthir al-naʿra al-diniyya wa yuhin al-Druz wal muslimin ʿamuman," *al-Bayan,* October 20, 1925.

50. "Kun rajul," *Mirʾat al-Gharb,* December 30, 1925.

51. "Kun rajul," *Mirʾat al-Gharb,* December 30, 1925.

52. I use the terms "patriot" and "nationalist" interchangeably as a translation for the Arabic word *watani* for this time period. As the confines of the nation-state were still in flux during the 1920s, more often than not the *mahjar* expressed a patriotic duty to homeland over the exclusive nationalism attached to a nation-state project. Even when *mahjar* activists clearly advocated for a specific nation-state project, the catch-all ethnicity of "Syrian" attached to their diaspora identities created ambiguities around the meaning of *watani.*

53. "Haʾulaʾ al-Lubnaniyyun," *al-Bayan,* January 7, 1926.

54. "Makhluq safil yuthir al-naʿra al-diniyya wa yuhin al-druz wal muslimin ʿamuman," *al-Bayan,* October 20, 1925.

55. "Makhluq safil yuthir al-naʿra al-diniyya wa yuhin al-druz wal muslimin ʿamuman," *al-Bayan,* October 20, 1925.

56. "Duʿat al-Istiqlal," *al-Bayan,* October 29, 1921.

57. "Al-shayʾ bil shayʾ yuthkar," *Mirʾat al-Gharb,* October 26, 1925.

58. For more on this, see Bailony, "From the Mandate Borders to the Diaspora.".

59. "Al-nahda tatabaraʿ," *al-Huda,* December 3, 1925.

60. "Al-nahda tatabaraʿ," *al-Huda,* December 3, 1925.

61. "Kahina wa Druz wa Muslim," *al-Huda,* December 12, 1925.

62. "Ghiwaya al-di ʿaya wa diʾaya al-ghiwaya," *al-Huda,* December 26, 1925.

63. "Dam yalum wa hibr yalum," *al-Huda,* January 30, 1926.

64. "Kahina wa Druz wa Muslim," *al-Huda,* December 12, 1925.

65. "Al-shawaʿir al-insaniyya al-wataniyya," *al-Huda,* January 28, 1926.

66. See Fahrenthold, *Between the Ottomans and the Entente.*

67. Fahrenthold, *Between the Ottomans and the Entente,* 52.

68. Fahrenthold, *Between the Ottomans and the Entente*, 52–54. As Fahrenthold demonstrates, in many cases World War I era disagreements also tended to split along sectarian lines. She writes, "The identification of Syrian and Armenian Christians as humanitarian subjects reinforced long-standing American stereotypes about Islam, but also offended Ottoman immigrants concerned about the sectarian character that some Syrian resistance work was taking."

69. Fahrenthold, *Between the Ottomans and the Entente*, 79.

70. "Muwadaf fransawi la na'ib lubnani," *Mir'at al-Gharb*, January 27, 1926.

71. "Muwadaf fransawi la na'ib lubnani," *Mir'at al-Gharb*, January 27, 1926.

72. "Liman tajma' al-Huda al-amwal?" *Mir'at al-Gharb*, January 14, 1926. The piece hints at possible embezzlement; however, the details are unclear. More research needs to be done on how diaspora support was collected in the name of the Maronite Church during World War I.

73. "Al-arajif wal akathib," *al-Bayan*, January 13, 1926.

74. "Nahnu wal bahlawan," *Mir'at al-Gharb*, February 13, 1926.

75. "Al-lamamun wal mankubun," *Mir'at al-Gharb*, February 23, 1926.

76. "Al-lamamun wal mankubun," *Mir'at al-Gharb*, February 23, 1926.

77. "Ila ma hatha al-tadlil wa hata mata hatha al-iftira'," *Mir'at al-Gharb*, March 2, 1926.

78. "I'anit mankubi Suriyya," *al-Bayan*, December 4, 1925.

79. This widespread slogan was popularized during the 1919 Egyptian revolution, and would be used across the Arab world in the post–World War I period.

Chapter 5

I gratefully acknowledge the Wenner-Gren Foundation for Anthropological Research for supporting part of this study.

1. Amira, conversation with the author, Beirut, July 15, 2016.

2. David Howes and Constance Classen, *Ways of Sensing: Understanding the Senses in Society* (London: Routledge, 2014), 66.

3. Ziad Fahmy, "Coming to Our Senses: Historicizing Sound and Noise in the Middle East," *History Compass* 11, no. 4 (2013): 311, https://doi.org/10.1111/hic3.12048.

4. The olfactory as a concept includes the act of smelling and smell-sources, together with their discursive, social, and spatial surrounds.

5. See Paul Rodaway, *Sensuous Geographies: Body, Sense and Place* (London: Routledge, 1994), 61–81.

6. The term "Rum" is derived from the Arabic word *al-rum*, meaning "Roman." It was used to denote the Christians under the Eastern Roman (or what came to be known as the Byzantine) Empire, and it later referenced an Ottoman millet. Today, "Rum" refers to the Arab-speaking Christians who follow the Rum Orthodox Patriarchate of Antioch and All the East. I choose not to use the alternative term, "Greek Orthodox," in order to avoid confusion and associations with Greek nationalist historiography.

7. One such organization is Harakat al-Shabiba al-Urthudhuksiyya, or Mouve-

ment de la Jeunesse Orthodoxe (MJO). Established in 1942, MJO is considered the result of a spiritual awakening in the Antiochian Orthodox Church. Spread across Syria and Lebanon, it has a community-based approach, organizing social and religious activities through and across parishes and dioceses in the two countries.

8. I use the term "laypersons" to mean members of a religious congregation who are not clergy.

9. Michel de Certeau, *The Practice of Everyday Life*, trans. Steven Rendall (Berkeley: University of California Press, 1988), 1–6.

10. See Mohamad Hafeda, *Negotiating Conflict in Lebanon: Bordering Practices in a Divided Beirut* (London and New York: I. B. Tauris, 2019), 211–57.

11. See Sami Hermez, *War Is Coming: Between Past and Future Violence in Lebanon* (Philadelphia: University of Pennsylvania Press, 2017); Joanne Randa Nucho, *Everyday Sectarianism in Urban Lebanon: Infrastructure, Public Services and Power* (Princeton, NJ: Princeton University Press, 2016).

12. Lara Deeb, *An Enchanted Modern: Gender and Public Piety in Shi'i Lebanon* (Princeton, NJ: Princeton University Press, 2006), 31.

13. Certeau, *The Practice of Everyday Life*, xix–xx. This approach finds inspiration in Certeau's notion of "tactics," which refers to the everyday operating modes of ordinary individuals. Their lived experiences imply creativity of movement in an urban geography, while underscoring the power of structural conditions of action.

14. Samir Kassir, *Beirut*, trans. M. B. DeBevoise (Berkeley: University of California Press, 2010), 441.

15. The English translation does not fully encompass the meaning of the Arabic term. While incense is restrictive to fumigatory practices, *bakhur* includes an array of material forms (soap, perfume, crystals) and a diversity of usages (burning, spraying, applying on skin).

16. See E. G. Cuthbert F. Atchley, *A History of the Use of Incense in Divine Worship* (London: Longmans, Green, 1909).

17. Glenn Bowman, introduction to *Sharing the Sacra: The Politics and Pragmatics of Intercommunal Relations around Holy Places*, ed. Glenn Bowman (New York: Berghahn Books, 2012), 1–9.

18. Anh Nga Longva, introduction to *Religious Minorities in the Middle East: Domination, Self-Empowerment, Accommodation*, ed. Anh Nga Longva and Anne Sofie Roald (Leiden, Netherlands: Brill, 2012), 1–23; Heather Sharkey, *A History of Muslims, Christians, and Jews in the Middle East* (Cambridge: Cambridge University Press, 2017), 1–10.

19. Tarek Mitri, "Christians in the Arab World: Minority Attitudes and Citizenship," *Ecumenical Review* 64, no. 1 (2012): 43–49, https://doi.org/10.1111/j.1758-6623.2012.00144.x.

20. Bassel F. Salloukh, "The Architecture of Sectarianization in Lebanon," in *Sectarianization: Mapping the New Politics of the Middle East*, ed. Nader Hashemi and Danny Postel (New York: Oxford University Press, 2017), 217.

21. Hiba Bou Akar, *For the War Yet to Come: Planning Beirut's Frontiers* (Stanford, CA: Stanford University Press, 2018), 24–34; Hermez, *War Is Coming*, 2–16.

22. See also Deeb, this volume.

23. See also Nucho, this volume; Judith Naeff, *Precarious Imaginaries of Beirut: A City's Suspended Now* (Cham, Switzerland: Palgrave Macmillan, 2018), 120–33.

24. Kelvin E. Y. Low, "Olfactive Frames of Remembering: Theorizing Self, Senses and Society," *Sociological Review*, 61, no. 4 (2013): 688–708, https://doi.org/10.1111/1467 -954X.12078.

25. David William Cohen, *The Combing of History* (Chicago: University of Chicago Press, 1994), 50–77.

26. "Abuna" is a title used to address a priest (*khuri*). It has a pastoral facet, and it literally translates as "our father." I use "Abuna" rather than "priest" or *khuri* because my respondents used it consistently, irrespective of the language they were speaking (Arabic, English, or French).

27. Abuna Nicola, interview with the author, Beirut, December 24, 2014.

28. Constance Classen, "The Odor of the Other: Olfactory Symbolism and Cultural Categories," *Ethos* 20, no. 2 (1992): 134, https://doi.org/10.1525/eth.1992.20.2.02a00010.

29. Bou Akar, *For the War Yet to Come*, 11–34.

30. Abuna Boulos Wehbe, interview with the author, Notre Dame University-Louaize, September 9, 2019.

31. Wehbe, interview.

32. Established in 1975, Harakat Amal, or the Amal Movement, is a major Shiʿi political party in Lebanon. It exercises political and sectarian control in the Mazraʿa sector of Beirut.

33. Wehbe, interview.

34. Hafeda, *Negotiating Conflict in Lebanon*, 71–90. Established in 2007 by former Prime Minister Saad Hariri, the Future Movement or Tayyar al-Mustaqbal is a political party with a mostly Sunni base. Hizbullah is a Shiʿi Islamic political party, officially established in 1985.

35. Roxana Maria Arāş, "Living in the Afterlife: Rum Christians of Mazraʿa" (unpublished manuscript, August 6, 2021).

36. Rita, conversation with the author, Beirut, June 20, 2018.

37. Dionigi Albera, "Combining Practices and Beliefs: Muslim Pilgrims at Marian Shrines," in *Sharing the Sacra*, 10–24.

38. This difference in titles does not necessarily imply a theological difference, as the virginity of Mary is not denied in Islamic exegetics.

39. Bruce Lincoln, "A Lakota Sun Dance and the Problematics of Sociocosmic Reunion," *History of Religions* 34, no. 1 (1994): 1, https://www.jstor.org/stable/1062976.

40. Webb Keane, "Anxious Transcendence," in *The Anthropology of Christianity*, ed. Fenella Cannell (Durham, NC: Duke University Press, 2006), 311.

41. Abuna Philip Said, "Introduction to the Liturgy" (class lecture in Arabic, Christian Education Department, Orthodox Archdiocese of Beirut, Ashrafiyya, Beirut, October 3, 2019).

42. Olivier Clément, *Corps de mort et de gloire: Petite introduction à une théopoétique du corps* (Paris: Desclée de Brouwer, 1995), 21–34; Peter Galadza, "Liturgy and Heaven in the Eastern Rites," *Antiphon: A Journal for Liturgical Renewal* 10, no. 3 (2006): 239–60, http://liturgysociety.org/journal/volume-10.

43. For a comprehensive historical perspective on the liturgical usage of incense in Eastern rites, see Atchley, *A History of the Use of Incense*, 269–82; E. Fehrenbach, "Encens," in *Dictionnaire d'archéologie Chrétienne et de liturgie*, ed. Henri Leclercq and Fernand Cabrol, vol. 5 (Paris: Letouzey et Ané, 1922), 2–21.

44. Said, "Introduction to the Liturgy" (class lecture in Arabic, October 10, 2019).

45. Saint Seraphim of Sarov, "On the Acquisition of the Holy Spirit", in *Little Russian Philokalia*, ed. and trans. Seraphim Rose, vol. 1 (Ouzinkie, AK: New Valaam Monastery, 1991), 109–14.

46. Saint John Chrysostom, "Homilies on the Gospel of Saint Matthew," 88, quoted in Atchley, *A History of the Use of Incense*, 200.

47. Abuna Porphyrios, interview with the author, Saint John of Damascus Institute of Theology, University of Balamand, June 13, 2016.

48. Constance Classen, David Howes, and Anthony Synnott, *Aroma: The Cultural History of Smell* (London and New York: Routledge, 1994), 140.

49. Clifford Geertz, *The Interpretation of Cultures: Selected Essays* (New York: Basic Books, 1973), 5.

50. On failure of rituals, see Matthew Engelke and Matt Tomlinson, eds., *The Limits of Meaning: Case Studies in the Anthropology of Christianity* (New York: Berghahn Books, 2006), 1–37.

51. Robert A. Orsi, "Everyday Religion and the Contemporary World: The Un-Modern, or What Was Supposed to Have Disappeared But Did Not," in *Ordinary Lives and Grand Schemes: An Anthropology of Everyday Religion*, ed. Samuli Schielke and Liza Debevec (New York: Berghahn Books, 2012), 150.

52. Low, "Olfactive Frames of Remembering," 694–98.

53. Nada, interview with the author, Beirut, December 23, 2014.

54. Nada, interview.

55. Said, "Introduction to the Liturgy" (class lecture in Arabic, October 3, 2019); John D. Zizioulas, *The Eucharistic Communion and the World*, ed. Luke Ben Tallon (London: T&T Clark, 2011), 12–24.

56. Daniel Corstange, "Religion, Pluralism, and Iconography in the Public Sphere: Theory and Evidence from Lebanon," *World Politics* 64, no. 1 (2012): 116–60, https://doi:10.1017/S0043887111000268.

57. See Alexander Schmemann, *For the Life of the World: Sacraments and Orthodoxy* (Crestwood, NY: St. Vladimir's Seminary Press, 1973).

58. Classen, "The Odor of the Other," 133–66; Classen, Howes, and Synnott, *Aroma*, 140.

59. Margaret E. Kenna, "Why Does Incense Smell Religious? Greek Orthodoxy and the Anthropology of Smell," *Journal of Mediterranean Studies* 15, no. 1 (2005): 57, https://www.muse.jhu.edu/article/677389.

60. Said, "Introduction to the Liturgy" (class lecture in Arabic, October 10, 2019).

61. Nadia Seremetakis, *The Senses Still: Historical Perception, Commensal Exchange and Modernity* (Boulder, CO: Westview Press, 1994), 6.

62. David Howes, introduction to *Empire of the Senses: The Sensual Culture Reader*, ed. David Howes (Oxford, UK: Berg Publishers, 2005), 10–11.

Chapter 6

1. This use of the term "intrasectarian" builds upon Ussama Makidisi's work in *The Culture of Sectarianism: Community, History, and Violence in Nineteenth-Century Ottoman Lebanon* (Los Angeles: University of California Press, 2000). He contends that the violence of 1860 took place not only between Maronite and Druze communities but also within them, all "in an attempt to define their own respective boundaries in an era of upheaval." Makdisi, *The Culture of Sectarianism*, 3. While Makdisi is "most interested in . . . the struggle over communal representation that was reflected in episodes of intracommunal social violence that constituted a fundamental part of broader religious violence *across* sectarian communities" (my emphasis), this story remains focused on how an intrasectarian Armenian conflict demonstrated new markers of political identity, namely affiliation to organized religion, or support of a particular church see. This meaning of religion was new, and would be replicated in different Armenian communities worldwide: namely in Istanbul in 1944–50, Jerusalem in 1956, and Beirut in 1956–57. See Talin Suciyan, *The Armenians in Modern Turkey Post-Genocide Society, Politics and History* (London: I. B. Tauris, 2016), 169–97; Ara Sanjian, "The Armenian Church and Community of Jerusalem," in *The Christian Communities of Jerusalem and the Holy Land: Studies in History, Religion, and Politics*, ed. Anthony O'Mahony (Cardiff: University of Wales Press, 2003), 71–84; Bedross Der Matossian, "The Armenians of Jerusalem in the Modern Period: The Rise and Decline of a Community," in *Routledge Handbook on Jerusalem*, ed. Suleiman A. Mourad, Naomi Koltun-Fromm, and Bedross Der Matossian (New York: Routledge, 2019), 400–402. Rather than looking at how Armenian institutions operated transnationally and linking this movement to their diasporic status, however, this story also suggests that it is sectarianism that traverses boundaries settled by Armenians, thus also reframing them as the local component.

2. The Armenian Church has two functioning Armenian Orthodox sees—one located in Lebanon, the other in Armenia—which trace their origins back to the Apostolic age of Saints Thaddeus and Bartholomew. Generally, neither church claimed jurisdiction over the other's congregations, each maintaining its own autonomy. Historically, the Armenian Church in Lebanon (also known as the Catholicosate of Cilicia or the Cilician See) was located in Sis (present day Kozan, in Turkey), which was the seat of the Armenian Church during the Armenian Kingdom of Cilicia (1198–1375). It remained in Sis until the genocide of Armenians under the Ottoman Empire during World War I. By 1936 the see had settled in Antelias, a northern suburb of Beirut, where it remains today. The other Armenian see, the Catholicosate of Echmiadzin (or the Echmiadzin See), was located in the village of Echmiadzin. In 1920, Echmiadzin became incorporated in the ASSR (which since 1991 is now the independent republic of Armenia). The first Armenian Church was established in the United States in 1890 in Worcester, Massachussetts, and was under the jurisdiction of the Istanbul Patriarchate. By 1898, it, along with all other Armenian Apostolic churches in the United States, was transferred to the jurisdiction of the Echmiadzin See. Oshagan Minassian, *A History of the Armenian Holy Apostolic Church in the United States* (New York: Mayreni Publishing, 2010), 65.

3. While some Armenians had migrated from Greater Syria, the vast majority at this time hailed from Anatolia. In addition, unlike many migrants who came from Mount Lebanon to the United States who were more reluctant to naturalize, this was not the case for Armenians from the Anatolian provinces. After 1897, Armenians were strictly forbidden from returning to the Ottoman Empire regardless of citizenship. In addition, the citizenship law in the United States until 1922 mandated that a wife's citizenship match that of her husband, allowing for Armenian migrants to extend their status to their wives and children and seek assistance of American diplomats back in the Ottoman Empire. For more on the politics of Armenian migration to North America, see David E. Gutman, *The Politics of Armenian Migration to North America 1885–1915: Migrants, Smugglers and Dubious Citizens* (Edinburgh: Edinburgh University Press, 2019). See also Anny Bakalian, *Armenian-Americans: From Being to Feeling Armenian* (New York: Transaction Publishers, 1993).

4. For more on the history of the Hnchak, Dashnak, and Ramgavar parties, see Razmik Panossian, *The Armenians from Kings and Priests to Merchants and Commissars* (New York: Columbia University Press, 2006), 200–227.

5. One does not have to begin with the death of Tourian to see how these actors engaged with one another in a bid for power. Nevertheless, I argue that sectarianism *traveled* with the death of Tourian. In one way this is particularly ironic, as it was Tourian's traversing of the United States while uncompromisingly supportive of Soviet Armenia in his capacity as prelate of the Armenian Church that generated and maintained controversy among many Armenians in the United States. While it may come as no surprise that his death transformed him into a martyr for those opponents of the Dashnak party, and that it legitimized claims against their supporters, it is how the entire incident created a new way of practicing sectarianism in the United States that interests me here.

6. Tsolin Nalbantian, "Going beyond Overlooked Populations in Lebanese Historiography: The Armenian Case," *History Compass* 11, no. 10 (2013): 821–32.

7. My emphasis. Makdisi, *The Culture of Sectarianism*, 3.

8. For example, Max Weiss, *In the Shadow of Sectarianism: Law Shi'ism and the Making of Modern Lebanon* (Cambridge, MA: Harvard University Press, 2010); Tamara Chalabi, *The Shi'is of Jabal 'Amil and the New Lebanon: Community and Nation-State, 1918–1943* (London: Palgrave, 2006), 60–62.

9. Fawwaz Traboulsi, *The History of Modern Lebanon* (London: Pluto Press, 2006), 109.

10. How this cleavage was maintained by various local and transnational Armenian actors and institutions, and the exploration of how this led to the bifurcation of the Armenian Apostolic sect, are topics of ongoing work by the author.

11. In this volume, Linda Sayed examines how members of the same *madhhab*, while citizens of different nation-states, used the sectarian institution of the Ja'fari courts *in* Lebanon to impact their daily lives there or in Iraq, Syria, and other countries. In that case, the *madhhab* is the transnational actor. In this chapter, sectarianism is the transnational actor instead.

12. In addition to "age-old," Ussama Makdisi notes the Ottoman officials' and European colonial and missionary uses of the terms "primordial passions," "ancient custom," and "a very old thing," in *The Culture of Sectarianism*, 5, 78, 67, and 146–65. Interestingly, the American press replicated this very terminology, and in so doing reinforced similar representations.

13. Diaspora Studies has challenged the nation-state as the normative frame in which to understand transnational populations, including Armenians. At the same time, due to their "classical" status, there is a tendency to forever cite Armenians as diasporic "reference." In recent years there have been innovative contributions to diaspora studies, especially by those adhering to Rogers Brubaker's call to consider diasporic stances, projects, claims, idioms, and practices, rather than a bounded analytical category. "The 'Diaspora' Diaspora," *Ethnic and Racial Studies* 28, no. 1 (January 2005): 13. See, for example, Sylvia Alajaji, *Music and the Armenian Diaspora: Searching for Home in Exile* (Bloomington: Indiana University Press, 2015); Der Matossian, "The Armenian of Jerusalem," 396–407; Sossie Kasbarian, "Between Nationalist Absorption and Subsumption: Reflecting on the Armenian Cypriot Experience," in *Cypriot Nationalisms in Context*, ed. Thekla Kyritsi and Nikos Christofis (Cham, Switzerland: Palgrave Macmillan, 2018), 177–98; and Khachig Tölöyan, "Elites and Institutions in the Armenian Transnation," *Diaspora: A Journal of Transnational Studies* 9, no. 1 (2000): 107–36. Still, there continues to be a propensity to understand Armenians through the lens of a diaspora. See, for example, Ulf Björklund, "Armenia Remembered and Remade: Evolving Issues in a Diaspora," *Ethnos* 58, no. 3-4 (1993): 335–60.

14. Perhaps a corollary to continued dependence upon the frame of diaspora studies, many scholarly works depend on comprehensive histories of Armenians that link them to a single (if imagined) homeland in an effort to demonstrate the linear development of the Armenian national subject. This inclination divorces them from local surroundings and prevents their inclusion in local historiographies. See, for example, George Bournoutian, *A History of the Armenian People, Vol. 1: Pre-History to 1500 AD* (Costa Mesa, CA: Mazda, 1993); Richard Hovannisian, *The Armenian People from Ancient to Modern Times, Volume I: The Dynastic Periods: From Antiquity to the Fourteenth Century; Volume II: From Dominion to Statehood: The Fifteenth Century to the Twentieth* (London: Macmillan, 1997); and Simon Payaslian, *History of the Armenian People* (Costa Mesa, CA: Mazda, 2002). The focus on the migratory movement of Armenians from Eastern Anatolia to the United States prior to World War I, David E. Gutman's *The Politics of Armenian Migration*, refreshingly situates the United States as a site of Armenian migration, and not one of the Armenian Diaspora. And while my own work on Armenians in Lebanon also challenges these linear, "comprehensive" histories, its aim was not to insert an Armenian story within a national Lebanese one, but rather, in demonstrating how Armenians created a center in Beirut, to also question overall conceptions about Lebanon. Tsolin Nalbantian, *Armenian beyond Diaspora: Making Lebanon Their Own* (Edinburgh: Edinburgh University Press, 2020). Similarly, my aim here is to challenge overall conceptions of the local and sec-

tarianism by noting how Armenians used sectarianism in struggles for power in the United States.

15. Works on Tourian's murder have overwhelmingly been limited to viewing the violence as an internal Armenian issue. See, for example, Sarkis Atamian and James H. Tashjian, *The Armenian Community: The Historical Development of a Social and Ideological Conflict* (New York: Philosophical Library, 1955), and Oshagan Minassian, *A History of the Armenian Holy Apostolic Orthodox Church in the United States (1888–1944)* (Monterey, CA: Mayreni, 2010).

16. Rather than being viewed as one location of a greater Armenian or Lebanese diaspora, therefore, the United States becomes one site of a sectarian diaspora. While most Armenian-Americans during this period had "originally" migrated from the Ottoman Empire, they had done so *not* from Lebanon, but from areas that had become the Republic of Turkey. Armenians in America created a new relationship between Lebanon and the United States, fashioning themselves as the metropole, and decisively *not* as the *mahjar* counterpart of Lebanon's *mashriq*. They did so to demonstrate their power not within a Lebanese nation but through an intrasectarian conflict, and claimed belonging in the United States vis-à-vis both Americans and Armenians. In addition, this intrasectarian conflict challenged the transnational authority of the Armenian Church located in the ASSR.

17. "Archbishop Assassinated in Procession to Altar; Laid to Old-World Feud," *New York Times*, December 25, 1933, 1.

18. "Nine Found Guilty in Church Murder: Two Convicted of Murder and Seven of Manslaughter in Armenian Prelate's Death," *New York Times*, July 14, 1934, 1.

19. "Nine Found Guilty in Church Murder," 1.

20. For more on the immediate aftermath of the murder on individual Armenian communities in the United States and attempts to broker peace, see Oshagan Minassian, "A History of the Armenian Holy Apostolic Church in the United States (1888–1944)," (PhD dissertation, Boston University, 1974), 512–78.

21. Newspapers began covering Archbishop Tourian as early as June 1, 1931, when he first arrived in the United States. "To Direct Armenian Church in US," *Boston Globe*, June 1, 1931, 4. But it is important to note that American newspapers followed the activities of Christian confessions on the front pages of their papers. For example, the *Brooklyn Citizen* on April 5, 1931, ran a United Press International article on the possibility of a union between the Anglican and Greek Orthodox churches. Coincidentally, that article also mentioned the Lambeth Conference of 1930, which called on worldwide Christian denominations to unite, and where Archbishop Tourian was the representative of the Eastern Churches. "Union of Anglican and Greek Churches Believed a Certainty," *Brooklyn Citizen*, April 5, 1931, 2.

22. "Armenian Church Ruler Will Visit Here Wednesday," *Kenosha Evening News*, December 8, 1931, 4.

23. "Armenian Church Ruler Will Visit Here Wednesday," 4.

24. "Armenian Church Ruler Will Visit Here Wednesday," 4.

25. "Bishop Tourian Will Sing Mass Here on Sunday," *Binghamton Press and Sun-Bulletin* (Binghamton, NY), November 14, 1931, 5.

26. "To Become Better Citizens," *Honolulu Advertiser*, January 4, 1932, 7.

27. "Radio Programs," *Brooklyn Times Union*, July 1, 1933, 8; "Radio Programs," *Daily Times* (Davenport, IA), July 1, 1933, 3; "Radio Programs," *Lancaster New Era* (Lancaster, PA), July 1, 1933, 17; *Daily Journal* (Vineland, NJ), July 1, 1933, 6; "Radio Programs," *Wisconsin State Journal* (Madison, WI), July 1, 1933, 6.

28. "Radio Programs," *Brooklyn Times Union*, July 1, 1933, 8.

29. "Soviets Blamed as Armenians Battle at Fair" *Daily News* (New York), July 2, 1933, 26.

30. "Soviets Blamed," 6.

31. "Soviets Blamed," 6.

32. "Riot Breaks Out at Fair," *Quad-City Times* (Davenport, IA), July 2, 1933, 2.

33. "Riot Breaks Out at Fair," 2.

34. "Riot Breaks Out at Fair," 2. The Associated Press version was also published in the *Fort Worth Star-Telegram*, July 2, 1933, 3, under the headline "Effort to Unfurl Flag Causes Riot."

35. "Riot Breaks Out at Fair," 2.

36. "New Arrests Likely after Outing 'Riot,'" *Boston Globe*, August 15, 1933, 15.

37. "New Arrests Likely," 15.

38. "New Arrests Likely," 15.

39. "New Arrests Likely," 15.

40. "New Arrests Likely," 15.

41. "New Arrests Likely," 15.

42. "Grape Crop Ritual Held Day Late," *Hartford Courant*, August 29, 1933, 12.

43. "Grape Crop Ritual," 12.

44. "Grape Crop Ritual," 12.

45. "Grape Crop Ritual," 12.

46. "Grape Crop Ritual," 12.

47. "Armenian Pastor Reinstated," *Hartford Courant*, September 5, 1933, 13.

48. "Armenian Pastor Reinstated," 13.

49. "Armenian Pastor Reinstated," 13.

50. "Armenian Pastor Reinstated," 13.

51. "Armenian Pastor Reinstated," 13.

52. "Armenian Pastor Reinstated," 13.

53. "Armenian Church Prelate Ousted at Stormy Convention" *Brooklyn Daily Eagle*, September 4, 1933, 13.

54. The court action sought to recover a suitcase containing two silk covers, two linen covers, seven songbooks, an Armenian Episcopal church seal, twenty robes, and a communion cap, all valued at two hundred dollars. This was clearly not solely a monetary issue, however. "Church Fight Gets to Court," *Kenosha Evening News*, December 21, 1933, 7.

55. "Church Fight," 7.

56. "Church Fight," 7.

57. "Church Fight," 7.

58. "Church Fight," 7.

59. Hagopian was represented by attorney Leo Vaudreuil, while Julius Goldstein was counsel for Bedroosian. "Church Fight," 7.

60. While murder is inherently a sensational act, the newspapers' depiction of the act and subsequent coverage of the trial highlighted gore and melee. See, for example, "Assassins Kill Head of Armenian Church," *Daily News*, December 25, 1933, 3; and "Slain 187th Street Church," *New York Times*, December 25, 1933, 1.

61. "Assassins Kill Head of Armenian Church," 3.

62. "Assassins Kill Head of Armenian Church," 3.

63. "Assassin Stabs Bishop in Aisle of High Church." *Chattanooga Daily Times*, December 25, 1933.

64. "Assassin Stabs Bishop."

65. "Assassin Stabs Bishop."

66. "Assassin Stabs Bishop."

67. "25 Assassins Plotted Death of Archbishop," *Daily News*, December 27, 1933, 8.

68. "25 Assassins Plotted Death," 8; "4 Thugs Kill Church Head at Services," *Daily News*, December 25, 1933, 4.

69. "Eight Plead in Tourian Slaying," *New York Times*, January 25, 1934, 9.

70. "Tourian Suspects Saved from Mob," *New York Times*, January 11, 1934, 42.

71. "Tourian Suspects Saved from Mob," 42.

72. "Tourian Suspects Saved from Mob," 42.

73. "Tourian Suspects Saved from Mob," 42.

74. "Slain Archbishop Mourned by 3,000," *New York Times*, January 29, 1934, 9.

75. "Slain Archbishop Mourned," 9.

76. "Slain Archbishop Mourned," 9.

77. "Five Hurt in Clash of Armenians Here," *New York Times*, February 26, 1934, 38.

78. "Five Hurt in Clash," 38.

79. "Five Hurt in Clash," 38.

80. "Five Hurt in Clash," 38.

81. "Five Hurt in Clash," 38.

82. "2 Tourian Slayers Condemned to Die," *New York Times*, July 25, 1934, 36. It should be noted that seventy-two hours before their scheduled execution, New York Governor Herbert H. Lehman commuted their sentences to life imprisonment. Lehman did this because of what he claimed to be the "most unusual circumstances of this case," most notably the prosecution's theory that all the defendants were engaged in a prearranged plan or conspiracy to kill the archbishop. "Lehman Spares Lives of Tourian's Slayers," *New York Times*, April 10, 1935, 12.

83. "2 Tourian Slayers," 36.

84. "2 Tourian Slayers," 36.

85. "2 Tourian Slayers," 36.

86. "2 Tourian Slayers," 36.

87. Ussama Makdisi, "Corrupting the Sublime Sultanate: The Revolt of Tanyus Shahin in Nineteenth-Century Ottoman Lebanon," *Comparative Studies in Society and History* 42, no. 1 (2000): 187.

88. "2 Tourian Slayers," 36.

89. "Armenians Gather in Church Assembly," *New York Times*, October 7, 1934, 35.

90. "Armenians Gather in Church Assembly," 35.

91. Makdisi, "Corrupting the Sublime Sultanate," 146–47.

92. For more on the election of Catholicos Zareh and the tension that surrounded it, see Nalbantian, *Armenians beyond Diaspora*, 126–66.

93. "Armenian Bishop Greeted by 600 Here," *Boston Globe*, October 18, 1957, 10. The first church consecrated by the Armenian Church in Lebanon was in Watertown, Massachusetts, a suburb of Boston. "Lebanon Archbishop Dedicates Armenian Church in Watertown," *Boston Globe*, October 21, 1957, 13.

94. "Lkʻuats Ēin Tēr Unetsʻan," *Aztag* (Beirut), October 18, 1957, 1.

95. "Bishop Guest of Armenians," *The Record* (Hackensack, NJ), November 16, 1957, 4. "Armenian Church Head Visits City," *Detroit Free Press*, November 7, 1957, 16.

96. "Armenian Archbishop to Visit New Britain," *Hartford Courant*, December 1, 1957, 20.

97. The Cold War was a factor, especially given the existence of the ASSR; but differences over Armenian nationalist ambitions (including debates over the ASSR) fundamentally drove these conflicts. Armenians used the Cold War to hash out their own internal Armenian struggles, in effect domesticating the global Cold War.

98. "Armenian Church Cuts Russian Link," *New York Times*, October 17, 1957, 55.

99. "Armenian Church Cuts Russian Link," 55.

100. "Armenian Church Cuts Russian Link," 55.

101. "Armenian Cleric Assails Prelate," *New York Times*, October 20, 1957, 78.

102. "Armenian Cleric Assails Prelate," 78.

103. "Armenian Cleric Assails Prelate," 78.

104. "Archbishop Paroyan Visits DC," *Washington Post and Times Herald*, October 29, 1957, 7.

105. "Bishop Guest of Armenians," *The Record*, November 16, 1957, 4.

106. "Khoren Srbazan Yrkushabtʻi Piti Endunui Amerikayi Pʻokh Nakhagahin Koghme," *Aztag*, October 27, 1957, 1.

Chapter 7

1. For more on the Armenian genocide, see Ronald Grigor Suny, *"They Can Live in the Desert but Nowhere Else": A History of the Armenian Genocide*. (Princeton, NJ: Princeton University Press, 2015).

2. Suad Joseph, "The Politicization of Religious Sects in Borj Hammoud, Lebanon." (PhD dissertation, Columbia University, 1975).

3. Julia Elyachar, "Phatic Labor, Infrastructure, and the Question of Empowerment in Cairo," *American Ethnologist* 37, no. 3 (August 2010): 452–64.

4. Sherene Seikaly, "The Matter of Time," *American Historical Review* 124, no. 5 (December 2019): 1681–88.

5. Sally Falk Moore, "Explaining the Present: Theoretical Dilemmas in Processual Ethnography." *American Ethnologist* 14, no. 4 (November 1987): 727–36.

6. Suad Joseph, "Working-Class Women's Networks in a Sectarian State: A Political Paradox." *American Ethnologist* 10, no. 1 (February 1983): 1–22.

7. Kathi Weeks, *Constituting Feminist Subjects* (London: Verso, 2018 [1998]), 153.

8. Julia Elyachar, *Markets of Dispossession: NGOs, Economic Development, and the State in Cairo* (Durham, NC: Duke University Press, 2005).

9. Hiba Bou Akar, *For the War Yet to Come: Planning Beirut's Frontiers* (Stanford, CA: Stanford University Press, 2018).

10. No official census has been conducted in Lebanon since 1932, so it is difficult to estimate the number of Armenians in Lebanon today. I have heard and read different figures from studies done by charities and NGOs, ranging anywhere from 100,000 to 150,000.

11. Suad Joseph, "Pensée 2: Sectarianism as Imagined Sociological Concept and as Imagined Social Formation." *International Journal of Middle East Studies*, 40, no. 4 (November 2008): 553–54.

12. Lara Deeb, *An Enchanted Modern: Gender and Public Piety in Shi'i Lebanon* (Princeton, NJ: Princeton University Press, 2006).

13. Max Weiss, *In the Shadow of Sectarianism: Law, Shi'ism, and the Making of Modern Lebanon* (Cambridge, MA: Harvard University Press, 2010).

14. Ussama Makdisi, *The Culture of Sectarianism: Community, History, and Violence in Nineteenth-Century Ottoman Lebanon* (Berkeley: University of California Press, 2000)

15. Tsolin Nalbantian, "Going beyond Overlooked Populations in Lebanese Historiography: The Armenian Case." *History Compass* 11, no. 10 (October 2013): 821–32.

16. Stuart Hall, "Reflections on 'Race, Articulation and Societies Structured in Dominance,'" in *Race Critical Theories: Text and Context*, ed. Philomena Essed and David Theo Goldberg (Malden, MA: Blackwell, 2002): 38–86.

17. Joanne Randa Nucho, *Everyday Sectarianism in Urban Lebanon: Infrastructures, Public Services, and Power* (Princeton, NJ: Princeton University Press: 2016).

18. Raymond Williams, *Marxism and Literature* (Oxford, UK: Oxford University Press, 1977).

19. Kathi Weeks, *Constituting Feminist Subjects* (London: Verso, 2018 [1998]).

20. Weeks, *Constituting Feminist Subjects*, 5.

21. Weeks, *Constituting Feminist Subjects*, 7.

22. Weeks, *Constituting Feminist Subjects*, 14.

23. Julia Elyachar, *Markets of Dispossession: NGOs, Economic Development, and the State in Cairo* (Durham, NC: Duke University Press, 2005).

24. Suad Joseph, "The Politicization of Religious Sects in Borj Hammoud, Lebanon." (PhD dissertation, Columbia University, 1975).

25. Julia Elyachar, "Next Practices: Knowledge, Infrastructure, and Public Goods at the Bottom of the Pyramid." *Public Culture* 24, vol. 24, no. 1 (January 1, 2012): 109.

26. Fawwaz Traboulsi, *A History of Modern Lebanon*, 2nd ed. (London: Pluto Press, 2012), viii.

27. Roxana Maria Arăş, this volume; Bou Akar, *For the War Yet to Come*; Sami Hermez, *War Is Coming: Between Past and Future Violence in Lebanon* (Philadelphia:

University of Pennsylvania Press, 2017); Joanne Randa Nucho, *Everyday Sectarianism in Urban Lebanon: Infrastructures, Public Services, and Power* (Princeton, NJ: Princeton University Press, 2016).

28. Keith David Watenpaugh, "Towards a New Category of Colonial Theory: Colonial Cooperation and the Survivors Bargain; The Case of the Post-Genocide Armenian Community in Syria," in *The British and French Mandates in Comparative Perspective*, ed. Nadine Meouchy and Peter Sluglett (Leiden, Netherlands: Brill, 2004), 619.

29. Watenpaugh, "Towards a New Category of Colonial Theory," 619.

30. Nicola Migliorino, *(Re)Constructing Armenia in Lebanon and Syria* (New York: Berghahn Books, 2008).

31. Nalbantian, "Going beyond Overlooked Populations," 821–32.

32. Keith David Watenpaugh, "Being Middle Class and Being Arab: Sectarian Dilemmas and Middle-Class Modernity in the Arab Middle East, 1908–1936," in *The Making of the Middle Class: Toward a Transnational History*, ed. A. Ricardo López and Barbara Weinstein (Durham, NC: Duke University Press, 2012).

33. Watenpaugh, "Being Middle Class and Being Arab," 274.

34. Tsolin Nalbantian, *Armenians beyond Diaspora: Making Lebanon Their Own* (Edinburgh: Edinburgh University Press, 2020).

35. Lara Deeb and Mona Harb, *Leisurely Islam: Negotiating Geography and Morality in Shiʿite South Beirut* (Princeton, NJ: Princeton University Press, 2013).

36. Joseph, "Working-Class Women's Networks," 1–22. For an important discussion on right-wing Christian political ideology, specifically through a psychoanalytic approach to nationalist and communitarian discourses within the Maronite Christian right, see Ghassan Hage. "Nationalist Anxiety or the Fear of Losing Your Other," *Australian Journal of Anthropology* 7, no. 2 (August 1996): 121–40.

37. Since then, it has been completely demolished.

38. Farha Ghannam, *Remaking the Modern: Space, Relocation, and the Politics of Identity in a Global Cairo* (Berkeley: University of California Press, 2002).

39. Julia Elyachar, "Phatic Labor, Infrastructure, and the Question of Empowerment in Cairo," *American Ethnologist* 37, no. 3. (August 2010): 452–64; Paul Kockelman, "Enemies, Parasites, and Noise: How to Take Up Residence in a System." *Journal of Linguistic Anthropology* 20, no. 2 (November 2010): 406–21.

40. Bou Akar, *For the War Yet to Come.*

41. The plural for *agoomp* is *agoompner*, but I add an *s* here to simplify the plural for the reader unfamiliar with Western Armenian.

42. "Tamar" is a pseudonym.

43. Melani Claire Cammett, *Compassionate Communalism: Welfare and Sectarianism in Lebanon* (Ithaca, NY: Cornell University Press, 2014).

44. Suad Joseph, "The Politicization of Religious Sects in Borj Hammoud, Lebanon." (PhD dissertation, Columbia University, 1975).

45. Mona Fawaz, "Beirut Madinati and the Prospects of Urban Citizenship," Century Foundation. April 16, 2019, https://tcf.org/content/report/beirut-madinati-prospects-urban-citizenship/.

Chapter 8

My gratitude to Joanne Nucho and my co-editors for their comments, to the Ruth Landes Memorial Fund and the Wenner-Gren Foundation for funding the field research, and to the American Council of Learned Societies and the Scripps College Sabbatical Fellowship for funding the writing.

1. Iliya Harik, *Politics and Change in a Traditional Society, Lebanon 1711–1845* (Princeton, NJ: Princeton University Press, 1968); Suad Joseph, "The Politicization of Religious Sects in Borj Hammoud, Lebanon" (PhD dissertation, Columbia University, 1975); Ahmad Beydoun, *Al-Jumhuriyya al-Mutaqati'a: Masa'ir al-Sigha al-Lubnaniyya ba'd Itifaq al-Ta'if* (Beirut: Dar An-Nahar, 1999); Ussama Makdisi, *The Culture of Sectarianism Community, History, and Violence in Nineteenth-Century Ottoman Lebanon* (Berkeley: University of California Press, 2000); Fawwaz Traboulsi, *A History of Modern Lebanon* (London, Pluto Press, 2007); Max Weiss, *The Shadow of Sectarianism: Law, Shi'ism, and the Making of Modern Lebanon* (Cambridge, MA: Harvard University Press, 2010); Karen Kern, *Imperial Citizen: Marriage and Citizenship in the Ottoman Frontier Provinces of Iraq* (Syracuse, NY: Syracuse University Press, 2011); Suad Joseph, ed. *Gender and Citizenship in the Middle East* (Syracuse, NY: Syracuse University Press, 2000); Paul Kingston, *Reproducing Sectarianism: Advocacy Networks and the Politics of Civil Society in Postwar Lebanon* (Albany: SUNY Press, 2013); Melani Cammett, *Compassionate Communalism: Welfare and Sectarianism in Lebanon* (Ithaca, NY: Cornell University Press, 2014); Bassel Salloukh et al., *The Politics of Sectarianism in Postwar Lebanon* (London: Pluto Press, 2015); Kristin Monroe, *The Insecure City: Space, Power, and Mobility in Beirut* (New Brunswick, NJ: Rutgers University Press, 2016).

2. Lara Deeb and Mona Harb, *Leisurely Islam: Negotiating Geography and Morality in South Beirut* (Princeton, NJ: Princeton University Press, 2013); Joanne Nucho, *Everyday Sectarianism in Urban Lebanon: Infrastructures, Public Services, and Power* (Princeton, NJ: Princeton University Press, 2016); Hiba Bou Akar, *For the War Yet to Come: Planning Beirut's Frontiers* (Stanford, CA: Stanford University Press, 2018).

3. I have interviewed more than two hundred people in mixed marriages, and some of their extended family members. The interviewees come from all major sects and class backgrounds, from every region in Lebanon, and from multiple generations. Their dates of marriage range from 1957 to 2018. I have also followed the experiences of multiple couples since 1999.

4. Suad Joseph, "Pensée 2: Sectarianism as Imagined Sociological Concept and as Imagined Social Formation," *International Journal of Middle East Studies* 40 (2008): 553–54.

5. Maria A. Kastrinou, *Power, Sect and State in Syria: The Politics of Marriage and Identity amongst the Druze* (London, I. B. Tauris, 2016), 231.

6. See especially Michelle Alexander, *The New Jim Crow: Mass Incarceration in the Age of Colorblindness* (New York: The New Press, 2010). My use of this analogy poses the question of the extent to which we can understand sectarianism as racism. My view is that we can, to the extent that people are attributing essentialized qualities to

people of other sects; because when they do so, they are racializing that form of social difference. This does not mean that discrimination works the same way in Lebanon as it does in the United States. And I am certainly not suggesting that there is any easy comparison between racism in the United States, with its history of enslavement and structural racism, and sectarian discrimination in Lebanon.

7. See, for example, the work of Faye V. Harrison, including "The Persistent Power of 'Race' in the Cultural and Political Economy of Racism," *Annual Review of Anthropology* 24 (1995): 47–74.

8. http://lcps-lebanon.org/featuredArticle.php?id=267.

9. Many of my interviewees described parents who readily accepted intermarriage as "open-minded" (*munfatih*). For an overview of marriage ideals in Beirut, see Barbara Drieskens, "Changing Perceptions of Marriage in Beirut," in *Les métamorphoses du mariage au Moyen-Orient* (Beirut: Presses de l'Ifpo, 2008). On religious endogamy and interreligious marriage, see Anne Françoise Weber, "Briser et suivre les normes: Les couples islamochrétiens au Liban," in *Les métamorphoses du mariage au Moyen-Orient* (Beirut: Presses de l'Ifpo, 2008). On the normativity of sectarian endogamy, see Sabiha Allouche, "Queering (Inter-Sectarian) Heterosexual Love in Lebanon," *International Journal of Middle East Studies* 51, no. 4 (2019): 547–65.

10. There are no good statistics on interreligious marriage in Lebanon. It seems more common in Lebanon than elsewhere in the Middle East, and it is increasing, though it is not a recent phenomenon. One way university structures have mattered is via the continued fragmentation of the public Lebanese University into multiple campuses during the civil war, which reduced opportunities for nonelite Lebanese to meet potential marriage partners.

11. Drieskens, "Changing Perceptions," 7. See also Weber, "Briser et suivre."

12. When women approach the age of thirty, parental opposition often begins to evaporate, betraying the relative strength of pronatalism and social pressures around unmarried daughters over those of endogamy. Drieskens suggests that women's inability to find the right spouses may be driving the increase in the average age of marriage for Lebanese women, from 24.1 in 1970 to (depending on the source) 28.8 or 30.1 in this century. Drieskens, "Changing Perceptions." While most unmarried Lebanese live with their parents, the financial ability to live independently shapes responses to spousal selection.

13. Drieskens, "Changing Perceptions;" Weber, "Briser et suivre." Nationality also factors into desirability. Intermarriage with non-Lebanese introduces new desires and discriminations—including, depending on the nationality in question, xenophobia, white/European supremacy, class, political histories, and racist hierarchies of civilization.

14. See Lara Deeb, "Beyond Sectarianism: Intermarriage and Social Difference in Lebanon," *International Journal of Middle East Studies* 52, no. 2 (2020): 215–28.

15. Ghassan Hage, *Is Racism an Environmental Threat?* (Cambridge, UK: Polity Press, 2017).

16. Hage, *Is Racism an Environmental Threat?* 98.

17. Deeb, "Beyond Sectarianism." See also Deeb and Harb, *Leisurely Islam*, on the "sect/class nexus"; Rima Majed, "The Political (or Social) Economy of Sectarianism in Lebanon," http://www.mei.edu/content/map/political-or-social-economy-sectarianism-lebanon; and Nucho, this volume.

18. This is akin to what is called the "mere exposure effect" or "familiarity principle" in psychology, in which initial exposure to something unfamiliar causes fear, and then with increased exposure and growing familiarity, positive responses develop. But exposure is not enough; and the context, prior ideas about different social groups, and the question of whether other forms of common ground can be established all play a vital role.

19. Lara Deeb, *An Enchanted Modern: Gender and Public Piety in Shi'i Lebanon* (Princeton, NJ: Princeton University Press, 2006).

20. https://youtu.be/ZJnZOlOHxFw.

21. Bou Akar, *For the War Yet to Come*. Anja Peleikis also shows how sect came to matter in new ways that linked it to class and neighborhood in a Lebanese village as a result of the civil war. Anja Peleikis, "Shifting Identities, Reconstructing Boundaries: The Case of a Multi-Confessional Locality in Post-War Lebanon," *Die Welt des Islams* 41 (2001): 400–429.

22. Bou Akar, *For the War Yet to Come*.

23. Wendy Cheng, *The Changs Next Door to the Diazes: Remapping Race in Suburban California* (Minneapolis: University of Minnesota Press, 2013).

24. Cheng, *The Changs Next Door to the Diazes*, 10.

25. Deeb, *An Enchanted Modern*. For my interlocutors at that time, this social landscape was a crucial part of their identity and practice as pious Shi'i Muslims committed to a politics of resistance. As Mona Harb and I described in *Leisurely Islam*, it also indicated a comfortable space within Beirut where certain norms were understood, taken for granted, and did not stand out as unusual, as they might in other neighborhoods. Bou Akar later (in *For the War Yet to Come*) observes the use of this term in 2009 among a different group of interlocutors, and also notes it as a key way in which identity and space intersect. Her discussion of the concept adds the key point that using the word *bi'a*, which literally means "environment," links the political and the natural in deeply problematic ways that can lead to justification for sectarian or discriminatory decision making and the entrenchment of sectarian boundaries in space.

26. Despite history telling us otherwise, some of these couples believed that their antisectarian views were relatively recent to Lebanese history (dating, at best, to the 1960s). Ussama Makdisi shows us instead that there has been a history of antisectarian discourse and practice from at least 1860 in the Ottoman Empire and the Middle East, and that it wasn't until the Mandate period that sectarianism was named as a problem in Lebanon. Ussama Makdisi, *Age of Coexistence: The Ecumenical Frame and the Making of the Modern Arab World* (Oakland: University of California Press, 2019).

27. Residency options can be limited by law; for example, in the Al-Hadath municipality's ordinance preventing Christians from selling land to Muslims. Village communities can be even more challenging. Ziad and Mona wanted to buy land in Mona's

village, but were strongly discouraged by Mona's family from doing so, because the village doesn't sell land to Muslims—not by ordinance, but because "it isn't done." Other mixed couples recounted actually trying to purchase village property and being stopped by village authorities.

28. When their cosmopolitan parents opposed their marriages, these interviewees were essentially confronted with what Sara Fregonese describes as Beirut's contradictory "double imaginary of openness and closure" which tacks between overlapping cosmopolitan and sectarian sensibilities. Sara Fregonese, "Between a Refuge and a Battleground: Beirut's Discrepant Cosmopolitanisms," *Geographical Review* 102 (2012): 318.

29. On alcohol as a marker of social distinction, see Deeb and Harb, *Leisurely Islam*.

30. Hage, *Is Racism an Environmental Threat?* 83.

31. Hage, *Is Racism an Environmental Threat?* 91.

32. Makdisi, *Culture of Sectarianism*.

33. Deeb and Harb, *Leisurely Islam*.

34. Deeb, "Beyond Sectarianism."

BIBLIOGRAPHY

Primary Sources
Aztag (Beirut)
Al-Bayan (New York)
Al-Mar'a al-Jadida (Lebanon)
Binghamton Press and Sun-Bulletin (Binghamton, NY)
Boston Globe (Boston)
Brooklyn Citizen (Brooklyn, NY)
Brooklyn Daily Eagle (Brooklyn, NY)
Brooklyn Times Union (Brooklyn, NY)
Centre des Archives diplomatiques de Nantes
Chattanooga Daily Times (Chattanooga, TN)
Daily Times (Davenport, IA)
Daily News (New York)
Daily Journal (Vineland, NJ)
Detroit Free Press (Detroit)
Fort Worth Star-Telegram (Fort Worth, TX)
Hartford Courant (Hartford, CT)
Honolulu Advertiser (Honolulu)
Al-Huda (New York)
Kenosha Evening News (Kenosha, WI)
Lancaster New Era (Lancaster, PA)
Al-mahfuthat al-wataniyya al lubnaniyya (Lebanese National Archives)
Al-maḥkama al-sharʿiyya al-jaʿfariyya fi Baʿalbek

Al-maḥkama al-sharʿiyya al-jaʿfariyya fī Bayrut
Al-maḥkama al-sharʿiyya al-jaʿfariyya fī Bint Jbeil
Al-maḥkama al-sharʿiyya al-jaʿfariyya fī Marjʿayun
Al-maḥkama al-sharʿiyya al-jaʿfariyya fī Ṣayda
Al-maḥkama al-sharʿiyya al-jaʿfariyya fī Sur
Mirʾat al-Gharb (New York)
New York Times (New York)
Quad City Times (Davenport, IA)
The Record (Hackensack, NJ)
Syrian World (New York)
Times-Herald (Washington)
Washington Post (Washington)
Wisconsin State Journal (Madison, WI)

Secondary Sources

Abdo, Geneive. *The New Sectarianism: The Arab Uprisings and the Rebirth of the Shiʿa-Sunni Divide*. Oxford, UK: Oxford University Press, 2017.

Abisaab, Rula, and Malek Abisaab. *The Shiʿites of Lebanon: Modernism, Communism and Hizbullah's Islamists*. Syracuse, NY: Syracuse University Press, 2014.

Abunnasr, Maria Bashshur. "The Making of Ras Beirut: A Landscape of Memory for Narratives of Exceptionalism, 1870–1975." PhD dissertation, University of Massachusetts at Amherst, 2013.

Agmon, Iris. *Family and Court: Legal Culture and Modernity in Late Ottoman Palestine*. Syracuse, NY: Syracuse University Press, 2006.

Alajaji, Sylvia. *Music and the Armenian Diaspora: Searching for Home in Exile*. Bloomington: Indiana University Press, 2015.

Alexander, Michelle. *The New Jim Crow: Mass Incarceration in the Age of Colorblindness*. New York: The New Press, 2010.

Ali, Nosheen. "Sectarian Imaginaries: The Micropolitics of Sectarianism and State-Making in Northern Pakistan." *Current Sociology* 58, no. 5 (September 2010): 738–54.

Alkifaey, Hamid. *The Failure of Democracy in Iraq: Religion, Ideology and Sectarianism*. New York: Routledge, 2020.

Allouche, Sabiha. "Queering (Inter-Sectarian) Heterosexual Love in Lebanon." *International Journal of Middle East Studies* 51, no. 4 (2019): 547–65.

Al-Rashoud, Talal. "Modern Education and Arab Nationalism in Kuwait, 1911–1961." PhD thesis, University of London, 2017.

AlShehabi, Omar. *Contested Modernity, Sectarianism, Nationalism, and Colonialism in Bahrain*. London: Oneworld, 2019.

Arondekar, Anjali. *For the Record: On Sexuality and the Colonial Archive in India*. Durham, NC: Duke University Press, 2009.

———. "In the Absence of Reliable Ghosts: Sexuality, Historiography, South Asia." *Differences* 25, no. 3 (2014): 98–122.

Arsan, Andrew. *Interlopers of Empire: The Lebanese Diaspora in Colonial French West Africa*. Oxford, UK: Oxford University Press, 2014.

———. *Lebanon: A Country in Fragments*. London: Hurst & Company, 2018.

Asad, Talal. *Formations of the Secular: Christianity, Islam, Modernity*. Stanford, CA: Stanford University Press, 2003.

Atamian, Sarkis, and James H. Tashjian. *The Armenian Community: The Historical Development of a Social and Ideological Conflict*. New York: Philosophical Library, 1955.

Atchley, Edward Godfrey Cuthbert Frederic. *A History of the Use of Incense in Divine Worship*. London: Longmans, Green, and Co, 1909.

Al-Ayyubi, Juhayna. "Jamʻiyyat al-Maqasid al-Khayriyya al-Islamiyya fi Bayrut." MA thesis, American University of Beirut, 1966.

Azoulay, Ariella. *Potential History*. London: Verso, 2019.

Bailony, Reem. "From Mandate Borders to the Diaspora: Rashaya's Transnational Suffering and the Making of Lebanon in 1925." *Arab Studies Journal* 26, no. 2 (2018): 44–73.

Bakalian, Anny. *Armenian-Americans: From Being to Feeling Armenian*. New York: Transaction, 1993.

Balibar, Etienne. "The Nation Form: History and Ideology." In *Race, Nation, Class: Ambiguous Identities*, edited by Etienne Balibar and Immanuel Wallerstein, 86–106. London: Verso, 1991.

Balloffet, Lily. "From the Pampas to the Mashriq: Arab-Argentine Philanthropy Networks." *Mashriq & Mahjar: Journal of Middle East and North African Migration Studies* 4, no. 1 (2017): 4–28.

Bashshur, Munir. *Education and the Secular/Religious Divide: The Case of Lebanon*. Los Angeles: G. E. von Grunebaum Center, 1992.

Bawardi, Hani J. *The Making of Arab Americans: From Syrian Nationalism to U.S. Citizenship*. Austin: University of Texas Press, 2014.

Beshara, Adel, ed. *The Origins of Syrian Nationhood: Histories, Pioneers and Identity*. London: Routledge, 2011.

Beydoun, Ahmad. *Al-Jumhuriyya al-Mutaqatiʻa: Masaʼir al-Sigha al-Lubnaniyya baʻd Itifaq al Ṭaʼif*. Beirut: Dar An-Nahar, 1999.

Björklund, Ulf. "Armenia Remembered and Remade: Evolving Issues in a Diaspora." *Ethnos* 58, no. 3-4 (1993): 335–60.

Bou Akar, Hiba. *For the War Yet to Come: Planning Beirut's Frontiers*. Stanford, CA: Stanford University Press, 2018.

Bournoutian, George. *A History of the Armenian People, vol. 1: Pre-History to 1500 AD*. Costa Mesa, CA: Mazda, 1993.

Bowman, Glenn W., ed. *Sharing the Sacra: The Politics and Pragmatics of Intercommunal Relations around Holy Places*. New York: Berghahn Books, 2012.

Brim, Matt. *Poor Queer Studies: Confronting Elitism in the University*. Durham, NC: Duke University Press, 2020.

Brownson, Elizabeth. *Palestinian Women and Muslim Family Law in the Mandate Period*. Syracuse, NY: Syracuse University Press: 2019.

Brubaker, Rogers. "The 'Diaspora' Diaspora." *Ethnic and Racial Studies* 28, no. 1 (January 2005): 1–19.

———. "Migration, Membership, and the Modern Nation-State: Internal and External Dimensions of the Politics of Belonging." *Journal of Interdisciplinary History* 41 (2010): 61–78.

———. *Nationalism Reframed: Nationhood and National Question in the New Europe.* Cambridge, UK: Cambridge University Press, 1996.

Burak, Guy. *The Second Formation of Islamic Law: The Hanafi School in the Early Modern Ottoman Empire.* Cambridge, UK: Cambridge University Press, 2015.

Cammett, Melani Claire. *Compassionate Communalism: Welfare and Sectarianism in Lebanon.* Ithaca, NY: Cornell University Press, 2014.

Cannell, Fenella, ed. *The Anthropology of Christianity.* Durham, NC: Duke University Press, 2006.

Certeau, Michel de. *The Practice of Everyday Life.* Translated by Steven Rendall. 2nd edition. Berkeley and Los Angeles: University of California Press, 2002.

Chalabi, Tamara. *The Shi'is of Jabal 'Amil and the New Lebanon: Community and Nation-State, 1918–1943.* London: Palgrave, 2006.

Charrad, Mounira. *States and Women's Rights: The Making of Postcolonial Tunisia, Algeria, and Morocco.* Berkeley: University of California Press, 2001.

Cheng, Wendy. *The Changs Next Door to the Diazes: Remapping Race in Suburban California.* Minneapolis: University of Minnesota Press, 2013.

Cioeta, Donald. "Islamic Benevolent Societies and Public Education in Ottoman Syria, 1875–1882." *Islamic Quarterly* 26 (1982): 40–55.

Clark, Janine, and Bassel Salloukh. "Elite Strategies, Civil Society, and Sectarian Identities in Postwar Lebanon." *International Journal of Middle East Studies* 45, no. 4 (2013): 731–49.

Classen, Constance. "The Odor of the Other: Olfactory Symbolism and Cultural Categories." *Ethos* 20, no. 2 (1992): 133–66.

Classen, Constance, David Howes, and Anthony Synnott. *Aroma: The Cultural History of Smell.* London and New York: Routledge, 1994.

Clément, Olivier. *Corps de mort et de gloire: Petite introduction à une théopoétique du corps.* Paris: Desclée de Brouwer, 1996.

Cohen, David William. *The Combing of History.* Chicago: University of Chicago Press, 1994.

Cohn, Bernard. *Colonialism and Its Forms of Knowledge: The British in India.* Princeton, NJ: Princeton University Press, 1996.

Conklin, Alice. *A Mission to Civilize: The Republican Idea of Empire in France and West Africa, 1895–1930.* Stanford, CA: Stanford University Press, 1997.

Conradson, David, and Deirdre McKay. "Translocal Subjectivities: Mobility, Connection, Emotion." *Mobilities* 2, no. 2 (2007): 167–74.

Corstange, Daniel. "Religion, Pluralism, and Iconography in the Public Sphere: Theory and Evidence from Lebanon." *World Politics,* 64, no. 1 (2012): 116–60.

Cortas, Wadad Makdisi. *Dhikrayat: 1917–1977.* Beirut: Mu'assassat al-Abhath al-'Arabiyya, 1982.

———. *A World I Loved.* New York: Nation Books, 2009.

Cvetkovich, Ann. *Archive of Feelings.* Durham, NC: Duke University Press, 2003.

Daher, Mas'ud. *Al-Judhur al-Tarikhiyya li-l-Mas'ala al-Ta'ifiyya al-Lubnaniyya, 1697–1861.* Beirut: Ma'had al-Inma' al-'Arabi, 1981.

———. *Lubnan, al-Istiqlal al-Sigha wa al-Mithaq, 1918–1946.* 2nd ed. Beirut: Dar al-Matbu'at, 1984.

———. *Tarikh Lubnan al-ijtima'i, 1914–1926.* Beirut: N.p., 1981.

Damluji, Mona. "'Securing Democracy in Iraq.' Sectarian Politics and Segregation in Baghdad, 2003–2007," *Traditional Dwellings and Settlements Review* 21, no. 2 (Spring 2010): 71–87.

Deeb, Lara. "Beyond Sectarianism: Intermarriage and Social Difference in Lebanon." *International Journal of Middle East Studies* 52, no. 2 (2020): 215–28.

———. *An Enchanted Modern: Gender and Public Piety in Shi'i Lebanon.* Princeton, NJ: Princeton University Press, 2006.

Deeb, Lara, and Mona Harb. *Leisurely Islam: Negotiating Geography and Morality in South Beirut.* Princeton, NJ: Princeton University Press, 2013.

Deeb, Lara, and Jessica Winegar. "Anthropologies of Arab-Majority Societies." *Annual Review of Anthropology* 41 (2012): 537–58.

Deguilhem, Randi. "Impérialisme, colonisation intellectuelle et politique culturelle de la Mission Laïque française en Syrie sous mandat," in *The British and French Mandates in Comparative Perspectives*, ed. Nadine Méouchy and Peter Sluglett, 321–44. Leiden, Netherlands: Brill, 2004.

Deleuze, Gilles, and Félix Guattari. *A Thousand Plateaus: Capitalism and Schizophrenia.* Bloomsbury, 1988.

Der Matossian, Bedross. "The Armenians of Jerusalem in the Modern Period: The Rise and Decline of a Community." In *Routledge Handbook on Jerusalem*, edited by Suleiman A. Mourad, Naomi Koltun-Fromm, and Bedross Der Matossian, 396–407. New York: Routledge, 2019.

Derrida, Jacques. *Archive Fever: A Freudian Impression.* Chicago: University of Chicago Press, 1996.

———. "Force of Law: The Mystical Foundation of Authority." In *Deconstruction and the Possibility of Justice*, edited by Drucilla Cornell, Michael Rosenfield, and David G. Carlson, 3–67. London: Routledge, 1992.

Dimechkie, Hala. "Julia Tu'mi Dimashqiyi and *al-Mar'a al-Jadida*, 1883–1954." MA thesis, American University of Beirut, 1998.

Drieskens, Barbara. "Changing Perceptions of Marriage in Beirut." In *Les Métamorphoses du Mariage au Moyen-Orient.* Beirut: Presses de l'Ifpo, 2008.

Dueck, Jennifer. *Claims of Culture at Empire's End.* Oxford, UK: Oxford University Press, 2010.

Eibner, John. *The Future of Religious Minorities in the Middle East.* Lanham, MD: Lexington Books, 2017.

El Shakry, Omnia. "History without Documents: The Vexed Archives of Decolonization in the Middle East." *American Historical Review* 120, no. 3 (2015): 920–34.

Elyachar, Julia. *Markets of Dispossession: NGOs, Economic Development, and the State in Cairo*. Durham, NC: Duke University Press, 2005.

———. "Next Practices: Knowledge, Infrastructure, and Public Goods at the Bottom of the Pyramid." *Public Culture* 24, no. 1 (January 1, 2012): 109–29.

———. "Phatic Labor, Infrastructure, and the Question of Empowerment in Cairo." *American Ethnologist* 37, no. 3 (August 2010): 452–64.

Engelke, Matthew, and Matt Tomlinson, eds. *The Limits of Meaning: Case Studies in the Anthropology of Christianity*. Oxford, UK, and New York: Berghahn Books, 2006.

Fahmy, Ziad. "Coming to our Senses: Historicizing Sound and Noise in the Middle East." *History Compass* 11, no. 4 (2013): 305–15.

Fahrenthold, Stacy. *Between the Ottomans and the Entente: The First World War in the Syrian and Lebanese Diaspora, 1908–1925*. New York: Oxford University Press, 2019.

———. "Transnational Modes and Media: The Syrian Press in the Mahjar and Emigrant Activism during World War I." *Mashriq & Mahjar: Journal of Middle East and North African Migration Studies* 1, no. 1 (2013): 30–54.

Farah, Caesar E. *The Politics of Interventionism in Ottoman Lebanon: 1830–1861*. London: I. B. Tauris, 2000.

Farha, Mark. "The Historical Legacy and Political Implications of State and Sectarian Schools in Lebanon." In *Rethinking Education for Social Cohesion: International Case Studies*, edited by Maha Shuayb, 64–85. London: Palgrave McMillan, 2012.

Ferguson, Susanna. "A Fever for an Education: Pedagogical Thought and Social Transformation in Beirut and Mount Lebanon, 1861–1914," *Arab Studies Journal* 16, no. 1 (2018):58–83.

Finkel, Eli J., Christopher A. Bail, Mina Cikara, Peter H. Ditto, Shanto Iyengar, Samara Klar, Lilliana Mason, Mary C. McGrath, Brendan Nyhan, David G. Rand, Linda J. Skitka, Joshua A. Tucker, Jay J. Van Bavel, Cynthia S. Wang, and James N. Druckman. "Political Sectarianism in America." *Science* 370, no. 6516 (2020): 533–36.

Firro, Kais. *Inventing Lebanon: Nationalism and the State under the Mandate*. London: I. B. Tauris, 2002.

———. "Lebanese Nationalism versus Arabism: From Bulus Nujaym to Michel Chiha." *Middle Eastern Studies* 40, no. 5 (2004): 1–27.

———. *Metamorphosis of the Nation (al-Umma): The Rise of Arabism and Minorities in Syria and Lebanon, 1850–1940*. Portland, UK: Sussex Academic Press, 2009.

Foucault, Michel. *The History of Sexuality: An Introduction*. New York: Vintage, 1990.

Foucault, Michel, and François Ewald. *"Society Must Be Defended": Lectures at the Collège de France, 1975–1976*. Vol. 1. New York: Macmillan, 2003.

Freeman, Elizabeth. *Time Binds: Queer Temporalities, Queer Histories*. Durham, NC: Duke University Press, 2010.

Fregonese, Sara. "Between a Refuge and a Battleground: Beirut's Discrepant Cosmopolitanisms." *Geographical Review* 102 (2012): 316–36.

Fuentes, Marisa J. *Dispossessed lives: Enslaved Women, Violence, and the Archive*. Philadelphia: University of Pennsylvania Press, 2016.

Galadza, Peter. "Liturgy and Heaven in the Eastern Rites." *Antiphon: A Journal for Liturgical Renewal* 10, no. 3 (2006): 239–60.

Gelvin, James. "'Arab Nationalism': Has a New Framework Emerged? Pensée 1: 'Arab Nationalism' Meets Social Theory," *International Journal of Middle East Studies* 41, no. 1 (February 2009): 10–12.

Ghannam, Farha. *Remaking the Modern: Space, Relocation, and the Politics of Identity in a Global Cairo.* Berkeley: University of California Press, 2002.

Gordon, Avery F. *Ghostly Matters: Haunting and the Sociological Imagination.* Minneapolis: University of Minnesota Press, 2008.

Gualtieri, Sarah. *Between Arab and White: Race and Ethnicity in the Early Syrian American Diaspora.* Berkeley: University of California Press, 2009.

Guirguis, Laure. *Copts and the Security State.* Stanford, CA: Stanford University Press, 2016.

Gupta, Radhika. "There Must Be Some Way Out of Here: Beyond a Spatial Conception of Muslim Ghettoization in Mumbai?" *Ethnography* 16, no. 3 (September 2015): 367–68.

Gutman, David E. *The Politics of Armenian Migration to North America 1885–1915: Migrants, Smugglers and Dubious Citizens.* Edinburgh: Edinburgh University Press, 2019.

Ha, Marie-Paule. "From 'Nos Ancêtres, Les Gaulois' to 'Leur Culture Ancestrale.'" *French Colonial History* 3 (2003): 101–17.

Hacking, Ian. *Rewriting the Soul: Multiple Personality and the Sciences of Memory.* Princeton, NJ: Princeton University Press, 1998.

Haddad, Fanar. "'Sectarianism' and Its Discontents in the Study of the Middle East." *Middle East Journal* 71, no. 3 (2017): 363–82.

———. *Sectarianism in Iraq: Antagonistic Visions of Unity.* Oxford, UK: Oxford University Press, 2014.

Hafeda, Mohamad. *Negotiating Conflict in Lebanon: Bordering Practices in a Divided Beirut.* London and New York: I. B. Tauris, 2019.

Hage, Ghassan. *Is Racism an Environmental Threat?* Cambridge: Polity Press, 2017.

———. "Nationalist Anxiety; or, the Fear of Losing Your Other." *Australian Journal of Anthropology* 7, no. 2 (August 1996): 121–40.

Hall, Stuart. "Reflections on 'Race, Articulation and Societies Structured in Dominance'" In *Race Critical Theories: Text and Context*, edited by Philomena Essed and David Theo Goldberg, 38–68. Malden, MA: Blackwell, 2002.

Hallaq, Wael. *Shari'a: Theory, Practice, Transformations.* Cambridge, UK: Cambridge University Press, 2010.

Hakim, Carol. *The Origins of the Lebanese National Idea, 1840–1920.* Berkeley: University of California Press, 2013.

Hamadeh, Najla. "*Bayna Dumu' al-'Ajz wa al-Muwatiniyya al-Fa'ila: Muqarana bayna Madrasatayn.*" In *Al-Muwatiniyya bayna al-Rajul wa al-Mar'a*, edited by Najla Hamadeh, Jean Said Makdisi, and Suad Joseph, 381–96. Beirut: Dar al-Jadid, 2000.

Hamoudi, Haider Ali. *Negotiating in Civil Conflict: Constitutional Construction and Imperfect Bargaining in Iraq.* Chicago: University of Chicago Press, 2014.

Hanssen, Jens. *Fin de Siècle Beirut*. London: Oxford Univerity Press, 2005.

Harik, Iliya. *Politics and Change in a Traditional Society: Lebanon 1711–1845*. Princeton, NJ: Princeton University Press, 1968.

Harrison, Faye V. "The Persistent Power of 'Race' in the Cultural and Political Economy of Racism." *Annual Review of Anthropology* 24 (1995): 47–74.

Hartman, Saadiya. *Lose Your Mother: A Journey along the Atlantic Slave Route*. New York: Macmillan, 2008.

——. *Wayward Lives, Beautiful Experiments: Intimate Histories of Social Upheaval*. W. W. Norton, 2019.

Hashemi, Nader, and Danny Postel, eds. *Sectarianization: Mapping the New Politics of the Middle East*. New York: Oxford University Press, 2017.

Haugbolle, Sune. *War and Memory in Lebanon*. Vol. 34. Cambridge, UK: Cambridge University Press, 2010.

Hermez, Sami. *War Is Coming: Between Past and Future Violence in Lebanon*. Philadelphia: University of Pennsylvania Press, 2017.

Hitti, Philip. *The Syrians in America*. New York: Doran, 1924.

Hovannisian, Richard. *The Armenian People from Ancient to Modern Times, Volume I: The Dynastic Periods; From Antiquity to the Fourteenth Century; Volume II: From Dominion to Statehood; The Fifteenth Century to the Twentieth*. London: Macmillan, 1997.

Howes, David, ed. *Empire of the Senses: The Sensual Culture Reader*. Oxford, UK: Berg Publishers, 2005.

Howes, David, and Constance Classen. *Ways of Sensing: Understanding the Senses in Society*. London and New York: Routledge, 2014.

Hull, Matthew S. *Government of Paper: The Materiality of Bureaucracy in Urban Pakistan*. Berkeley: University of California Press, 2012.

Human Rights Watch. "Why They Died: Civilian Casualties in Lebanon during the 2006 War," in Human Rights Watch, *World Report*, 2007.

Hurd, Elizabeth Shakman. "Politics of Sectarianism: Rethinking Religion and Politics in the Middle East." *Middle East Law and Governance* 7 (2015): 61–75.

International Center for Transitional Justice. "Failing to Deal with the Past: What Cost to Lebanon?" 2014.

International Crisis Group. *The Central Sahel: The Perfect Sandstorm*. Brussels: International Crisis Group, 2015.

Joseph, Suad, ed. *Gender and Citizenship in the Middle East*. Syracuse, NY: Syracuse University Press, 2000.

——. "Pensée 2: Sectarianism as Imagined Sociological Concept and as Imagined Social Formation." *International Journal of Middle East Studies* 40, no. 4 (November 2008): 553–54.

——. "The Politicization of Religious Sects in Borj Hammoud, Lebanon." PhD dissertation, Columbia University, 1975.

——. "The Public/Private: The Imagined Boundary in the Imagined Nation/State/Community: The Lebanese Case." *Feminist Review* 57 (1997): 73–92.

———. "Working-Class Women's Networks in a Sectarian State: A Political Paradox." *American Ethnologist* 10, no. 1 (February 1983): 1–22.

Karam, George. *Al-Jinsiyya al-Lubnāniya bayna al-qānūn wal-wāqiʿ*. Beirut: Maṭbaʿat Joseph al Hājj, 1993.

Kasbarian, Sossie. "Between Nationalist Absorption and Subsumption: Reflecting on the Armenian Cypriot Experience." In *Cypriot Nationalisms in Context*, edited by Thekla Kyritsi and Nikos Christofis, 177–98. Cham, Switzerland: Palgrave Macmillan, 2018.

Kassab, Selim. *Our Inspector's Story*. Gloucester, UK: John Bellows, n.d.

Kassir, Samir. *Beirut*. Translated by M. B. DeBevoise. Berkeley: University of California Press, 2010.

Kastrinou, Maria A. *Power, Sect and State in Syria: The Politics of Marriage and Identity amongst the Druze*. London: I. B. Tauris, 2016.

Kayyali, Randa. "Race, Religion and Identity: Arab Christians in the United States." *Culture and Religion* 19, no. 1 (2018): 1–19.

Kenna, Margaret E. "Why Does Incense Smell Religious? Greek Orthodoxy and the Anthropology of Smell." *Journal of Mediterranean Studies* 15, no. 1 (2005): 51–70.

Kern, Karen. *Imperial Citizen: Marriage and Citizenship in the Ottoman Frontier Provinces of Iraq*. Syracuse, NY: Syracuse University Press, 2011.

Khater, Akram. *Inventing Home: Emigration, Gender, and the Middle Class in Lebanon, 1870–1920*. Berkeley: University of California Press, 2001.

———. "Phoenician or Arab, Lebanese or Syrian: Who Were the Early Immigrants to America?" *Khayrallah Center for Lebanese Diaspora Studies Blog*, September 20, 2017, https://lebanesestudies.news.chass.ncsu.edu/2017/09/20/phoenician-or-arab/.

Khoury, Phillip. *Syria and the French Mandate: The Politics of Arab Nationalism, 1920–1945*. Princeton, NJ: Princeton University Press, 1987.

Khuri-Makdisi, Ilham. "The Conceptualization of *the Social* in Late Nineteenth- and Early Twentieth-Century Arabic Thought and Language," in *Global Conceptual History: A Reader*, edited by Margrit Pernau and Dominic Sachsenmeier. London: Bloomsbury, 2016.

Kingston, Paul. *Reproducing Sectarianism: Advocacy Networks and the Politics of Civil Society in Postwar Lebanon*. Albany: SUNY Press, 2013.

Kockelman, Paul. "Enemies, Parasites, and Noise: How to Take Up Residence in a System." *Journal of Linguistic Anthropology* 20, no. 2 (November 2010): 406–21.

Latour, Bruno. *The Making of Law: An Ethnography of the Conseil d'État*. London: Polity, 2010.

Lattouf, Mirna. *Women, Education, and Socialization in Modern Lebanon*. Lanham, MD: University Press of America, 2004.

Léon, Antoine. *Colonisation, Enseignement, et Education*. Paris: L'Harmattan, 1991.

Lincoln, Bruce. "Lakota Sun Dance and the Problematics of Sociocosmic Reunion." *History of Religions* 24, no. 1 (1994): 1.

Longrigg, Stephan. *Syria and the French Mandate*. Oxford, UK: Oxford University Press, 1958.

Longva, Anh Nga, and Anne Sofie Roald, eds. *Religious Minorities in the Middle East: Domination, Self-Empowerment, Accommodation.* Leiden, Netherlands: Brill, 2012.

Low, Kelvin E. Y. "Olfactive Frames of Remembering: Theorizing Self, Senses and Society." *Sociological Review* 61, no. 4 (2013): 688–708.

Luehrmann, Sonja, ed. *Praying with the Senses: Contemporary Orthodox Christian Spirituality in Practice.* Bloomington: Indiana University Press, 2017.

Machlis, Elisheva. *Shiʿi Sectarianism in the Middle East: Modernization and the Quest for Islamic Universalism.* London: I. B. Tauris, 2014.

Majed, Rima. "In Defense of Intra-Sectarian Divide: Street Mobilization, Coalition Formation, and Rapid Realignments of Sectarian Boundaries in Lebanon." *Social Forces* 1 (2020): 1–26.

———. "The Political (or Social) Economy of Sectarianism in Lebanon." *MEI@75*, November 7, 2017. http://www.mei.edu/content/map/political-or-social-economy-sectarianism-lebanon.

Makdisi, Ussama. *Age of Coexistence: The Ecumenical Frame and the Making of the Modern Arab World.* Oakland: University of California Press, 2019.

———. "Corrupting the Sublime Sultanate: The Revolt of Tanyus Shahin in Nineteenth-Century Ottoman Lebanon." *Comparative Studies in Society and History* 42, no. 1 (2000): 180–208.

———. *The Culture of Sectarianism: Community, History, and Violence in Nineteenth-Century Ottoman Lebanon.* Los Angeles: University of California Press, 2000.

Maktabi, Rania. "The Lebanese Census of 1932 Revisited: Who Are the Lebanese?" *British Journal of Middle Eastern Studies* 26, no. 2 (1999): 219–41.

Matthews, Roderic D., and Matta Akrawi. *Education in Arab Countries of the Near East.* Washington: American Council on Education, 1949.

Matthiesen, Toby. *Sectarian Gulf: Bahrain, Saudi Arabia, and the Arab Spring That Wasn't.* Stanford, CA: Stanford University Press, 2013.

Mawani, Renisa. "Law's Archive." *Annual Review of Law and Social Science* 8 (2012): 337–65.

Mbembe, Achille. "The Power of the Archive and its Limits." In *Refiguring the Archive*, 19–27. Dordrecht, Netherlands: Springer, 2002.

McCallum, Fiona. "Christian Political Representation in the Arab World." *Islam and Christian-Muslim Relations* 23, no. 1 (2012): 3–18.

Mermier, Frank. "The Frontiers of Beirut: Some Anthropological Observations." *Mediterranean Politics* 18, no. 3 (2013): 376–93.

Migliorino, Nicola. *(Re)Constructing Armenia in Lebanon and Syria.* New York: Berghahn Books, 2008.

Mikdashi, Maya. "The Magic of Mutual Coexistence: The Taif Accord at Thirty." *Jadaliyya*, October 2019. https://www.jadaliyya.com/Details/40134.

———. "Sex and Sectarianism: The Legal Architecture of Lebanese Citizenship." *Comparative Studies of South Asia, Africa and the Middle East* 34, no. 2 (2014): 279–93.

———. "Sextarianism: Notes on Studying the Lebanese State." In *The Oxford Handbook of Contemporary Middle Eastern and North African History.* Oxford, UK: Oxford University Press, 2020.

———. *Sextarianism: Sovereignty, Secularism, and the State in Lebanon*. Stanford, CA: Stanford University Press, 2022.

Minassian, Oshagan. "A History of the Armenian Holy Apostolic Church in the United States (1888–1944)." PhD dissertation, Boston University, 1974.

———. *A History of the Armenian Holy Apostolic Orthodox Church in the United States (1888–1944)*. Monterey, CA: Mayreni Publishing, 2010.

Mitchell, Timothy. *Colonising Egypt*. Berkeley: University of California Press, 1991.

———. "Society, Economy, and the State Effect," in *The Anthropology of the State: A Reader*, edited by Aradhana Sharma and Akhil Gupta, 169–86. Oxford, UK: Blackwell Publishing, 2006.

Mitri, Tarek. "Christians in the Arab World: Minority Attitudes and Citizenship." *Ecumenical Review* 64, no. 1 (2012): 43–49.

Monroe, Kristin. *The Insecure City: Space, Power, and Mobility in Beirut*. New Brunswick, NJ: Rutgers University Press, 2016.

Moore, Sally Falk. "Explaining the Present: Theoretical Dilemmas in Processual Ethnography." *American Ethnologist* 14, no. 4 (November 1987): 727–36.

Naeff, Judith. *Precarious Imaginaries of Beirut: A City's Suspended Now*. Cham, Switzerland: Palgrave Macmillan, 2018.

Nalbantian, Tsolin. *Armenians beyond Diaspora: Making Lebanon Their Own*. Edinburgh: Edinburgh University Press, 2020.

———. "Going beyond Overlooked Populations in Lebanese Historiography: The Armenian Case," *History Compass* 11, no. 10 (2013): 821–32.

Nucho, Joanne Randa. *Everyday Sectarianism in Urban Lebanon: Infrastructure, Public Services and Power*. Princeton, NJ: Princeton University Press, 2016.

Panossian, Razmik. *The Armenians from Kings and Priests to Merchants and Commissars*. New York: Columbia University Press, 2006.

Pastor, Camila. *The Mexican Mahjar: Transnational Maronites, Jews, and Arabs under the French Mandate*. Austin: University of Texas Press, 2017.

Payaslian, Simon. *History of the Armenian People*. Costa Mesa, CA: Mazda, 2002.

Pearlman, Wendy. "Competing for Lebanon's Diaspora: Transnationalism and Domestic Struggles in a Weak State." *International Migration Review* 48, no. 1 (2014): 34–75.

Peirce, Leslie. *Morality Tales: Law and Gender in the Ottoman Court of Aintab*. Berkeley and Los Angeles: University of California Press, 2003.

Peleikis, Anja. "Shifting Identities, Reconstructing Boundaries: The Case of a Multi-Confessional Locality in Post-War Lebanon." *Die Welt des Islams* 41 (2001): 400–429.

Pitts, Graham Auman. "The Ecology of Migration: Remittances in World War I Mount Lebanon." *Arab Studies Journal* 26, no. 2 (2018): 102–29.

Provence, Michael. *The Great Syrian Revolt and the Rise of Arab Nationalism*. Austin: University of Texas Press, 2005.

Qato, Mezna. "Forms of Retrieval: Social Scale, Citation, and the Archive on the Palestinian Left." *International Journal of Middle East Studies* 51, no. 2 (2019): 312–15.

Quraishi, Asifa, and Frank E. Vogel. *The Islamic Marriage Contract: Case Studies in Islamic Family Law*. Boston: Harvard University Press, 2008.

Rayburn, Joel. *Iraq after America: Strongmen, Sectarians, Resistance.* Stanford, CA: Hoover Institution Press, 2014.

Rodaway, Paul. *Sensuous Geographies: Body, Sense and Place.* London: Routledge, 1994.

Salloukh, Bassel F. "The Architecture of Sectarianization in Lebanon." In *Sectarianization: Mapping the New Politics of the Middle East,* edited by Nader Hashemi and Danny Postel, 215–34. New York: Oxford University Press, 2017.

——. "The Autumn of Sectarianism." Lebanese Center for Policy Studies, February, 2020. https://www.lcps-lebanon.org/articles/details/1802/the-autumn-of-sectarianism.

Salloukh, Bassel F., Rabie Barakat, Jinan S. Al-Habbal, Lara W. Khattab, and Shoghig Mikaelian. *Politics of Sectarianism in Postwar Lebanon.* London: Pluto Press, 2015.

Sanjian, Ara. "The Armenian Church and Community of Jerusalem." In *The Christian Communities of Jerusalem and the Holy Land: Studies in History, Religion, and Politics,* edited by Anthony O'Mahony, 57–89. Cardiff: University of Wales Press, 2003.

Sayej, Caroleen Marji. *Patriotic Ayatollahs: Nationalism in Post-Saddam Iraq.* Ithaca, NY: Cornell University Press, 2018.

Sayigh, Rosemary. *Too Many Enemies: The Palestinian Experience in Lebanon.* London: Zed Books, 1994.

Sbaiti, Nadya. "'If the Devil Taught French': Strategies of Language and Learning in French Mandate Beirut." In *Trajectories of Education in the Arab World,* edited by Osama Abi-Mershed, 59–83. London: Routledge, 2010.

Schatkowski, Linda. "The Islamic Maqasid of Beirut: A Case Study of Modernization in Lebanon." MA thesis, American University of Beirut, 1969.

Schayegh, Cyrus, and Andrew Arsan, eds. *The Routledge Handbook of the History of the Middle East Mandates.* New York: Routledge, 2015.

Schielke, Samuli, and Liza Debevec, eds. *Ordinary Lives and Grand Schemes: An Anthropology of Everyday Religion.* Oxford, UK, and New York: Berghahn Books, 2012.

Schmemann, Alexander. *For the Life of the World: Sacraments and Orthodoxy.* New York: St. Vladimir's Seminary Press, 1973.

Schumann, Christoph. "'The Generation of Broad Expectations': Nationalism, Education and Autobiography in Syria and Lebanon 1930–1958." *Die Welt des Islams* 41, no. 2 (July 2001): 174–205.

——. "Nationalism, Diaspora and 'Civilisational Mission': The Case of Syrian Nationalism in Latin America between World War I and World War II." *Nations and Nationalism* 10, no. 4 (2004): 599–617.

Seikaly, Sherene. "How I Met My Great-Grandfather: Archives and the Writing of History." *Comparative Studies of South Asia, Africa and the Middle East* 38, no. 1 (2018): 6–20.

——. "The Matter of Time." *American Historical Review* 124, no. 5 (December 2019): 1681–88.

Seremetakis, Nadia. *The Senses Still: Historical Perception, Commensal Exchange, and Modernity.* Boulder, CO: Westview Press, 1994.

Shahine, Fouad. *Al-Ta'ifiyya fi Lubnan Hadirha wa Judhurha al-Tarikhiyya al-Ijtima'iyya*. Beirut: Dar al-Hadatha, 1986.

Sharkey, Heather. *A History of Muslims, Christians, and Jews in the Middle East*. Cambridge, UK: Cambridge University Press, 2017.

Shepard, Todd. "'Of Sovereignty': Disputed Archives, 'Wholly Modern' Archives, and the Post-Decolonization French and Algerian Republics, 1962–2012." *American Historical Review* 120, no. 3 (2015): 869–83.

Sleiman, Hana. "The Paper Trail of a Liberation Movement." *Arab Studies Journal* 24, no. 1 (2016): 42–67.

Steedman, Carolyn. *Dust: The Archive and Cultural History*. New Brunswick, NJ: Rutgers University Press, 2002.

Stoler, Ann Laura. "Colonial Archives and the Arts of Governance." *Archival Science* 2, nos. 1–2 (2002): 87–109.

Suciyan, Talin. *The Armenians in Modern Turkey Post-Genocide Society, Politics and History*. London: I. B. Tauris, 2016.

Suny, Ronald Grigor. *"They Can Live in the Desert but Nowhere Else": A History of the Armenian Genocide*. Princeton, NJ: Princeton University Press, 2015.

Tarhini, Mohammad. *Al-Usus al-Tarikhiyya li-Nizam Lubnan al-Ta'ifi, Dirasa Muqarina*. Beirut, Dar al-Afaq, 1981.

Theodorelis-Rigas, Haris. "Model Citizens or a Fifth Column? Greek Orthodox (Rum) Communities in Syria and Turkey between Secularism and Multiculturalism." In *Diasporas of the Modern Middle East: Contextualizing Community*, edited by Anthony Gorman and Sossie Kasbarian, 31–69. Edinburgh: Edinburgh University Press, 2015.

Thompson, Elizabeth. *Colonial Citizens. Republican Rights, Paternal Privilege, and Gender in French Syria and Lebanon*. New York: Columbia University Press, 2000.

Tibawi, A. L. *Islamic Education: Its Traditions and Modernization into the Arab National Systems*. New York: Crane, Russak & Company, 1972.

Tölöyan, Khachig. "Elites and Institutions in the Armenian Transnation." *Diaspora: A Journal of Transnational Studies* 9, no. 1 (2000): 107–36.

Traboulsi, Fawwaz. *A History of Modern Lebanon*. London: Pluto Press, 2012.

Trouillot, Michel-Rolph. *Silencing the Past: Power and the Production of History*. Boston: Beacon Press, 1995.

Tucker, Judith. *In the House of the Law: Gender and Islamic Law in Ottoman Syria and Palestine*. Berkeley: University of California Press, 1998.

United Press International. "Rocket Strikes Beirut Justice Palace, Destroys Files." *Los Angeles Times*, 1985.

Vejdani, Farzin. *Making History in Iran: Education, Nationalism and Print Culture*. Stanford, CA: Stanford University Press, 2015.

Waldinger, Roger, and David Fitzgerald. "Transnationalism in Question." *American Journal of Sociology* 109, no. 5 (2004): 1177–95.

Watenpaugh, Keith David. "Being Middle Class and Being Arab: Sectarian Dilemmas and Middle-Class Modernity in the Arab Middle East, 1908–1936." In *The Making of the Middle Class: Toward a Transnational History*, edited by A. Ricardo López and Barbara Weinstein. Durham, NC: Duke University Press, 2012.

———. *Being Modern in the Middle East: Revolution, Nationalism, Colonialism and the Arab Middle Class*. Princeton, NJ: Princeton University Press, 2012.

———. "Towards a New Category of Colonial Theory: Colonial Cooperation and the Survivors Bargain; The Case of the Post-Genocide Armenian Community in Syria." In *The British and French Mandates in Comparative Perspective*, edited by Nadine Meouchy and Peter Sluglett. Leiden, Netherlands: Brill, 2004.

Weber, Anne Françoise. "Briser et Suivre les Normes: Les Couples Islamochrétiens au Liban." In *Les métamorphoses du mariage au Moyen-Orient*. Beirut: Presses de l'Ifpo, 2008.

Wedeen, Lisa. *Peripheral Visions: Publics, Power and Performance in Yemen*. Chicago: University of Chicago Press, 2008.

Weeks, Kathi. *Constituting Feminist Subjects*. London: Verso, 2018 [1998].

Wehrey, Frederic M. *Sectarian Politics in the Gulf: From the Iraq War to the Arab Uprisings*. New York: Columbia University Press, 2016.

Weiss, Max. "The Historiography of Sectarianism in Lebanon," *History Compass* 7, no. 1 (2009): 141–54.

———. *In the Shadow of Sectarianism: Law Shi'ism and the Making of Modern Lebanon*. Cambridge, MA: Harvard University Press, 2010.

Weld, Kirsten. *Paper Cadavers: The Archives of Dictatorship in Guatemala*. Durham, NC: Duke University Press, 2014.

Williams, Raymond. *Marxism and Literature*. Oxford, UK: Oxford University Press, 1977.

Wittgenstein, Ludwig. *The Blue and Brown Books*. Vol. 53. Oxford, UK: Blackwell, 1958.

Womack, Deanna Ferree. "Syrian Christians and Arab-Islamic Identity: Expressions of Belonging in the Ottoman Empire and America." *Studies in World Christianity* 25, no. 1 (2019): 29–49.

Zachs, Fruma. "Toward a Proto-Nationalist Concept of Syria? Revisiting the American Presbyterian Missionaries in the Nineteenth-Century Levant." *Die Welt des Islams* 41, no. 2 (2001): 145–73.

Zamir, Meir. *Lebanon's Quest: The Road to Statehood, 1926–1939*. London: I. B. Tauris, 1997.

Zeuge-Buberl, Uta. *The Mission of the American Board in Syria*. Translated by Elizabeth Janik. Stuttgart, Germany: Franz Steiner Verlag, 2017.

CONTRIBUTORS

ROXANA MARIA ARĀŞ is a PhD candidate in the doctoral program in anthropology and history at the University of Michigan, Ann Arbor, with research interests in religious studies, sensorial aesthetics, and multimedia ethnography. Since 2014 she has been doing research in Lebanon, where she currently resides. She is writing her doctoral dissertation on Orthodox Christian communities in the Middle East.

REEM BAILONY is an assistant professor of Middle East history at Agnes Scott College, and formerly an American Druze Foundation postdoctoral fellow at Georgetown University's Center for Contemporary Arab Studies. She is currently working on her monograph titled "Syria's Transnational Rebellion: Diaspora Politics and the Revolt of 1925–1927."

LARA DEEB, professor of anthropology at Scripps College, is the author of *An Enchanted Modern: Gender and Public Piety in Shi'i Lebanon* (Princeton University Press, 2006); coauthor, with Mona Harb, of *Leisurely Islam: Negotiating Geography and Morality in Shi'ite South Beirut* (Princeton University Press, 2013); and coauthor, with Jessica Winegar, of *Anthropology's Politics: Disciplining the Middle East* (Stanford University Press, 2016).

MAYA MIKDASHI is an associate professor in the Department of Women, Gender, and Sexuality Studies at Rutgers University. She is an anthropologist and an interdisciplinary scholar of state power. Maya is a cofounding editor of *Jadaliyya*, and the author of *Sextarianism: Sovereignty, Secularism and the State in Lebanon* (Stanford University Press, 2022).

TSOLIN NALBANTIAN, associate professor of modern Middle East history at Leiden University, is the author of *Armenians beyond Diaspora: Making Lebanon Their Own* (Edinburgh University Press, 2020). She is also the series coeditor of *Critical, Connected Histories* (Leiden University Press).

JOANNE RANDA NUCHO, an anthropologist and filmmaker, is the author of *Everyday Sectarianism in Urban Lebanon: Infrastructures, Public Services, and Power* (Princeton University Press, 2016) and associate professor of anthropology at Pomona College.

LINDA SAYED is an assistant professor at James Madison College at Michigan State University. She is an interdisciplinary scholar of the Middle East and its diaspora, focusing on issues of citizenship, power, and health inequality as it relates to marginalized and minority communities.

NADYA SBAITI is assistant professor in the Center for Arab and Middle Eastern Studies at the American University of Beirut, and visiting assistant professor at Georgetown University–Qatar's History Department. She is an historian of the modern Middle East, with research interests focusing on education, gender, colonialism, and tourism. She is the author of a number of articles, book chapters, and essays, and is a coeditor of *Jadaliyya*.

INDEX

Abisaab, Malek, 189n9
Abisaab, Rula Jurdi, 189n9
Ahliyya School for Girls *(al-madrasa al-ahliyya li al-banat),* 18, 20–23, 25–27
AlShehabi, Omar, 4
antisectarianism, 12–13, 157–60, 165, 171, 177–79, 216n26
Arāş, Roxana Maria, 6–9, 98, 158, 164, 233
archives: account of fire in, 66–69; as assemblages, 57, 196n58; Barbir Bridge and, 66; Barbir Tunnel and, 67; Bourj Hammoud and, 139; challenges posed by rereading of, 7, 9, 14, 17, 57–58, 196n58; citizenship and, 63, 72; civil war and, 63–69, 72–75, 194n30; coexistence through, 65; community and, 72–73; Court of Cassation archive, 57, 59–69, 62*fig,* 192n1; destruction of, 55, 59–69; digital transparencies and, 69–71; education and, 14, 17, 20, 23, 29; ethnography and, 7, 58–60, 75–80; fever for, 60–61; history-making through,

59–60; Jaʿfari shariʿa courts and, 32, 52, 195n40; legal uses of, 71–74; life in, 56–61; memory and, 59–60, 65, 71–74, 77; narrative and, 7, 9, 14, 17, 57–58, 196n58; overview of, 52–53; power and, 60–61; sextarianism and, 52–54; violence and, 58–59, 65, 73–80, 195–96n53

Armenian community: aftermath of Tourian murder and, 120–21; Cilician See in, 116–19, 133–37, 205n2; citizenship and, 122, 124, 206n3; contemporary situation of, 136–37; Dashnak party and, 117, 122, 125, 128–30, 132–33, 206n5; development of, 116–17, 144, 207nn13–14, 208n16; Echmiadzin See in, 116–18, 120–28, 134–35, 205n2; enacting of sectarianism in, 123–26; entrenchment of sectarianism in, 132–36; identity and, 37, 116–18, 136–37; *mahjar* (diaspora) and, 9, 118, 119, 149, 207n14; nationalism and, 118, 120–24, 207nn13–14; newspaper coverage of, 121–35;

Printed in the USA
CPSIA information can be obtained
at www.ICGtesting.com
LVHW092022230923
758990LV00003B/494